Out-of-print -

$25—
1ᵉ Editᵘ

Books by Ruth Painter Randall

MARY LINCOLN: BIOGRAPHY OF A MARRIAGE

LINCOLN'S SONS

THE COURTSHIP OF MR. LINCOLN

COLONEL ELMER ELLSWORTH

For Young People

LINCOLN'S ANIMAL FRIENDS

I MARY

Colonel Elmer Ellsworth

Colonel
Elmer Ellsworth

*A biography of Lincoln's friend
and first hero of the Civil War*

by

RUTH PAINTER RANDALL

WITH ILLUSTRATIONS

Little, Brown and Company · Boston · Toronto

Published simultaneously in Canada
by Little, Brown & Company (Canada) Limited

PRINTED IN THE UNITED STATES OF AMERICA

To Jim
who never knew about this book
yet helped to write it

FOREWORD

In writing *Mary Lincoln: Biography of a Marriage* and *Lincoln's Sons*, I necessarily gave some attention to Colonel Elmer E. Ellsworth because he was so loved by the Lincolns that he was involved in their story. Becoming interested in his personality, I later began a further study of him. Soon I came upon some remarkable statements which John Hay, at the time he was private secretary to President Lincoln, made about Ellsworth. "No man ever possessed in a more eminent degree the power of personal fascination," wrote Hay. "That faculty . . . of winning, fettering, moving and commanding the souls of thousands till they move as one, he enjoyed, in a measure, of which the world will forever remain ignorant." Hay was himself under that magnetic spell; he deeply loved Ellsworth and called him "one of the dearest of the friends of my youth."

Young Hay also said in 1861 that Colonel Ellsworth was "the most talked-of man in the country," and that President Lincoln "mourned him as a son."

Another of my discoveries was that today people in general know nothing of Ellsworth. When I spoke of him the result was usually the question, "Who was Colonel Ellsworth?" The occasional exception came from those who had a progenitor who had been among the hundreds of babies named for him, and usually all they knew about him was that "Grandfather was named Elmer Ellsworth." Even professors of American history (unless their specialty was the Civil War period) sometimes asked "Who was he?"

This situation seemed ironic in view of the judgment of his own time. At Ellsworth's death sermons and editorials outdid themselves in mid-Victorian eloquence on the subject of his immortal fame. Two extracts from editorials late in May 1861 will serve as examples. The *New York World* on the day after Ellsworth's death said: "The day last gone has added a knightly name to our list of heroes — one which will not be blurred so long as the record of our war of liberty survives." The *New York Times* ended a long eulogy: ". . . long after the Rebellion shall have become a matter of history, his death will be regarded as a martyrdom and his name will be enrolled upon the list of our country's greatest patriots."

His death gave a tremendous impetus to the war effort of the North in the initial stages of the Civil War. On all sides was heard the slogan "Remember Ellsworth!" This became the battle cry of the volunteer regiment he had raised from the New York firemen. Shouts of "Remember Ellsworth!" rose from the battlefield at the First Battle of Bull Run.

The time came when in my study I held in my hands the very letters Ellsworth had written his fiancée. There are approximately a hundred of his letters in the Illinois State Historical Library, most of them to his "Darling Carrie," such satisfactory letters that his story from 1858 to 1861 can be made almost autobiography by quoting them. They unfold an appealing love story. Their sparkle and originality come down through the years to give telling glimpses of the magnetic man who lived a century ago.

In this book I have wanted to recover Ellsworth's intriguing personality. The unusually personal nature of the source material lends itself to this. I have tried to give a full account of his remarkable life, so closely bound up with the history of his time and so intimately connected with Abraham Lincoln. There is too much of human interest and poignant history in Ellsworth's story to allow it to remain forgotten.

My purpose has been to write an authentic biography of Colonel Ellsworth for the general reader. It has been considered best not to have footnotes but my original manuscript has the references to the sources used, and these sources are given in the Bibliographical Note at the end of the book.

R. P. R.

Acknowledgments

I WISH first to acknowledge my great indebtedness to Louis Ellsworth Laflin of Lake Forest, Illinois. An Ellsworth writer and collector, Mr. Laflin has done everything possible to assist in my research for this book. Incidentally, his Ellsworth play was one of the first things to give me the feel of the subject. I have had the use of Mr. Laflin's Ellsworth Collection and he has found, out of his own knowledge and generosity, many ways to give invaluable and deeply appreciated assistance.

I also wish to express my profound thanks to Miss Carolyn Godfrey (niece of Ellsworth's fiancée, Carrie Spafford) for permission to use the Godfrey collection and for answering many questions in letters and in our visit together. Miss Godfrey's nephew, Warren Godfrey, has also been responsive to requests for help. I am extremely grateful for this co-operation from Carrie Spafford's relatives.

Two friends of Albany, New York, Mr. Harlan Hoyt Horner, Lincoln author and collector, and Mrs. Horner, devoted much time and effort to getting and sending me information about Malta and Mechanicville, Ellsworth's birthplace and boyhood home. I deeply appreciate their most generous assistance.

Those pleasant people who have charge of libraries and

historical societies have been wonderful as usual. I found working in the Ellsworth letters at the Illinois State Historical Library a happy as well as a fruitful experience. There Dr. Clyde C. Walton, Miss Margaret Flint, S. Ambrose Wetherbee, and Thomas Felt did everything possible to forward my research. Margaret Flint, in addition to her other indispensable assistance, has read the Bibliographical Note of this book in manuscript.

The Chicago Historical Society, which has a fine exhibit of Ellsworth and Zouave relics, has furnished pictures and other important material. At this Society, Paul Angle, Mrs. Phyllis Healy, Miss Blanche Jantzen, and Mrs. Mary F. Rhymer have all given the best of expert help.

Dr. R. Gerald McMurtry of the Lincoln National Life Foundation provided photostats of valuable letters in the Ellsworth story. Juliet Wolohan of the New York State Library, Lucile Kane of the Minnesota Historical Society, Norma Cuthbert of the Huntington Library, and Josephine Harper of the Wisconsin Historical Society have all been most helpful about the material under their charge.

Ralph Newman of the Abraham Lincoln Book Shop has given excellent suggestions. Dr. Wayne C. Temple of Lincoln Memorial University sent valuable notes and Dr. LeRoy Fischer of Oklahoma State University gave useful references. Martha Swain Carlson supplied helpful information. President Raymond Dooley of Lincoln College furnished a photostat of Ellsworth's last orders to his men, and the late Dean Robert B. Browne of the University of Illinois answered military questions.

Alice Harnish has again let me read my chapters to her and has made encouraging suggestions. Helen Hart Metz once more has demonstrated her skill in making the index of this book.

In the final phases of the manuscript I am especially indebted to Ned Bradford of Little, Brown and Company for his wise and skillful editing and to Mrs. Mary Rackliffe, Head Copy Editor, for her helpfulness which made proof-reading a pleasure.

R. P. R.

Contents

List of Illustrations

(between pages 140 and 141)

Colonel Elmer Ellsworth

1

Mr. Lincoln Chooses a Student-at-Law

On Monday the 13th of August, 1860, the town of Spring-field, Illinois, was in a pleasant state of excitement. An event which had been eagerly awaited was scheduled to take place that day. As a sort of overture there was the sound of band music that morning as the Springfield Greys, the local military company, paraded around the public square in the center of the town. Then the booming of a cannon was heard. People had grown accustomed to these sounds in the political rallies which had been taking place ever since Mr. Abraham Lincoln had been nominated for President the previous May, but today's attraction was not a matter of politics. It concerned the military.

A much heralded military company was coming to town to give its new spectacular drill, the Zouave drill, it was called. This strange word "Zouave" had been splashed in newspaper headlines all during July and August and was a current topic of conversation from Illinois to the Atlantic seaboard. Its spelling and pronunciation, incidentally, were giving the average citizen a bit of trouble, but it was a word clothed in glamour.

The company scheduled to arrive on the eleven o'clock train was called the U. S. Zouave Cadets. It was carrying a huge blue and white flag which signified that it was the champion military company of the nation. The Zouave Cadets were a picked group of young men from Chicago and just now they were returning from a triumphant tour of the East in which they had challenged any company of the United States or Canada to compete for that champion flag.

Their commandant, the man who had trained them, was twenty-three-year-old Colonel Elmer E. Ellsworth. His name too had been appearing in headlines and reporters had been saying some unusual things about him. His picture had become familiar in the newspapers and it was said that at the moment he was the most talked-about young man in the country.

Colonel Ellsworth was not coming to Springfield for the first time. He had spent some weeks in the town the previous winter and had made warm friends, Mr. Lincoln among them. One of these friends, General John Cook, commander of the Springfield Greys, was in a position to know that Mr. Lincoln had a special interest in Ellsworth and was making every effort to have him settle down in Springfield to study law in the Lincoln law office. After his stay in Springfield the previous January, Ellsworth had exchanged letters with General Cook, who had written him in March: "You ask me if I have seen our friend Lincoln. I answer yes repeatedly and never without the conversation turning upon you and his expressing an earnest desire that you should make this place your home & his office your head quarters. He has taken in you a greater interest than I ever knew him to manifest in any one before." There was no doubt that Mr. Lincoln would be among the thousands who would watch Colonel Ellsworth put his company through the Zouave drill at three o'clock that Monday afternoon at Major Iles's open lot on South Sixth Street.

Shortly before eleven General Cook with the Springfield Greys arrived at the depot to welcome the guest company. Promptly at eleven the Zouaves stepped lightly from the train platform and, under the direction of their leader, quickly formed themselves into line. Spectators who had assembled at the station stared curiously at the young colonel of whom they had heard so much. They saw a somewhat boyish figure of five feet six, quick-motioned, and with a spirited poise of the head. Ellsworth's hair was almost black, his features were clean-cut, his eyes dark hazel, and his complexion (though undoubtedly deeply tanned at the moment) was naturally fair with a tendency to ruddiness. His face was lively and expressive and he gave the impression of unusual energy and strength.

The Springfield Greys escorted the Zouaves to the armory. People lined the streets as they paraded by to the music of the Union Silver Band. At the armory Adjutant General Thomas S. Mather, in his speech of welcome, spoke of their "great and glorious work of placing our State militia on a firm and enduring basis." Thoughtful men in 1860 feared that their country was threatened with war, and these words were a recognition of Colonel Ellsworth's known purpose to build up the military strength of the nation. Referring to the championship flag, the Adjutant General continued: "You nobly won it; you have still more nobly kept it; and on its starlit folds should now be inscribed the words: This belongs to the Champion Company of the Continent."

Long before three o'clock carriages and pedestrians were moving in an excited procession toward Major Iles's field until, as a Springfield paper reported, there were five or six thousand people assembled on the ground in a state of "feverish expectancy." Along with the tall-hatted gentlemen in the crowd was a surprising number of hoop-skirted ladies, or, as the *Illinois State Journal* put it in the more formal language of the period, "the predominance of crinoline was particularly noticeable." The *Illinois State Register* was equally stately in its phrasing: "All that was fair and beautiful in our city," it said, "had gone forth to witness, to honor, to encourage by their smiles this gallant band of citizen soldiers." It did not diminish the feminine interest to know that, exactly nine days before, the performance they were about to witness had been given by special invitation on the White House lawn with President Buchanan and his niece, Miss Harriet Lane, and Washington dignitaries in attendance.

It was hot in Springfield on that afternoon of August 13 and Mr. Lincoln watched the show as he stood in the shade of a cottonwood tree in a yard on Sixth Street. Few scenes could have blazed with more color than the one before him. In the bright sunshine stood some fifty fine young Americans dressed in gorgeous uniforms of red, blue, and gold. Each man wore loose scarlet trousers, high gaiters, a collarless blue jacket trimmed with gold braid, a shirt of lighter blue, and a jaunty red cap with gold or orange decorations. Their knapsacks were on their shoulders and the rolled scarlet blankets on top of the knapsacks made red the dominant color.

The crowd had to be pushed back to make room and the drill began. With an incredible quickness of motion the Zouaves went through the maneuvers of war: marching, retreating, rallying by fours, firing at halt, firing while kneeling, loading while lying on the back, taking every conceivable position. They demonstrated bayonet practice, the parry, the lunge, the thrust. Their movements were so swift and elaborate that unmilitary onlookers found it difficult to follow what was being done. When the company stacked arms it seemed like a trick of sleight of hand.

The feats plainly required young men of superb physical strength who had been trained to perfection. As one of the Springfield papers remarked, "It is not easy for one man to go through their singular and difficult performances; indeed, a great many men would find it entirely beyond their power to go through one-half of them." The program was varied by forming such figures as squares, triangles, double crosses, pyramids, and revolving circles, one formation dissolving into the next like the bright-colored designs of a kaleidoscope.

The crowd was going wild with applause and cheers. It was a blood-stirring spectacle as graceful in movement and as beautiful as an elaborate ballet. The spectators could hardly take their eyes off the young officer who was calling out the orders in a ringing voice. They sensed a magnetic bond between him and his men, who obeyed him as if their muscles were his own. Every command was executed with faultless precision.

Mr. Lincoln watched the two-hour drill with kindling eyes. He too centered his attention upon the boyish-looking commander. Afterwards he said of Colonel Ellsworth, "He is the greatest little man I ever met."

With the final hurrahs ringing in their ears the U. S. Zouave Cadets took the train to Chicago the following morning. A month later Elmer Ellsworth returned to Springfield to enter Mr. Lincoln's law office as his student-at-law.

◇
◇◇
◇◇◇
◇

2

"Oyster Kegs" and Other Complications
for a Small Boy

Elmer Ellsworth wrote in his diary on his twenty-second
birthday that his life up to that time had been "a jumble of
strange incidents." To go back to the beginning of his
story takes one eastward from Illinois to the little village
of Malta in Saratoga County, New York. It was there, on
April 11, 1837, that a son was born to a young tailor and
his bride of a year, Mr. and Mrs. Ephraim D. Ellsworth.

Ephraim had been making an adequate living by his
tailoring when they were married, and they were living in
a simple but pleasant story-and-a-half frame cottage. It has
been called "the low-browed cottage" because two narrow
horizontal windows in the short upper story suggested
two eyes peeping out from under the eaves. The Ellsworths
were nice young people well liked by their friends, who
doubtless shared in neighborly fashion their joy and excitement over the birth of their first child.

There was perhaps a bit of discussion about what to
name the baby, which is usual; what was unusual in this
case was that the discussion did not end with the bestow-
ing of the name. The parents decided upon the first name
Ephraim after the father and the middle name Elmer for
their friend Mr. John Thompson Elmer. So the boy was to

grow up as Ephraim Elmer until he was about fifteen or sixteen, and he was so listed in the directory of Troy, New York, where he was then living. By that time he knew his name was often confused with that of his father, so he decided to reverse the order and be Elmer Ephraim. Just to make doubly sure, he usually wrote it Elmer E., thus leaving his father in undisputed possession of the second name. (There were to be scores of babies named Elmer Ellsworth after the popular hero in the early part of the Civil War, but few, if any, knew how narrowly they had escaped being called Ephraim!)

The change in the order of the names has resulted in some confusion in writings about Ellsworth and occasionally in print he has been referred to as Ephraim Elmer. But in her manuscript recollections of his childhood, his mother gave his name as Elmer Ephraim.

Elmer's father, as the name Ellsworth indicates, came of English ancestors. He had been born in Halfmoon, New York, in 1809, the same year in which a baby named Abraham Lincoln had been born in Kentucky. The name of the town was evidently from the good ship *Half Moon* in which Henry Hudson, the explorer, had long before sailed up the river which bears his name. The historic Hudson River ran close to the people living in that part of New York and was strong in their consciousness, as it was to be in Ellsworth's.

Ephraim D. Ellsworth learned the tailor's trade at Waterford and settled in Malta in 1836, the year in which he married an attractive young woman named Phoebe Denton. He was described in later life as a man of medium height, solidly built, with dark eyes, a fair complexion, and a hearty voice. Letters written by him indicate his degree of education — or the lack of it: they have a forceful, unhesitating handwriting and are intelligible, but contain such misspellings as "pleas" for "please," "grate" for "great" and such a phrase as "wile I was thare." He had evidently grown up with few advantages but was spoken of as a kind, intelligent, honest, hard-working man, well respected by all who knew him. He was a pleasant man judging by the likable face in his daguerreotype.

Phoebe Denton Ellsworth, by her own statement, had an English father and a "Scotch Presbyterian" mother. Phoebe was a little woman with dark brown eyes and a bright, loving disposition. These are the few bare bones of facts about Ellsworth's parents; what brings them to life are the things he said about them, the love and devotion in his letters to them, and his passionate longing to improve their circumstances. When he was twenty-one, he was to put into a letter to them a comment which tells a great deal: "Poor as we are and have been," he wrote, "I am thankful that I cannot recollect of an instance where my father or mother have been guilty of a mean spirited or ungenerous action." In the same letter he was to speak gratefully of "the care and affection so lavishly bestowed" upon him by his "dear parents."

Mr. Lincoln had a rule for bringing up children: "Love," he said, "is the chain whereby to bind a child to its parents." This was evidently the rule of the Ellsworths too, for never was such a chain more strongly forged than the one in the little "low-browed cottage" at Malta.

Ellsworth had a special closeness to his mother. "All the good in my nature I owe to her," he wrote the girl with whom he was in love. Again one is reminded of Lincoln who said, "All that I am, or hope to be, I owe to my angel mother." There is fine character to be read in the face of Phoebe Ellsworth's picture. A neighbor who lived beside her for many years called her "a noble woman," and another friend referred to her as one "whose heart is always full of tenderness." Ellsworth inherited many qualities, including his small stature, from his mother.

With such understanding between them, it is doubly interesting to have her manuscript recollections of him as a small boy. Although she could write and did write him letters, the recollections are not in her handwriting. By the time she came to record them, she had had an illness which rendered her hand unsteady. She dictated these memories to a dear friend and, if one may judge by the well-chosen language, she was better educated than her husband. She paints a vivid picture of the curly-haired, earnest, lovable, hardheaded little boy that Elmer had been.

One of the earliest incidents she tells brings into focus the misfortune which soon took away the security of the close-knit little family. The year Elmer was born, 1837, was also the year of a severe financial panic which threw many people out of employment and caused terrible hardship. A great, long-lasting depression settled over the country like a blight. People wear their old clothes in a depression; they do not go to a tailor for new ones. As a result Ephraim Ellsworth soon found himself out of a means of livelihood. Years later Elmer Ellsworth was to tell John Hay how this depression ruined his father.

The young parents met the situation pluckily. Mr. Ellsworth undertook various odd jobs which promised to bring in a little money. He peddled kegs of oysters on commission, helped with butchering, and even netted pigeons to sell, evidently the abundant wild passenger pigeons which are now extinct. The mother took in a boarder and worked hard to do her part. Though they always had an adequate home and did not lack for food, life was to be a laborious struggle for the couple until that far-off time when President Lincoln, out of his love for their son, would give Ephraim, then in his fifties, a government appointment which brought them a regular income and security.

Poverty had a far-reaching effect upon the boy. It was not only that he himself had to grow up deprived of many things he longed for and needed, but there was also his constant worry about his parents. This was especially true when he grew to realize that they were breaking under the strain of hard physical work. "Throughout his childhood as well as manhood," said his mother, "it seemed the one wish of his life to gather riches, that he might place his parents above the necessity of labor." She added that it might be said to have been the wish of his babyhood, for she remembered an incident that happened when he was still using baby words. She was "suffering greatly with the toothache," she went on, but she had work which must be done and kept at it. The little fellow watched her with his face full of distress and sympathy and finally said, "It's too bad muver, to have the teefache and have to work too, but never mind, when I'm a man I'll work and earn money, and you shall ride in a carriage."

To ride in a carriage seemed, his mother said, "the climax of prosperity to him." For this there was a reason. The hamlet of Malta was near Saratoga Springs, the fashionable watering place. A road to this resort ran through Malta, and one can almost see the little boy, poorly dressed and barefooted, watching by the roadside as the stately coaches rumbled through the town. There would be a coachman in livery in front and the passengers would be beautifully dressed ladies, and gentlemen with tall hats and long coattails, who seemed to come from another world. The child passionately wanted these things for his parents; he wanted his mother to "be as big a lady as any of them." He was by nature unselfish and would always think of others. John Hay would one day say that Ellsworth had only "two faults." One was that he was "too generous." What the other was will be seen later.

The lowly situation of his parents pursued Elmer at school. He attended the district school at Malta and also at Mechanicville, New York, after the family moved to that nearby village when he was a young boy. Aside from this early schooling he had to be self-educated.

The exact date of the move to Mechanicville is hard to pin down — accounts differ — but it seems to have been when Elmer was ten or eleven years old. The new home was a pleasant one in a beautiful part of New York. The Hudson River flows through Mechanicville, and from the Ellsworth grounds the Green Mountains could be seen in the far distance. The family had a larger house here, with land enough around it for domestic animals — dogs, pigs, a horse named Mink, and assorted poultry. Raising chickens and pigs may have been a source of income as well as of food and a horse was certainly necessary for peddling those oyster kegs.

Years later, at a time when he was in deep trouble, Ellsworth let his thoughts wander back for comfort to this beloved home. He wrote in his diary a longing passage about it which incidentally shows the command of language which was to be his at twenty-two — and also his tendency to omit punctuation. "In my fancy," says the diary page, "I saw a dear old home stead embosomed in gloriously old trees whose wide spreading branches seemed to wave to & fro with gentle dignity as if conscious of their noble beauty, the river with its islands — the green clad hills afar off — the great dutch barn & its denizens all — the poultry dogs & even old Mink with his soft eyes beaming with almost human intelligence were as patent to my imagination as when oft in boy hood I have gazed upon them & tried to picture to myself the great world beyond & the part I should play in it." But his pleasure in this picture vanished with the recollection of his father and mother "prematurely aged working & slaving for existence" in that home.

Some of the children at school taunted Elmer with his father's lowly occupations and limited means. Mrs. Ellsworth remembered well the day he came home fighting mad because another boy had twitted him with the fact that his mother wore "patched shoes." Torn by his fury at the boy and his helpless pity for her, he again tried to comfort her by saying that some day he would earn money and she should ride in a carriage.

He was, as she said, "proud spirited." He would need that sustaining pride of self-respect and courage in the years ahead.

"Patched shoes" was not the only insult that Elmer had to endure at school. He was "uncommonly small, or at least short for his age," his mother said, and "a boy much larger than himself used to take particular delight in calling him 'oyster keg.'" It was perhaps a double-barreled taunt, referring both to his size and to his father's peddling oysters. "He would get so angry at this," continued his mother, "that it seemed almost impossible for him to control himself; but his father told him if he touched the boy he would give him a sound whipping as soon as he found it out." This created an almost impossible situation for Elmer, who, though short, was very muscular and quick and was as fearless and ready for a good fight as any high-spirited boy would be under the circumstances.

So the taunts went on until one day Elmer came home "highly wrought up and indignant" and, his father being absent, poured out his troubles to the man who boarded with them. The man heard the story out and then asked, "Why don't you lick him?" Elmer explained that his father had forbidden him to do so.

"Well," said the boarder, "if your father won't let you lick him, *I will;* so the next time he calls you 'oyster keg' do you give him a good whipping."

That was all Elmer wanted to hear. The following day after school the bully yelled the hated words "oyster keg." The next thing he knew, he was knocked flat on the ground. Something that must have seemed to him like a cross between a boy and a wildcat was on top of him giving him the beating of his life. Elmer fought with the accumulated fury of days of taunting and the victory was complete.

The schoolteacher, unknown to the boys, had watched the fight from the doorway with quiet satisfaction. After it was over, he called the belligerents in and asked each to state his case. Then he said, "I have noticed what was going on for some time, and think *now*, you are about square." He added that he wanted no more fighting — but this was unnecessary; neither the big boy nor anyone else had anything to say about oyster kegs from that time on!

When Elmer was about three, another son had been born to the Ellsworth family whom they called Charley. Elmer was enchanted with the new arrival. He wanted that baby for his very own — could he buy him? It is pleasant to imagine the scene of that bargaining: the tiny lad's eagerness and the mother's smiling questions about how much he would pay for the baby. The price finally agreed upon was six shillings (shillings not being obsolete in New York around 1840), and Elmer had to negotiate a loan. He paid his debt later "in good faith," continued his mother, but she did not tell by what small tasks he earned the money.

Before long Elmer had his moments of disillusionment about babies, finding out that they cried a great deal and had other disconcerting and irresponsible habits which made a lot of work. Then he would say that "he had got cheated" and made "a poor bargain." But, Mrs. Ellsworth added, "he always assumed and seemed to feel a sort of ownership and supervision over him [Charley], which matured into almost paternal care." Though entirely different, the brothers were to grow up completely devoted to each other, but Elmer had a strong sense of responsibility, a quality in which Charley seemed to be somewhat lacking.

The baby was an involuntary assistant in a philosophical experiment which Elmer made when he was about four. The incident grew out of Mrs. Ellsworth's early attempts to teach him about God and good and evil. She was a sincerely religious woman, belonging to the Presbyterian church like her mother. Her husband attended church with her but did not join it. (Possibly he was one of those who, like Mr. Lincoln, did not unite with a church because he could not honestly accept some of the narrow orthodoxy of the mid-nineteenth century.) But it is clear that Elmer was growing up in a religious home and that he developed a deep trust in God.

Early religious instruction, however, presented problems, with a young child of inquiring mind. His mother said of Elmer: "A spirit of inquiry and investigation, and a disposition to take nothing on assertion that could be demonstrated by proof was . . . a childhood characteristic." One day she told him that "the Lord knew and saw all that he thought and did, and when he was naughty would put down a black mark, and when he was good would put down a good mark, and then if he got the most black ones he would be punished."

This was an exciting idea to the little boy. What did those marks look like and how would God punish him? Would he spank him? This was something worth finding out.

Elmer sat down beside the baby's cradle and began to rock it, meanwhile gazing innocently out of the window. Suddenly the baby gave a sharp cry. His mother at once asked Elmer what was the matter. "Oh, nothing," was the answer, and as the baby was quiet again she did not investigate further. Presently the baby gave another yell. His father, becoming suspicious, said to Elmer, "What are you doing to your brother?" "Nothing," replied Elmer, "I guess he is saying his prayers."

In a few minutes Charley cried out a third time and Elmer felt that his experiment had proved conclusive. "There mother," he said, "the Lord has told a lie himself, — for I've been naughty — I've pinched my little brother, and I've told a lie, 'cause I told you I hadn't done any thing to him — and the Lord hasn't seen me, nor done any thing to me for it, so he's lied himself for you say, he says he will punish naughty boys." Mrs. Ellsworth failed to tell just how she answered that reasoning.

She had worked out a special way of disciplining Elmer. She was, she said, dealing with a boy "of great energy and decision of character, as well as indomitable pride." She did not whip him but she made him sit on the floor and keep perfectly still, doing nothing. "He would beg of me," she continued, "to whip him and release him, for *that* he could bear, but to sit in disgrace on the floor in constant expectation that some of the neighbors would come in and see him there, was more than his philosophy could cope with."

When he was older he told his mother that when she punished him in this manner he had a dark suspicion that she must be his stepmother, not his real one. He had, she explained, received the idea that a stepmother meant "something dreadful, from my youngest brother who lived with us and was unpleasantly situated in that respect." This was doubtless Chester Denton, her half-brother, who was to give his own recollections of Elmer's boyhood.

That "The child is father of the man" was certainly true in Elmer's case. The incidents told by his mother show the same qualities in him as a boy which he would have when grown up: sympathy, affection, unselfishness, independence of thought and action, enterprise and fearlessness. His mother's words are like gentle brush strokes painting the portrait of a personality.

There is, fortunately, a photograph of Elmer. At the

time he was born people did not know how to take pictures, but about two years later the photographic process was worked out. As a result men and women in the 1840s were undergoing the new experience of sitting rigid before the strange machine which photographed them.

Dressed in his best, the boy one day sat for the photographer. His curly hair had been well brushed in an attempt to make it smooth but a few locks had refused to submit to such discipline. He was sitting very still, as he had been told, and there was a look of wonder in the big hazel eyes.

◇
◇
◇

3

"Gun and 'Cussion Cap to Shoot the Devil"

Mrs. Ellsworth in her recollections spoke of Elmer's early "military propensity." She remembered a remark her father had made about the boy. "That child will be a great military character if he lives," he said, adding impressively, "remember what I tell you." Grandfatherly predictions of greatness for their grandsons are rather common and are usually forgotten unless they happen to hit the target. Then Grandfather is credited, as here, with the gift of prophecy.

Small boys are normally interested in soldiers who wear striking uniforms, use fascinating guns, and are called brave. But in Elmer's case there were special strong influences at work to turn his mind to things military. Malta was in a part of the country which was soaked in historic associations with the American Revolution. When Elmer was six, the definitive treaty of peace which brought American independence was only sixty years in the past. Men and women were still living who could remember and tell about the intensity of feeling in that struggle for liberty and the fervor of making a great experiment, a new kind of government called a democracy, where the people ruled themselves. Love of country was instilled in Ellsworth at an early age.

At the Ellsworth fireside Elmer heard thrilling stories about an ancestor of his who had fought in that war for independence. His great-grandfather, George Ellsworth, was a youth of fifteen living at Halfmoon, New York, when General John Burgoyne invaded the country. Fired by patriotism, he joined the Continental Army, fought gallantly, and was present at the surrender of Burgoyne at the Battle of Saratoga, a triumphant event which has been called the turning point of the American Revolution.

The very battlefield where his great-grandfather had fought was near Malta and there is no doubt that Elmer was taken over it when he was very young. Perhaps the ardent little boy envied his great-grandfather George for being part of so patriotic a war. He heard much too about another soldier named George — George Washington, who had been the leader in the fight for independence, and General Washington became one of his heroes. It is no wonder Elmer became convinced it was the most glorious thing in the world to be a soldier and fight for one's country.

When he reached the mudpie stage, Elmer made little mud breastworks or collected bricks to make a fort. His aunt remembered that he used little blocks to represent soldiers and that they were "American soldiers fighting the British or Indians." Later, when he went to school, he began to organize his playmates into a small company of which he was the captain. It seemed to trouble his mother that he always took command, but she noticed that "he showed no wish or tendency to domineer" and that the other boys accepted his leadership cheerfully.

Having an inquiring mind, Elmer learned easily at school, where, as one of his schoolmates remembered, he sat on a front seat because of his small size. He would quickly mas-

ter the required lesson and then have time to draw pictures of soldiers in his own book or the books of other pupils. He delighted so much in drawing it is surprising that
no one predicted he would be an artist.

Loving color, of course he wanted to make his drawings
into paintings. But he had no materials for this, neither
paints nor canvas. One day he discovered he could get some
paints at a wagon or carriage shop. Casting about for something to paint on, he decided a window shade would be
just the thing. So Elmer, aged nine, it is said, painted
his hero, General George Washington, and his staff on his
mother's window shade. Perhaps Mrs. Ellsworth had only
one shade to donate to her son's artistic impulses, for he
used the reverse side for his next juvenile masterpiece,
General Andrew Jackson with his staff.

Attending the district school on weekdays, he went to
"Sabbath School" on Sundays, his mother remembered,
adding that it was in the Methodist church, not the Presbyterian, to which she belonged. To explain how this happened she told of this incident. One day Elmer and his father went to a camp meeting four miles from their home.
Mr. Ellsworth "had a refreshment stand near the ground,"
which was evidently another method of making a little
money. They had presumably driven out in a wagon drawn
by old Mink, and Elmer probably found the activities of a
camp meeting very entertaining.

When it was over the father said he must "go after some
stock to butcher" and told Elmer to go out to the road and
ask a ride home on some wagon coming by — or, in modern terms, to hitchhike. Elmer did as he was told and
waited by the roadside. By and by a wagon came along but
it was so full that he said nothing. After another long period a second wagon appeared. Elmer noticed the horses
pulling this wagon seemed thin and overworked and he did
not have the heart to add his weight to their burden.

After some more waiting a third wagon approached and the boy thought this was it. The man driving it taught in the Sunday school of the Presbyterian church to which his mother belonged. He had only his small son with him and the horse was big and fat, so Elmer asked for a lift. He was curtly refused. Possibly there was an element of snobbishness involved in this refusal to take the poorly dressed son of a man who did odd jobs like butchering; at all events, as Elmer trudged the four miles home, his resentment knew no bounds.

From then on he told his mother he would go to Sunday school, yes, but to the one at the Methodist church, not the one where this man taught. "Mother," he said indignantly, "don't ever ask me to go to Sabbath school to that man, for it won't do me any good." Mrs. Ellsworth did not argue the matter.

Later, the teacher at the Methodist Sunday school told her Elmer asked so many searching questions that he, the teacher, was in a tight spot, often because he found it difficult to keep a straight face. Perhaps, like many teachers before and since, he was hard put to it to explain certain forthright Biblical phrases to the juvenile mind.

Elmer liked his weekday school especially because it had a library and he could take books home with him. He loved to read and was never without a book, his mother remembered, and she told a story showing his concentration when he read.

She and his father had to be absent from home one day from eight until four to attend a funeral. Possibly they took Charley with them, as Elmer was to be left at home alone. Mrs. Ellsworth told him he could spend his time reading but he must be sure to feed the pigs at noon when he ate his own dinner. The boy, in pure bliss at the prospect, pulled the shades down so that nobody would come in to disturb him, sat down on the floor in a corner with a treasured book in his lap, and buried himself in its pages.

At four his parents returned and were somewhat surprised to see the shades down and the house looking deserted. When his mother opened the door, Elmer looked up in astonishment and asked, "Why Ma, what are you back for?" When she told him it was four o'clock, he started up, exclaiming, "I didn't think it was noon, let me run and feed the pigs." He had read eight hours straight.

School and reading were not the whole of life for the growing boy. He was, according to his mother, "cheerful" and "happy" by nature and he found so much to interest him. He loved, as he always would, all kinds of sports and activities. There were many lakes near Malta, including Lake Saratoga, and he learned the dip and pull of rowing a boat on their waters. At Mechanicville there was the Hudson River, which was no doubt as fascinating to him as the great Mississippi was at that time to a boy named Sam Clemens, born two years before Elmer and growing up in the little town of Hannibal, Missouri.

When Ellsworth was twenty-one he described the ideal home he wished to achieve for his parents and himself — near a town or city "situated on the bank of a fine river or lake." Something vital would be missing without the endless variety and charm of riverside life.

When he was not drawing or painting soldiers, he liked to do pictures with water in them. There exists today in the Illinois State Historical Library a painting which, according to the account passed down about it, he made with paints from the wagon shop. It shows a sweeping river with a sailboat in the right foreground and hills rising on the far side. The model for the river was doubtless the Hudson. On the hills beyond are turreted castles such as might come out of books about King Arthur and the age of chivalry — or from the daydreams of a nine-year-old boy.

Ellsworth, after he had grown up, described his young days on that lordly river. By that time he had had a disillusioning experience which shook his faith in people for a while and he was looking back to the sweet, unspoiled fancies of boyhood. "With mind free from care," he wrote, "I wandered away into the green old hills, or in my boat drifted slowly down the Hudson and dreaming of the future, built castles in the air, and longed for the time to come when I could commence the battle with the world. And I . . . with the generosity of boyhood, peopled the world with the brave the good — the noble hearted."

Elmer was twice blessed with waterways at Mechanicville; he had a canal too. It was the Champlain Canal, part of the system of which the Erie Canal (completed twelve years before his birth) was the great artery. The boy undoubtedly heard much talk of this wonderful canal which opened up a water highway from the Atlantic Ocean to the Great Lakes. He could not realize what this new means of travel and transportation meant to the development of the West or how it was building up a place called Chicago to which he would one day go. This was the time when canals were in their heyday.

The home-town canal was a thing of wonder and delight to him. He and his uncle Chester Denton (who was apparently near his age), used to play together on its towpath. Chester wrote later of Elmer as a companion that he was "cherful good natured" and always "ready where thare was any fun going on." One incident which happened as the two played on the towpath came very near being anything but funny. Firearms always fascinated Elmer, and to his great joy one day he found "an old horse pistol." Of course he wanted to know whether it would shoot or not, so he experimented with pulling the trigger and narrowly missed ending Chester's career then and there.

Elmer's brother Charley had soon grown to an age when he also could be a companion in school and play; in fact Charley, the six-shilling baby, was growing bigger than Elmer! Various recollections show glimpses of Charley, a bright, lovable boy, somewhat happy-go-lucky, and quite a tease.

A story told by one who had lived with Mr. and Mrs. Ellsworth for many years brings the two brothers vividly to life. Elmer was twelve at the time, which would make Charley around nine. The scene of the following dialogue was the Ellsworth home one evening, with one or both of the highly amused parents listening in.

"Charley," Elmer said suddenly, "did you ever realize that you would soon be a man?"

"Well," replied Charley, "I haven't given much serious thought to that subject."

"You must not treat the subject lightly," Elmer said earnestly, "for it is one of great importance to every one; Charley have you decided on your profession in life?"

"Yes, Elmer," answered Charley, doubtless with a spark of mischief coming into his eyes, "I have."

"Oh I am so glad," exclaimed Elmer looking highly pleased. "For my part I intend to be a military man. Now Charley if there is any thing I can say or do to encourage you, I shall be only too glad."

"Well I don't know," replied Charley with a sober face, "my work will be in the large cities, amongst the crowds."

"Why I don't understand you at all," said Elmer, looking puzzled, "Do tell me what your chosen life work is."

"Well Elmer, I will tell you, and I hope that you will help and encourage me all you can, I intend to be a *pick-pocket*." And Charley discreetly made a quick exit!

The boarder added what will become evident later, that the two brothers were so devoted they did not like to be separated. Charley too undoubtedly played with Elmer and Chester on that beloved towpath beside the Champlain Canal.

In the winter months the canal would freeze over and then, as an old-timer of Mechanicville recalled, Elmer would go skating on it. It must have been a favorite pastime, for it offered opportunity for several things very much to his liking: vigorous exercise, graceful motion, and "stunts." But the canal would have been most interesting in milder weather, when the canal boats came through — great, blunt boats drawn by horses who walked along the towpath. Some of them would be for freight only, but the "packet" boats would carry passengers like the people who rode in those splendid carriages to Saratoga Springs, fine ladies and gentlemen in elegant clothes.

To the small boy on the towpath, horses and boat would appear out of the far distance. Gradually they would draw nearer and nearer until the boat with those ladies and gentlemen sitting on the deck, which was on top of the long cabin or "saloon," would be so close that they could call to him, if they wished, to ask him what was the name of his town. Then the boat would go on by and slowly pass into the distance again, leaving him gazing after it and wondering once more about the great world beyond.

Elmer would have been as familiar with the banks of the Hudson as he was with the towpath. He had to explore them as a matter of business enterprise. Two older friends of his were engaged in trapping muskrats and they employed him to make the rounds of the traps. Elmer loved the outdoors and the beautiful river scenes in the keen morning air; he carried out the job with joyful energy.

Elmer even had a taste of a sport usually reserved for the sons of well-to-do fathers, riding a pony. The Ellsworths had the neighborly, sterling qualities that lead to long-lasting friendships. Near them in Mechanicville, in a fine house, lived Mr. Robert Sears, whose family included a son Charles, a daughter Mattie, and an unnamed but important pony. The children played together, and it was Mattie who later told how Elmer and his brother learned to ride on the Sears pony.

In all these activities of a normal, happy boyhood, Elmer was not losing sight of his determination to earn money so that his parents would not have to work so hard. "In his tenth year," said Mrs. Ellsworth, "he went to live with a man who kept a saloon and grocery together." It was common in those days for groceries to sell liquor, but the situation presented a dilemma to the boy.

Drunkenness was very prevalent at the time and Elmer had inevitably seen on the streets the sad spectacles which drunkards made of themselves in small towns. Such weakness and degradation were distressing to him. As a very little fellow he had been taken to a temperance lecture to which he listened attentively. Shortly thereafter he was urgently trying "to borrow a 'gun and 'cussion cap' to shoot the devil." Naturally there were parental inquiries about where he was going to find his "lordship," the devil, if he got the gun and 'cussion cap. Elmer explained that the temperance lecturer had said the devil was in a cider barrel. And he knew where he could find a cider barrel.

When he was nine he joined the temperance society, proudly reported his mother, "and promised me he would never drink." So it was quite a problem to work in a store which sold liquor. Elmer solved it by making a bargain beforehand "that he should not be required to wait on liquor customers, wash their glasses, or in any way have any thing to do with liquor." It was a bargain he kept to the last degree. About liquor, his mother said, his motto was "touch not, taste not, handle not." It is said he was employed about a year in this general store at Malta and then it was that the family moved to Mechanicville. This was the first of several store jobs he would hold in his attempt to get started toward affluence.

John Hay would one day write of Ellsworth: "His parents were plain people, without culture or means; one cannot guess how this eaglet came into so lowly a nest." (Hay did not stop to consider that Abraham Lincoln, the great statesman whom he knew so well, came out of a wilderness log cabin beside which the Ellsworth home in Mechanicville would have looked positively luxurious.) Though Ellsworth did miss the education he so longed for, he was nevertheless having a good American upbringing in the world of the 1840s.

He was in a home where the parents were gentle, upright people who loved and enjoyed their children. He was in a section which stimulated his pride in and loyalty to his country. He was assembling a set of ideals to live by, as children do, and they were the highest ideals of the time. He was absorbing a religious faith that would sustain him all his days. His standards would make his life one of strict integrity and he would never fail to fight for what he believed was right.

In other words, wherever and whenever he would encounter wrongdoing, he would always be ready to get a "gun and 'cussion cap" to shoot the devil!

4

❖
❖
❖
❖

"Sport and Foot-ball of Fortune"

His mother's recollections make a rich source from which to reconstruct Elmer's boyhood. And from the time he was twenty-one his own letters, the best of all sources, tell in remarkable detail what he was doing and thinking. These many letters, most of them written to the girl he loved, bring him so close you can almost touch him. They tell about his progress so faithfully that they are the very answer to a biographer's prayer. Warm, sparkling, confidential, they also unfold a most engaging love story.

In addition, his diary, covering more than four months in a crucial year, reveals intimate details that he never put into his letters.

There is, however, no comparable material for the years between, the teen-age years; they are difficult to recover except in general outline. To picture young Ellsworth between the early 1850s and 1858 is like trying to operate with a camera which will not focus clearly except for a few momentary flashes. Occasionally a casual recollection of someone who met him will show him more or less closely in such and such a situation; then the image will blur again with its details lost in the out-of-focus view. He was too obscure during these years to leave many traces. Fortunately, his letters often contain flashbacks as he tells his "Darling Kitty" of his life before he met her.

Mechanicville was blessed with an early railroad as well as a canal. The primitive little cars and the engine with its flaring smokestack looked like a prehistoric ancestor of the streamliner of today. The people of Mechanicville, however, felt very modern and progressive because they could travel by train from their village to Troy, New York. Railroads were in their infancy in the early 1850s but the infant was destined to grow prodigiously in the next ten years.

The passengers on one of these trains noticed the winning face and manner of the boy who was carrying the New York newspapers up and down the aisle, cheerfully offering them for sale and making quick and accurate change. Elmer had become a railroad newsboy. He was taking his first step into the great world.

He felt that he must work to relieve his parents of his support. With his great longing for a military career, he wanted desperately to go to West Point, but in the little town of Mechanicville, which had only about eight hundred inhabitants, there was no opportunity to prepare himself for entrance. In fact, in Mechanicville there was no opportunity for getting any work with a future. Ambitious to make something of himself and to help his father and mother, he had to get out of the town, and selling papers on the train gave him his first chance.

He probably enjoyed being a train newsboy. It was not a sitting-still job and he met interesting people. One incident of a chance meeting was remembered. An elderly gentleman one day, drawn to the boy, it is said, by "his frank, bright and manly appearance," engaged him in a long conversation. The gentleman was a merchant who had a dry-goods store in New York City and he evidently realized that this newsboy had unusual qualities. They discussed young Ellsworth's future and, judging by what happened later, the gentleman may have brought up the subject of his working in his store. No plans, however, were made and they parted without Elmer's getting his address.

On the train he inevitably met people from Troy and it was possibly some casual contact like this which led to an offer, when he was around fifteen, of a job as clerk in a linen store there. It is plain that anyone, watching him selling papers efficiently, tactfully, and with the gay boyish charm that would always be his, recognized that he would make an excellent salesman anywhere. Elmer worked for Corless & House about a year.

An incident that occurred about this time was related by an old-timer of Mechanicville. Ellsworth's military yearnings simply had to have an outlet. He was reading and studying all the books on military drills and tactics he could get his hands on. He found them so absorbing that one suspects the eight-hour reading session, when he forgot to feed the pigs, had been spent with a book about something military. Of course he wanted to put his growing knowledge of military drill into action. So he found a group of interested youths at the village of Stillwater, about three miles from Mechanicville, organized them into a military company, and became their drillmaster.

The high-sounding name chosen for this company was the Black Plumed Riflemen of Stillwater. This was the first of the many military groups which Ellsworth was to train, and its members soon developed that enthusiasm for doing stunts to show their physical prowess which would characterize his later trainees. This fact led one day to the great bewilderment of Mr. F. D. Hatfield, who kept a general store in Mechanicville. The store was, of course, on the street floor, but there was an outside door on the second story through which goods for storage were taken in by tackle.

Unknown to the storekeeper, the Black Plumed Rifle-

men of Stillwater had come to Mechanicville that day. One
of the lively young band, or perhaps Ellsworth himself,
noticed the door on the second floor and evidently felt it
would be too bad if that door was left idle. Wouldn't it be
a bright idea to use that door to enter the building instead
of the usual humdrum method of walking in through the
street entrance? How about forming a human ladder and
climbing up over themselves?

Inside, the unsuspecting Mr. Hatfield was suddenly
transfixed. There was a curious bumping on the outside
wall, while overhead a great commotion was breaking out,
with tramping, laughter, and shouts of jubilant young
voices. What in the world was going on up there? He had
not seen anyone going up the stairs. He dashed out front to
investigate just as the last man was pulled through the upstairs doorway. His dumfounded expression doubtless
added the final glee to what the Riflemen felt had been a
most successful day.

This was the first of the exuberant pranks of Ellsworth's
companies which would one day have a climax in his soldiers' suspending themselves from the lofty dome of the
United States Capitol at Washington.

Evidently young Ellsworth saved some money while
he was working for Corless & House at Troy; at least he
managed early in the 1850s to get out into the world beyond his own state. He made a trip West to Wisconsin,
which seemed very remote to New Yorkers in those days.
It is possible he traveled on one of the passenger canal
boats which he used to watch on the Champlain Canal at
Mechanicville. He may have gone by canal as far as Lake
Erie, perhaps sleeping at night on the gentleman's side of
the long, narrow saloon whose lighted window squares
had looked so alluring when the boats passed by at night-
fall. He could, however, have worked his way West, for he

was in his teens already well able to take care of himself.

Satisfactory details again are lacking. But years later in the 1900s, an elderly gentleman named Charles H. Goffe wrote that he had met the teen-age Elmer Ellsworth at Kenosha, Wisconsin, in 1852 or 1853. They were both staying at the same boardinghouse — "Mrs. Bell's," he said — and a rivalry soon developed between them about which had the more expert penmanship. Mr. Goffe, when eighty, still prided himself on his former skill. "I followed Penmanship teaching," he wrote, "while yet in my teens."

Ellsworth, too, in his process of educating himself, had developed into a fine penman. He would later earn his livelihood for a time by copying legal papers. What might be called his dress-parade handwriting was painstaking and artistic, but when he was scribbling a letter in a hurry he used many abbreviations and omitted much punctuation, and the writing varied greatly with his moods. Sometimes it became difficult to read.

He was handwriting-conscious at this time, perhaps because he was still perfecting his art. As a boy will, he practiced writing his name on scraps of paper and even, according to Mr. Goffe, "on the weatherboards of the house, and on gate and fence posts." Both boys bragged about their skill and Elmer challenged Charles to write the name "Elmer E. Ellsworth" "without taking off the pencil." The elderly Mr. Goffe recorded with relish that Ellsworth "was forced to admit I could lay over him."

The two proud teen-agers evidently rubbed each other the wrong way. Charles Goffe thought Ellsworth was standoffish. What Ellsworth thought of Charles it would be interesting to know.

Goffe said in a letter to a newspaper that Ellsworth had been adopted by the Ottawa Indians who lived near Muskegon, Michigan. He was also under the impression that Ellsworth attended the Kenosha High School for a while. But these recollections of a chance encounter were given sixty-four or sixty-five years after the event.

Not long after this incident, Ellsworth returned to Mechanicville and began looking for a job. He then recalled the elderly New York gentleman who had talked with him when he was a train newsboy and who had a store in New York City which might offer opportunities. So the resourceful youth inserted a "personal" in the *New York Herald* and by good fortune the gentleman saw it. He answered it with a letter and the result was that Ellsworth became a clerk in his store.

One joy of living in New York City was that he could learn more about military tactics by attending the drills of the Seventh Regiment, which he did whenever possible. Finally clerking proved too confining and inactive for his taste, so he left the store to join a group of engineers who were working on the improvement of the channel at Hell Gate. With his skill at drawing, it has been suggested that his duties may have been those of a draftsman, but on the other hand he could probably have endured any amount of hard physical labor.

There were, however, almost irresistible forces pushing him back to the West he had visited, that young, new, opening-up country where there might be a better chance to build a future. Going West was in the very air. It was embodied in the well-known counsel of an odd-looking man with a pink, babylike face framed in whiskers who was editor of the *New York Tribune* at this time. His name was Horace Greeley and his usual advice to the ambitious was "Go West, young man."

The idea of heading westward may have lodged in Ellsworth's mind when he was a boy and heard the excited talk in Mechanicville about gold being discovered in California. Few tales could have been more thrilling to the twelve-year-old than those of the gold rush and the forty-niners who could wash out nuggets in troughs and pans and become rich overnight. Youth properly has its visions of a wonderful future and young Ellsworth was more given than most boys to dreams of glory and fortune. And it was a propitious time for adventure.

Ellsworth made his decision to go West. The engineers with whom he had worked on the channel at Hell Gate were going to Chicago and he went with them. He visited the "dear old home stead" in 1854, when he was seventeen, and for a little while his parents had the joy of gazing on the face which was now developing into the handsomeness of young manhood. Then there were tender good-bys and he was gone, not to return for four years.

Chicago became his headquarters, though scraps of rec-ollections indicate he knocked around considerably in these years. An old friend from Mechanicville, Merritt Hutchins, who worked in a railroad office in Chicago in the middle '50s, remembered how Ellsworth came to see him and told him of the deer he had shot in Wisconsin. Ellsworth, who, like Mr. Lincoln, had much curiosity and ingenuity about machinery and devices, had invented a train window-catch or spring and wished to borrow seven dollars from Mr. Hutchins to promote it or sell the patent. Mr. Hutchins was glad to lend him the money.

Possibly it was in connection with this patent that young Ellsworth made the acquaintance of a New Englander about a year older than himself, Arthur F. Devereux, who had also come to Chicago to seek his fortune. The two were especially congenial because Devereux also was in-tensely interested in military matters. He had a patent-soliciting business in Chicago and soon offered Ellsworth a position as clerk in his office.

One wonders a little if Ellsworth had not come to hate

the word "clerk." When he was twenty-one he was to write an intimate friend named Henry Parks about the mental conflict that was always pulling him in opposite directions. "My life has been a constant struggle between duty and inclination," wrote Ellsworth. "My parents . . . should ever be my first care." He mentioned in this same letter that the health of both was "broken," and that they could not stand much adversity. "I want to see them placed beyond the reach of want — relieved from the necessity of future exertion. Now how am I to accomplish this, is it my duty to settle down to some business and plod along till I can realize the accomplishment of my desires or shall I follow my inclination & make a bold push for fortune where I can experience but one of two things success or death."

Duty would always come first with Ellsworth. An opportunity in hand seemed worth two in far-off places, so he went into the patent-soliciting business with Arthur Devereux. They had come to be and would remain devoted friends, both through the disaster which was ahead for them and later through a glorious day of triumph. Ellsworth worked so faithfully he became a partner in the business. It prospered, and he had hopes of accumulating enough money to set himself free. ". . . if I possessed to day ten thousand dollars," he wrote, "I would give every cent to my parents bid them good by and go abroad to earn the right to come home & make *myself* and *another* happy."

These quotations from a letter Ellsworth wrote in 1858 give a number of sidelights on his development. Like Lincoln, he had had to educate himself and to begin by training himself in the use of language. He had learned to speak and write naturally and most effectively, though (again like Lincoln and most of humanity) he would slip up occasionally on the spelling of a word.

He had had an intensive course in the school of experience. He wrote his brother Charley in that same year of 1858, "For four years I have seen every variety of life, and every class of persons; in that time I have lived in experience twenty years." He had matured and realized his own full-grown strength of body and mind and his remarkable ability to lead and influence others. When telling Mr. Parks of his conflict between duty and inclination, he wrote, "Ambition — consciousness of inate power, resistless energy bid me go where it would seem I am most likely to succeed."

So gradually Ellsworth's own letters begin to throw some light back on the period of his life for which information is meager. Help comes too from another source. As many sentimental young people do, he kept invitations and programs as souvenirs of happy occasions. There exists today a little stack of these mementos, faded and discolored with age but each having the touch of his fingers and telling its own story.

An ornamental folded card with tarnished gilt cord and tassels is a dance program of the First Grand Military and Civic Ball of the Cadets of the National Guard. It is dated November 12, 1856, and it reveals a good deal. The Committee of Arrangements includes those two business partners A. F. Devereux and "Capt. E. E. Ellsworth." Captain? If Ellsworth had become a captain, he evidently had formed a military connection. One of the "Managers" of the ball was "Col. R. K. Swift" (later Brigadier General), who in the following year would appoint Ellsworth an aide on his staff with the rank of major. This recognition of the abilities of a nineteen-year-old youth indicates considerable social progress.

This impression is strengthened by another souvenir of three months later. It is an engraved invitation (adorned with an elaborate picture in which soldiers, flags and scrolls are gracefully intertwined) to the Anniversary Ball at the

Light Guard Armory in February, 1857, which suggests that Ellsworth was fairly well situated at this time.

Then, in a letter to his "Friend Parks," already quoted, he poured out his story of a disaster which overwhelmed him. He had been working unmercifully hard — "how I labored," he said, "what I suffered & what privation I endured God & myself only knew." A point had almost been reached where he expected to have enough for his parents' protection; he could soon "place them in circumstances which would leave me at liberty." In "an evil hour," he wrote, he had put his trust in "an infernal scound[rel]" and was "robbed" of everything. He continued, in an agitated handwriting. In one moment, he said, he "saw the reward of the years' toil fade . . . when about to grasp it." The name of the thief is not given. He has been referred to as "an agent" and the supposition is that Devereux and Ellsworth entrusted their accumulated funds to him, only to have him steal them. The firm was ruined. Suddenly Ellsworth found himself without a position and with no means.

It was a terrible shock to young Ellsworth, with his ideals of honor, to have one in whom he had placed his confidence betray him. The psychological effect was to make him very bitter, moody, and for a while, suspicious of everyone. "I hardly dare to trust myself to form an ardent friendship," he wrote Mr. Parks. To another he later described his state of mind after this great disillusionment: ". . . I acknowledged no friend, and within myself held all at defiance, and goaded on almost to madness by disappointment and misfortune bid fate do its worst. This was not the result of *trivial disappointment or trouble*, but in consequence of *suffering most terrible* rendered more *poignant* by a pride which forced me to bear in silence and alone, what now seems utterly impossible."

The material effect was as devastating as the psychological. He was not only penniless; he was left in debt, an intolerable situation to one of his strict integrity. He explained that when "fortune seemed about to smile on me . . . I cursed myself with a paltry debt." He had been denying himself everything in the way of comfort, but when prospects looked so bright he had borrowed enough "to live like a human being for a few days." He had promised to repay the loan at a definite time, then the crash of his business came and he could not.

His creditors gave him rough treatment. He was exposed, he wrote, "to the insults & infernal stare of those who did not know me," who thought "that I had no right to hold up my head or look like other men," and "attacked me like a pack of hungry wolves." Language in those days was inclined to be melodramatic.

These words and other comments he made suggest that people may have associated him with the dishonesty of the villain in the case. He was possibly left in a false position and it is certain that in the months that followed he had to fight slanders accusing him of all kinds of vices. There may be special significance in the strong warning he gave his brother Charley the following year about the dangers of running around with people of bad traits because he would then by association be thought guilty of the same evil qualities.

At all events, the experience was a long-drawn-out nightmare to him. He would pay his debts if he had to starve — which he very nearly did. The recollection of the years which reached a climax with this disaster would always be bitter; he felt, as he wrote, that he had been "the *sport* and *foot-ball* of fortune."

Ellsworth defended himself for being so resentful and gloomy, which may indicate he felt guilty about harboring such emotions. "Let some one," he wrote ". . . who prates so learnedly of the happiness of success, let such a one sacrifice *every thing* for some great purpose, *commit no wrong* & receive in return the treatment I have *borne* & see how quickly it will destroy philosophy."

He was only twenty when he received this shock, and the unexpected heartwarming influence which would help bring him back to a happier outlook was still a year in the future.

5

❖
❖

An Invitation with Hidden Importance

One immediate effect of Ellsworth's financial downfall is
clear in an incident which later in his diary he described
as having happened in 1857. Disillusioned, penniless, and in
debt, he resolved not to accept any hospitality or favors
which he was not able to return. It seems a foolish, youthful
resolution, for he was almost starving and had many genuine friends who would have been only too glad to help
him. But that unyielding pride would not let him reveal
his situation to them.

There was no barrier of pride between Ellsworth and his
diary, however; he made it his confidant. On April 12,
1859, he wrote in it: ". . . two years ago, when I was so
poor — one day went into an eating house on some errand
while there Clybourn & several friends came in." James A.
Clybourn was to be a member of that company which in
almost exactly sixteen months would give the brilliant
Zouave drill in Major Iles's vacant lot on South Sixth Street
in Springfield.

Ellsworth's diary continues: ". . . as I started to go out
they stopped me & insisted upon my having an Oyster stew
with them I refused — for I always made it a principle
never to accept even an apple from any one because I
could not return like courtesies — while they were clamoring about the matter & I trying to get away from them, the

waiter brought on stews for the whole party — having
taken it for granted that I was going to stay." Clybourn
told Ellsworth that he could go, if he wished, but that he,
Clybourn, would pay for the stew anyway, "so," Ellsworth
wrote, "to escape making my self any more conspicuous by
further refusal I sat down. How gloriously every morsel
tasted — the first food I had touched in three days &
nights."

When he again had funds, as he tells in his diary, "I
sought James out & told him I owed him half a dollar he
said I did not." Ellsworth, who of all men delighted in being generous to his friends with no thought of any return,
would not see James's point of view and made him take the
money.

The shock of his disillusionment had left its mark on
him. He himself, two years later, had some mature reflections on the results of such a psychological jolt. It has one
of two effects, he wrote, it either "breaks all principles of
good, — eradicates all the better feelings from the heart of
man, and if he be possessed of strong passions, make him a
very demon in human form," or it "while it tortures, makes
him self-reliant, — the very extent of his suffering makes
him more readily sympathize with others, and the hollow-
hearted selfishness of the majority of the world in which he
moves thus made apparent to him, without dispossessing
him of his better impulses and feelings, makes him *lock
them* in *his heart*, as the only tie which binds him to his
God."

In the four years from 1854 to 1858 young Ellsworth
thought he had "lived in experience twenty years." During
these years in Chicago he had not forgotten for a moment
his longing for a military career. That was one thing that
made his work with Arthur Devereux in the patent-soliciting business, otherwise so intolerable to him. Any occupa-

tion not connected with the military was frustrating to this youth, "who," as John Hay once said, "knew that God had made him a soldier."

He had continued studying the leading books on military tactics until he knew them by heart. One, the first standard set of American drill regulations, was by General Winfield Scott, then a sort of elder statesman of the military world who was usually called "Old Fuss and Feathers." The other leading book, Hardee's *Tactics*, became the textbook for the United States Army about this time; its author, Colonel William J. Hardee, was the commandant of cadets at West Point. Ellsworth, bent intently over these two volumes, did not know that one day he would stand at West Point before those well-known author-officers and put his famous company through their drills for them. And the time was to come when he would write his own *Manual of Arms*.

He had been able to drill the Black Plumed Riflemen of Stillwater when he was about fifteen, and when he came to Chicago and continued to enlarge his military knowledge, he was inevitably to come into demand as a drillmaster for volunteer military companies.

The uniformed volunteer company was a remarkable institution of this period and its conspicuous presence in every town and city had been a strong influence in stimulating Ellsworth's military propensity. Its members were not the minuteman type of militia, who were citizens subject to call in an emergency. The military companies were composed of men who enjoyed the things that go with soldiering and therefore voluntarily formed these companies. They wore striking uniforms, practiced intricate drills, and were called upon by their own town or city to parade on every possible occasion. There was a distinct social cast to the organizations; as a general thing only young men from families of social standing belonged. Their armories were much like men's clubs and, as seen from Ellsworth's souvenir invitations, they gave most elaborate balls. To belong required a certain amount of money (alas for Ellsworth!), since they paid their own expenses, and their uniforms and other accoutrements were costly. Ellsworth was too poor to join such a company — his connection was to come in another way.

The impressive titles which these companies selected usually included the name of their town — the "Elgin Continentals," the "Rockford City Greys," the "Springfield Cadets." Each town was proud of its company and watched its public drills with great applause and yells of approval. Contests in drills between the companies of different towns became very popular and drew the same sort of huge, wildly enthusiastic crowds seen today at baseball and football games. Any new, exciting feature in drilling, any special expertness, drew a throng of admiring spectators. The military companies furnished a lot of entertainment to the public in the 1840s and 1850s.

And, in addition, they constituted a trained and equipped militia which would be available in time of crisis or war. Each state was supposed to have its own militia but these had for the most part fallen into such disorganization and neglect that for practical purposes they amounted to very little. In emergencies there might be a genuine need for these volunteer companies — the forerunners, incidentally, of our National Guard.

Naturally each of these companies needed someone to train it, a man who was an expert in military tactics and preferably one who was a magnetic leader. Ellsworth qualified eminently on both counts. In those years in Chicago his interest soon drew him into military circles. This explains why, as early as 1856, he was attending the First Grand Military and Civic Ball of the Cadets of the National Guard. There was to be a mention in Ellsworth's *Manual of*

Arms that he drilled these same cadets in July of the following year, 1857.

His drawings of soldiers in his schoolbooks had revealed Ellsworth's love of uniforms. Furthermore, he liked uniforms that had style and color. It was part of the romantic approach to warfare; war was glamourized and poetized with such trappings as sweeping plumes, flowing sashes, golden spurs, and flashing sabers.

The Civil War, only four years in the future when Ellsworth was twenty, has been called the last romantic war, fought in the grand manner. Many of its ideas and ideals seem more closely related to the age of chivalry than to those of today. Though patriotism and heroism remain the same, the approach to mechanized warfare has to be different. In the performance of his duties the leader of a tank corps does not, as did General J. E. B. Stuart, wear a ribbon love knot in his lapel and a hat with a long sweeping plume. Ellsworth, growing up in the taste patterns of his time, absorbed a sense of honor and chivalry which was to make him, on some occasions, seem like one of King Arthur's knights born into the wrong century.

It is not strange that the terms "knightly" and "knight errant" have been frequently applied to Colonel Ellsworth. He was definitely influenced by the legends of King Arthur and his Knights of the Round Table. In the late '50s, Tennyson was publishing his first *Idylls of the King* which became immediately popular. Ellsworth read and loved the stately measures of Tennyson's *Idylls*.

Another influence, a far-reaching one, also came from abroad — the newspapers had much to say between 1854 and 1856 about the Crimean War. It was probably in newspaper accounts of this war that Ellsworth saw for the first time the name Zouave. The name came from a mountain tribe in Algeria, the Zouaves, whose soldiers had a special method of fighting which made them remarkably effective.

They were so successful, in fact, that regiments of French soldiers adopted their system and were also called Zouaves. These French Zouave regiments distinguished themselves in the Crimean War and became famous, especially the one called the Chasseurs de Vincennes.

The Zouave regiments had two striking features, their brilliantly colored uniforms and their special system of military tactics. The Zouave drill, which required superb physical fitness and perfection of training, was a spectacular performance calculated to surpass all other drills. Ellsworth's mounting excitement can be imagined: oh, if he could only find out more about this marvelous drill and introduce it in the United States! He must learn more about these Zouaves.

Unknown to him, fate was bringing across the ocean and to Chicago itself the very person who could answer all his questions, Charles A. DeVilliers, who had served as surgeon in a French Zouave regiment in the Crimean War. Possibly the two first met because Ellsworth wanted to take fencing lessons and DeVilliers was an expert swordsman. Under DeVilliers' instruction Ellsworth did become one of the most skillful fencers in Chicago and at the same time he learned innumerable details about the Zouaves. Why were those scarlet trousers so loose and baggy and why did the dark blue, gold-trimmed jacket and blue shirt have no collars? The answer was that no one could do the exacting Zouave drill in a stiff, tight uniform; a Zouave had to have complete freedom of motion to go through his maneuvers. This fact was possibly the starting point in Ellsworth's mind that there was need for some kind of dress reform in the United States, a conviction which was to have an amusing aspect when this intrepid young man came to reflect upon the unwholesome fashion by which women then laced themselves into tight corsets.

After talking with DeVilliers, Ellsworth, sent to France

for books about the Zouave system. He studied French long enough to read them, probably having DeVilliers' help in both the study and the reading. By this time it is evident that young Ellsworth had an unusual mind and ceaseless energy; it will be seen that he also budgeted his time almost to the minute. The result was amazing accomplishment in a short period.

Ellsworth mastered the intricate Zouave drill as he had already mastered those of Hardee and Scott. One striking characteristic of the drill was the division of companies into squads of four men each, thus forming an unusual fighting unit. The squad was rather like an individual with eyes and arms on all four sides. It could act as a formidable whole in attack and, when defending itself, it could face in all directions at once. When Ellsworth came to write his book on the Zouave tactics, he began the first lesson thus: "The Manual of arms will be taught to four men, at first in one rank. . . . After causing the squad of four men to execute one command several times, until they comprehend it, cause another squad to take their place, and in turn execute the same command."

The system required a training for the four comrades in battle which was far beyond that usually given to soldiers. Studying the movements given in the *Manual,* one understands why those bright-colored uniforms had to be as unimpeding as gymnasium suits. The drill was in truth the most strenuous of gymnastic exercises. The Zouaves were taught to load and fire on the run, while lying down, or kneeling — in short, in every possible position. They must also be perfect in the deadly art of using the bayonet, an art that took endless practice in itself. And all these maneuvers must be executed with incredible rapidity.

For the public exhibitions so dear to the military companies, Ellsworth was to drill his men in formations which, while they undoubtedly helped to build up muscles of steel, were meant to be mainly spectacular. Such were the double crosses, the revolving circles and the pyramids already mentioned. These figures, dissolving one into another, were beautiful and graceful in themselves and thus a means of delighting the crowds and arousing interest in military matters.

Having learned all he could about the Zouave drill, Ellsworth tried it out on classes in the gymnasium. Word of this new, exciting drill and its interesting young advocate got around in military circles in whch he was now fairly well established.

By December, 1857, he was being addressed as Major Ellsworth, for that devoted friend General R. K. Swift, whom he once affectionately described as "bluff, hearty, and good natured," had appointed him an aide on his staff with this rank. Military companies were accustomed to having banquets as well as balls, and in that month the Rockford City Greys decided to give a banquet, inviting military men from neighboring towns and cities in northern Illinois. So there came to Major Ellsworth an invitation to attend a fine banquet at the Holland House in Rockford. It was for him an invitation with hidden importance.

One can take a close look at Major Ellsworth as he stood among those assembled in the Holland House on that December evening more than a century ago. This can be done through the eyes of a member of the Rockford Greys who was present and later wrote about the event.

The name of this particular Grey was Frank E. Peats. In his account of the occasion he uses the phrases dear to the period: there were present "fair women and brave men" who could "trip the light fantastic" while they were enjoying a "flow of soul." Frank Peats speaks of Ellsworth in a tone of affection, as he was to come to know him well shortly thereafter. "Let me present him as he appeared to me that evening," he says, and then in flowery language he gives the details which bring the "boyish figure" to life: "a well-balanced head crowned by a wealth of dark brown hair that fell in careless clinging curls about his neck, eyes of dark hazel, that sparkled and flashed with excitement or melted with tenderness," the generous mouth with "lips full and red" and "teeth of dazzling whiteness" that were revealed by the quick, winning smile or laugh. "Thus stood Major Ellsworth as I saw him then," wrote Mr. Peats of the Rockford Greys.

He also told what happened at the banquet. At one point in the ceremonies, "according to an ancient precedent . . . the captain of the 'Greys' tendered the command of his company to either of the numerous guests present, but they all declined by saying 'We beg to be excused while Major Ellsworth is present.' " (Judging by what happened later, they may have been trying the young man out.) Ellsworth accepted the captain's invitation and, turning to the Rockford Greys, who were lined up in readiness, he began to give his commands. A little start of astonishment went over the whole group at the power of his voice, "which," Mr. Peats said, "Could have been distinctly heard at a distance of four blocks away."

That banquet was probably the pleasantest thing that had happened to Ellsworth for quite a while. The Rockford Greys were captivated with him and invited him to spend several months as their drillmaster the following summer, an invitation he was glad to accept.

It was in this way that Ellsworth came to Rockford, Illinois, which was to be the city of his romance.

❖
❖❖
❖

6

Enter Carrie

THE New Year of 1858 came in with Ellsworth's problems unsolved. He was still torn between his overwhelming desire for a military career and the obligation to get established in some regular position where he could care financially for his parents. At times he was not even able to take adequate care of himself, though he earned something with his gymnastic classes and by giving fencing lessons. This new year, when he would be twenty-one, was to add another complication to his situation. While it was to be the most glorious thing that had happened to him, it was nonetheless a complication which would deflect him further from the route he wanted to take.

A young man trying to choose and start his life work is likely to dream of various rosy possibilities. His ideas are, of course, conditioned by "the world in which he moves," to use Ellsworth's own expression. He is necessarily limited by the thought patterns, circumstances, and events of the period in which he exists. Many a man's life is an epitome of the history of his time and this is extraordinarily true in the case of Elmer Ellsworth.

Beginning in 1858 and continuing into 1860, one finds various references in Ellsworth's letters to what might be called his Mexican dream. This was what he was referring to when he spoke of "a bold push for fortune" in his letter to his friend Parks. Following that phrase he explained, "I go — say to Mexico in two or three years realize a competency & a name [and] return & make my parents happy."

Many a youth was thinking along these lines at the time; it was an age for adventurous young men to make their fortunes in a young country which was rapidly expanding. In the 1840s Texas had been annexed and the settlement of the Mexican War had resulted in the United States acquiring California and New Mexico. Even as the treaty of peace was ratified, gold was discovered in California and fortune-hunters began pouring West.

Expansion was in the air. A new term arose, "manifest destiny." People had come to believe that it was the manifest destiny of the young United States to expand its territory. Coupled with this was a strong feeling that it was also the mission of the United States to take over Mexico and thus fulfill its expansionist destiny, while at the same time satisfying a certain missionary zeal by civilizing a poor and backward people. Following the Mexican War many adventurers had gone to Mexico, seeking their fortunes.

Ellsworth did not explain all this when he spoke of going to Mexico in his letters — his correspondents knew what he meant. But he did explain his plan in detail to John Hay later, when it became full-fledged, and John Hay put the explanation in an article he wrote for the *Atlantic Monthly* of July, 1861. Nothing could plunge one more quickly into the mental atmosphere of the time than Hay's words describing Ellsworth's Mexican dream: "His clear, bold, and thoroughly executive mind planned a magnificent scheme of commercial enterprise, which, having its centre of operations at Guaymas, should ramify through the golden wastes that stretch in silence and solitude along the tortuous banks of the Rio San José. This was to be the beginning and ostensible end of the enterprise. Then he dreamed of the influence of American arts and American energy penetrating into the twilight of that decaying nationality, and saw the natural course of events leading on, first, Emigration, then Protection, and at last Annexation. Yet there was no thought of conquest or rapine. The idea was essentially American and Northern." And, it might be added, it was considered a very patriotic idea in the '50s.

The Mexican plan was in Ellsworth's mind when he was twenty-one, living sketchily in Chicago and trying hard to get a foothold on some kind of ladder which would lead upward to success. Probably the most satisfying subject he had to think of on his twenty-first birthday, April 11, 1858, was the prospect of drilling the Rockford Greys that summer. That would be a military activity. It would be fine if he could somehow make a quick fortune in Mexico, but nothing could give him complete fulfillment but a military career. He looked forward to Rockford especially because he was going to teach the new Zouave drill.

Major Ellsworth went to Rockford probably around the first of June. Fortune was still using him as a "foot-ball," giving him a very disagreeable experience shortly after he arrived. According to a newspaper account written some years later, a journalist friend took him to a reception at a young ladies' seminary. (This was doubtless the Rockford Seminary which had a student destined to become important in this story.) At one point, Ellsworth, who loved fresh air, trees, and flowers, went outside to look around the grounds, "which were very handsomely laid out." As he walked along he accidentally brushed against a farmer who had come into town that day. A few minutes after they passed each other the farmer discovered that his watch was not in its accustomed pocket. He at once jumped to the conclusion that the young man who had just passed had robbed him so he promptly fetched the sheriff, who arrested Ellsworth. Ellsworth, very indignant, demanded to be taken before the proper authorities, where he identified himself and was cleared. The Justice discharged him, whereupon he demanded an apology from the farmer. The farmer refused in a "most offensive style." Ellsworth then turned to the Justice and asked, "Squire, how much will it cost to whip this man?" The Squire looked from Ellsworth's five feet six "to the farmer's stalwart six feet of stature and replied while he smiled, 'Oh, I wouldn't do anything of that kind, Major,' adding significantly, however: 'It won't cost much, though.'"

Ellsworth then told the farmer he would give him until sundown to apologize. The six-footer sneered and walked out. Ellsworth rejoined his journalist friend (who may well have been the one who wrote about the incident) and the two went to the sheriff to ask if he had heard anything about the farmer's watch.

"Yes," said the sheriff, "the fact is he never lost his watch; I met him just now, and he told me it was all right; he had dropped it into the pocket in the side of his trousers instead of the watch pocket and he found it there, all right. I told him he ought to hunt you up and make a public apology to you, but he swore he wouldn't."

Ellsworth and his friend started off to see the farmer again. They found him with a crowd of his friends. Ellsworth again asked him to apologize. "The big fellow looked down upon the little man with contempt, and again declined to do what was demanded. The next instant he was sprawling in the gutter; he got up but 'took another tumble,' and still a third, and in less than five minutes and before his astonished friends could interfere, he was a badly whipped countryman." He could have sympathized with the schoolboy who called Elmer an "oyster keg."

The Rockford City Greys had rented an armory on South Main Street. Knowing that it would take prolonged, intensive practice to master the Zouave drill, Major Ellsworth first exacted a promise from the Greys that they would sacrifice all else to their desire to learn it. He was proving a very strict disciplinarian. "All summer long," said the *Rockford Register-Gazette* later, in an article on "The Old City Greys," "they drilled in that hot room every week night, except Saturday night."

This was the summer when people were much excited over attempts to lay the Atlantic cable. Efforts to complete it the year before had failed and now in June the cable broke again. To have a cable across the ocean seemed a very wonderful thing and public interest was intense. So there was much jubilation when word came to Rockford in August that the Atlantic cable had been successfully completed. England and America rejoiced, and Queen Victoria and President Buchanan exchanged greetings by telegraph. As its part of that rejoicing Rockford planned to have an evening celebration with speeches, cheers, and the firing of cannon.

Would the Greys get that evening off from drill to attend the festivities? They would not. A military man carries out his duties regardless of his personal wishes. The Greys went through their perspiring drill within hearing of the cheers and the booming of the cannon. It took unremitting work like this to perfect the Zouave drill, a fact which becomes clear when one studies the involved movements described in Ellsworth's *Manual of Arms*.

It was soon apparent that the drills were ruining the social life of Rockford. How could young ladies go to summer evening parties without escorts? How could there even be parties when the pick of the town's young masculine eligibles were tied up every night with drilling? Major Ellsworth was soon encountering a subtle force he had not met before, the power of feminine revolt. Dire reprisals were threatened unless something was done to alleviate the manless situation of the town.

Something was done. A corner of the armory was fitted up as a reception room and here the ladies and all others interested were invited to watch the drills. This, continued the *Rockford Register-Gazette*, proved to be the most popular corner in the city from then on. Major Ellsworth now had an added problem in discipline. With this lovely audience of girls in the corner, of course the eyes of the Greys would occasionally turn in that direction, but the commanding officer would immediately recall those straying eyes with "Come, look around here and tend to business."

It is likely that before long he became more sympathetic to the Greys whose eyes were drawn toward that magnetic corner. The fifteen-year-old daughter of a Rockford banker whose family was prominent in the social life of the town could hardly have failed to attend those fascinating drills. It is even possible she had been among the "fair women" present at the banquet of the Rockford Greys the previous December and had, like Mr. Peats on that occasion, gazed with irresistible attraction at the soldierly form and handsome face of young Major Ellsworth.

Her name was Caroline Spafford, but her family and friends called her "Carrie" or "Kitty." Like Ellsworth himself, she was not entirely satisfied with the way her parents had arranged her name. They had neglected to give her a middle name, so she had adopted a middle initial "M."

It is not possible to know the exact occasion on which Ellsworth first met Carrie Spafford. She would have been prettily dressed in the tight-waisted bodice and wide-spreading skirts of the period. Her daguerreotype shows a beautiful young face, sensitive and intelligent. There is sincerity in the gaze of the large blue eyes and a girlish sweetness about the mouth. Her complexion is fair and her cheeks have scarcely lost the roundness of childhood.

She was dainty and small, just the right height to walk beside a fine military figure of five feet six. One suspects that young Major Ellsworth would not have lingered long in the company of a girl who towered above him. His artistic sense, his instinct for the fitness of things, not to mention his pride, would all have rejected such a situation. Everything about Carrie was satisfactory and winsome.

After Ellsworth became acquainted with her he was to be seen frequently at the hospitable Spafford home at 220 South Madison Street. It was a large, comfortable-looking house with a pleasing little cupola on top. It was just such a home as would be expected of a well-to-do banker like Charles H. Spafford, who had a young growing family. Carrie, born December 2, 1842, was the eldest; she had a sister Mary and a brother Charles. The fourth child, as yet unsuspected, would be a baby girl born in April, 1860. Ellsworth by that time was to be so much a member of the family that he would have the privilege of naming the baby — he named her Eugenia.

The Spaffords had the kind of home that Ellsworth would have wished for his overworked, ailing parents at Mechanicville. It held the kind of family he could well have wished he might have been born into. The Spaffords were sterling, warmhearted, interesting people who had all the privileges of money, culture, social position, and everything that makes up a gracious mode of living.

There were distinguished ancestors. Carrie's mother had been Miss Abigail Warren of Boston, a granddaughter of Dr. John Warren, famous surgeon in the American Revolution. This made her the grandniece of Dr. Joseph Warren who fell at the Battle of Bunker Hill. Undoubtedly Carrie and Ellsworth had much to say to each other about their Revolutionary ancestors. Mrs. Spafford was a very able and warmly understanding woman to whom Ellsworth was soon to give his complete confidence and affection. Of Carrie's father he was to write, "He is certainly a noble hearted man

if one lives on earth." These fine people soon took young
Major Ellsworth to their hearts.

He saw much of Carrie that summer and learned much
more about her. She was a student at the Rockford Seminary, which Ellsworth highly approved. This was still an
age when many people thought that "females" should not
trouble their weak little minds with anything intellectual —
that they should have no interests outside of woman's domestic sphere. There was none of this belief in Ellsworth;
he had a strong conviction that girls should study and develop their mental powers to the fullest extent. Nothing
bored him more, as he was to state in somewhat vigorous
language in one of his letters, than a tête-à-tête with a fluffy-
minded, affected, coquettish female.

Two years later Ellsworth told Carrie how she impressed
and interested him when they first met. If he sounds a bit
stilted and somewhat analytical, this was in accordance
with the taste of the age. "I studied your character as far as
possible," he wrote, "and my conclusion was that in the
*happy combination of the natural qualities that form the base
of a perfect character you were superior to any one I had
ever met.* I thought you *embodied the elements* of a *true
woman.*" Carrie being so very young, he continued, "I *pictured to myself* what you *might* become." Such was the
way in which this lover of the mid-nineteenth century told
his girl that she had everything!

With the Rockford Greys becoming more and more pro-
ficient in the Zouave drill and with Ellsworth in and out at
the Spaffords' until their house seemed a second home, it
was a wonderful summer. And it was to have a glorious
finale. When a military company had made itself perfect in
a spectacular new drill, of course some other companies
must be invited to come and see it perform.

The Rockford Greys planned to go into camp at the fair
grounds in September, invite military guests, and hold a

celebration of four days as a grand finale to their training under Major Ellsworth. Elaborate programs were printed for the event.

Carrie saved a copy of that program. It is one of a great mass of papers preserved by her and her family, now called the Godfrey Collection, which is so useful today in recovering Ellsworth's personality and story. The program is headed *Camp Sinnissippi* and is adorned with a picture of the American eagle against a background of eight banners. The dates are September 22, 23, 24, and 25, 1858. Beneath the dates is the name "MAJOR E. E. ELLSWORTH COMMANDANT." The "Companies from abroad" are the National Guard Cadets of Chicago and the Washington Continental Artillery of Elgin. Their arrival on the first day is to be celebrated by a "Grand Full Dress Parade through the city."

Rockford had an exciting time during those four days. The "Battalion Drill" came on Thursday, September 23. The climax came on Friday, when (here the program changed to large red letters) the Rockford Greys went through the entire Zouave drill of the "Chasseurs de Vincennes of the French Army."

That thrilling Friday ended with a party. Folded into another copy of the program is a note of invitation in a small, ladylike handwriting which strongly resembles Carrie's. The note is addressed to "Major E. E. Ellsworth Commandant of Camp Sinnissippi" and "respectfully" invites him and the company under his command to a party "to be given by the Ladies of this City at Metropolitan Hall on Friday evening" at eight o'clock. There is no signature; merely "By order of the Committee of Invitations." It must have been quite a festive occasion, with the girls in their lovely party dresses, the young men in their dazzling uniforms, and over all youth, gaiety, and romance.

One of the visiting companies was evidently honored in a special fashion. The story has come down in Carrie's family that she presented a flag to the Chicago Cadets of the National Guard, from the porch of the Spafford home on Madison Street, and the evidence seems to pin the time down to that gala four days in September, 1858, when the Cadets were in Rockford. The story pictures a delightful scene, the company in bright uniforms drawn up in front of the Spafford home, the lovely young girl on the porch making her graceful little speech of presentation, the handsome Major Ellsworth giving an eloquent response.

This is preserved in a scribbled manuscript without date and addressed only to "Lady." It thanks her for the gift of a "rich and beautiful flag" to the "Cadets of the National Guard." It continues: "Believe me that it will always be cherished . . . as the flag . . . without a blot upon its fair escutcheon of the country to which we are proud to owe our birth." After a further patriotic passage, the manuscript ends with the promise "never to dishonor the gift of the *fair donor.*"

Major Ellsworth at Rockford may well have had an increasing sense of the importance of his work in military training. He may by 1858 have recognized, as he assuredly did later, that his country was drifting toward civil war. People in the latter part of that summer were much excited about the public debates between two prominent politicians in Illinois, Mr. Abraham Lincoln and Mr. Stephen A. Douglas. These two had much to say about slavery and the extension of slavery in the territories and the United States was obviously dividing over the question of slavery.

Ellsworth could not have failed to read in the papers about a speech Mr. Lincoln made on June 16. He had said at Springfield: " 'A house divided against itself cannot stand.' I believe this government cannot endure, permanently half *slave* and half *free.*"

Was the government Ellsworth's great-grandfather had fought for to fall? If it became necessary for the United

States to fight to preserve their union, trained soldiers would be needed. Ellsworth knew that the regular state militia was so badly disorganized at this time as to be of little use in case of war and that it was a vital service to train volunteer military companies.

The Rockford Greys had come to respect their young commander. To show their appreciation of what he had done for them, they decided in October to present him with a handsome gold watch "as a token of their regard for him as a gentleman and a soldier." One can imagine what a glow this brought to the responsive face of the young man who had been so embittered and disillusioned the year before.

Several things had happened in Rockford which were affecting Ellsworth's spirit. One was his feeling of triumph and fulfillment when he saw the Greys whom he had trained give his Zouave drill to the applause and cheers of the watching crowd. Another was being accepted so warmly into the household of the Spaffords, who treated him, as he said that fall, like "a son or brother." The third was knowing Carrie; Carrie, who was so pretty, bright, and understanding. There may well have been a telltale light in the eyes of those two young people who had stood on the Spafford porch at the time the flag was presented and made such a fine picture together that day.

Ellsworth's work with the Rockford Greys was now finished. When the last heart-tugging good-bys had been said as he left Rockford, it is not clear how far the romance had progressed. But Ellsworth and Carrie were entering — to use a line from their current poet, Mr. Tennyson — "In that new world which is the old."

7

"Should Your Father Be Displeased"

November of 1858 found Ellsworth in a new city. The time has at last been reached when one can follow his thoughts and activities through his letters, and from now on he practically tells his own story. Appropriately the first letter is to Carrie and it is headed "Capitol House Madison Wis. Nov. 6th, 1858."

Much can be gathered about the status of the romance from the self-conscious beginning. He is not sure what salutation to use. He writes first in sweeping letters "Miss Carrie Sppafford" — with two *p*'s. This is followed by a hesitating, unflourished "Miss — Carrie —"; then, below this, and evidently with his mind made up, he writes firmly "My Dearest Friend." Comparing these terms with the ardent ones later to be used in his letters, one can feel quite sure they were not yet engaged.

Ellsworth undoubtedly realized that this new interest in his life was one of which he should have steered clear. Without a permanent occupation, and so far failing to establish himself firmly enough to help his parents, he was certainly in no position to marry, especially to marry one like Carrie, who was used to everything a girl could wish for. This love interest was adding a tremendous complication to the "constant struggle between duty and inclination" which was already with him.

He was even not sure that he ought to be writing to Carrie, for he says, "Should your Father be displeased at my writing this letter, I trust you will tell me so frankly, I would not willingly do aught, which to him, might appear like a disposition to take advantage of his kindness." A young man in those days had to get a father's permission to court his daughter and he was even supposed to get the father's consent to correspond with her.

The fear of Mr. Spafford's displeasure, however, is not stopping Ellsworth. He is not only writing this letter (which is a very long one), but he mentions to Carrie that about ten days before he had written a letter to her which she had evidently not received. "In making another attempt," he continues, "I must confess, that I do so, with the conviction that I shall be unable to interest you, as I exhausted all my store of originality in my first attempt."

Ellsworth reveals that his spirits are low. It had rained almost continually since he arrived and as for Madison, "a more unloveable place can scarcely be imagined. At least, that is the opinion of a stranger, who spends his valuable time in his own room, in study, or in the armory, teaching the adult idea how to shoot." He concedes that the town "must be very beautiful in mid summer," but he can find nothing good to say about it on a rainy day in November.

The trouble with Madison was plainly that Carrie was not in it. Ellsworth comes as near as he dares to saying that: "Perhaps, if I were . . . surrounded by pleasant friends — and all my hopes centered here, I might fancy, Madison a Paradise, while standing six inches deep in the mud."

He gives a full account of what he is doing. As Carrie is aware, it had been his intention to go to Indiana, and he would have done so "had I not received a proposition, so advantageous to myself, that it would have been folly to refuse; and in consequence of which, I am located here untill the 1st of January." Just why he had planned to go to Indiana he does not state; probably after his success as drillmaster at Rockford he was receiving other offers. "I leave you to judge," he continues, "whether I am busy or not, when I tell you, I am instructing the Governor's Guards, a Cavalry company, and giving ten fencing lessons every day, besides filling up odd moments by drilling a company of cadets. . . . Two months more of such work will make me look like the ghost of tribulation."

Madison had recently had the excitement and oratory of an election and Ellsworth had been getting what was perhaps his first close-up view of politics in action. He waxes somewhat sarcastic as he speaks of "low political tricksters" and their humbug. "However," he says, "election is concluded — candidates have descended from their lofty flights to the realms of reason. . . . All seem to have awakened to the fact, that they have something else to do, besides holding half drunken sovereigns by the button hole, and inquiring with the most affecting solicitude, after the welfare of their interesting families; and paying endless sums for *refreshments*, by way of procuring their disinterested devotion to the cause of Liberty, Truth, and justice."

What irked Ellsworth particularly was that politics had invaded military affairs. Under the militia laws of Wisconsin all appointments above the rank of captain were in the hands of the governor. This resulted in the appointment of officers who had little or no military knowledge or training, a situation which it was very hard for Ellsworth to endure.

He did not like the emphasis on rank and position that he was encountering either. He was staying at a hotel when he started the letter and was getting acquainted, as he says, "with any quantity of Honorables, Judges, Generals etc. It is a slight peculiarity of this place, that every man sports a title, of more or less magnitude; and members of the state

Legislature, (pardon the expression) are *lying* about loose, so that one is almost afraid, to address a stranger by the old fashioned title of Mister."

It is not to be wondered at that Ellsworth, with his overcrowded schedule, had to write this letter "at odd moments" over three days. During this time, he says, "the Regiment" had to move into camp under a most disagreeable rain. The next item is more cheerful: "Immediately after our arrival at the Camp, I received a very flattering invitation, to assume the command of the encampment." Overworked he was, but he adds, "I have the satisfaction of knowing that I am laboring for a worthy purpose."

There is a self-conscious quality to this letter which was soon to disappear in his correspondence with Carrie. He accuses himself of "dull loquacity" and makes an effort to be light and humorous about it. "If any of your acquaintances, are ambitious of becoming renowned in the medical world," he says, "cut this letter in small slips, and give it to them with directions to administer as a narcotic, in doses, to suit patients, and their reputation is made."

On the last page his homesickness for Carrie and her family spills over. "I should like very much, to pay a flying visit to Rockford," he begins. "But at present it is impossible as I cannot leave here, excepting on sundays." He seemed to be afraid Carrie might not understand how hard-driven he was. What did the young girl know of the hardships he had been through and how much she and her family meant to him? "To you Carrie," he says, "whose good fortune it is, to be surrounded by kind friends, who are ever ready to soothe your slightest sorrow and chase away with loving hands the semblance of a care, It may seem impossible, that others, who to all casual observers, wear a happy, careless expression, go through the world perhaps, separated from friends, experiencing none of those invaluable pleasures, and privileges of home: which are never appreciated untill lost, alone in the most desolate sense of the word: so seldom experiencing any symphathy, that the slightest act of *unselfish* kindness, goes straight to the heart, and is treasured up, and an importance attached to it, which you cannot understand, untill you in time have had (what God grant you may never know) . . . experience of the dark side of life." He tells her that if she had known desolation like this, "you would then understand how I treasure up the remembrance of the kindness of yourself, your Mother and Father, and how gladly, I shall avail myself of every opportunity to prove the depth of my gratitude."

As with the salutation, he seems uncertain just how much warmth to put into the closing of the letter. He decides to use restraint and concludes: "I hope to hear from you very soon. Till then adieu, Ellsworth."

Nine days after he wrote thus to Carrie he received a letter from his mother which cut him to the quick. Some busybody had taken it upon herself to tell Mrs. Ellsworth it did seem that, if her eldest son had the proper respect for his parents, he would come to see them occasionally. His mother told Elmer what this woman had said and he could read between the lines her hurt feelings and longing to see him. Already perplexed by many problems, working on a schedule that kept him occupied every minute from eight in the morning to ten or eleven at night, and committed to staying in Madison until January 1, he could not possibly respond to that plea for some time. He knew that, with her limited horizon, she could not understand his situation, especially as he was careful not to put any of his troubles into his letters to Mechanicville.

He replied the same day he received her letter, November 15, 1858. His answer is charged with feeling. "My mother," he wrote tenderly, "If you knew how I long to meet you again, how bitterly I regret that circumstances over which I have no control have prevented me from following the dictates of my affection, and kept me almost four long years, which to me have seemed so many ages, an exile from home: and with what eager anticipation I look forward to a reunion with you, Father and brother, you would not, never again permit yourself to think it possible for my affection for home to become lessened by absence, even though I were absent a century."

He went on to tell her that all his other ambitions and wishes, "no matter how important, sink into insignificance beside the dearest wish of my heart, to see you placed in the position you deserve to occupy — your old age rendered comfortable and happy by the possession of every thing heart can desire." This was the very purpose for which he was working so far away: "I speak from the heart, and you have the whole secret of my absence from home, and the key to all my actions."

Then he described the home he intended to give them, "a neat comfortable unpretending house, such a one as would please and content you, dear mother, and tickle father so hugely that he would not speak for a month." He had even drawn the plans for it, he said; it should have "two nice parlors, a generous old fashioned hall and a pleasant family room, fitted up with every appliance for comfort that could be procured, well stocked with books and pictures." There should be "a nice cozy sleeping room" for her and "a good kitchen, dining room, washing room, wood shed etc."

It is an interesting description of what was considered a comfortable, unpretentious home in the 1850s. One wonders a little what were called "appliances for comfort" in those days before electricity and push-button conveniences. Ellsworth planned another desirable feature: ". . . last though not least I would find a couple of middle aged colored people, to whom I would promise a home for life on condition of their serving you faithfully."

This "little home," as he called it, should be located two

or three miles from a pleasant town or city situated on a fine river or lake. Near the house he wanted "some stately old trees" and the grounds should include "one hundred and fifty or two hundred acres, bordered by a heavy growth of timber." His mother should have "a fine garden (which should be your special charge)," he told her, and his father a work shop well stocked with tools "over the carriage house." A "regular New York state barn," a horse "as like poor dead Mink as possible," plenty of farm animals and poultry complete the dream. His brother Charley was to take charge of this establishment.

It is evident that Ellsworth had a taste for an ample and gracious way of living. Perhaps this planning of a fine home was an old game between him and his mother; at least he knew she would express her doubts about their ever having this dream house, for he continued, "Yes you say but shall we ever realize it? Yes, my dear parents, I've enumerated nothing very extensive after all — nothing but what a stout heart, strong arm and steady perseverence can, and with God's blessing shall obtain."

As part of his effort to comfort her he told his mother how fine and generous-spirited she and his father had always been. His letter overflows with his affection for them. "As for the person who takes the advantage of my absence to make such unkind remarks" (about his absence from home) ". . . the act only proves the littleness of her mind."

He knew every bit of news about himself was precious to her and he had some high hopes about "a number of projects" of which to tell her. "My prospect for the adjutant generalship is good, as I am sure of the unanimous support of the state Militia whenever a vacancy occurs." (A letter to Carrie later makes it clear that he meant the adjutant generalship in Illinois.) Also he had had a most complimentary letter from General Swift of Chicago congratulating him upon his achievement at Rockford. He quoted for his mother a passage from General Swift's letter: "I shall ever take pleasure in pointing to you as a bright example of what may be accomplished by energy and ceaseless application to study."

Ellsworth had made it clear in his letter to Carrie that he did not like certain politicians in Madison. To his mother he could tell details which he would not have written to the girl. With the companies under his instruction consisting of young businessmen, lawyers, and others of Madison's leading families, he was in a position to hear all the current scandal and he was outraged at the graft and immorality among those who were considered the most respectable citizens. One wealthy man, he wrote, though sixty years old and the father of a family, was "guilty of the most glaring infidelity." Another, he continued indignantly, was "living on the proceeds of 3000 acres of school lands obtained by the sale of his wife to a member of the state legislature, these are facts and well known here."

Ellsworth, of course, wanted to tell his mother about the Spaffords and how good they had been to him. He refrained, however, from mentioning their name or the fact that they had a lovely fifteen-year-old daughter named Carrie who was very much in his thoughts. "I met some kind friends at Rockford," he wrote, "who, could you know them, you would love with your whole heart."

His letter ends: "Write immediately, and let your letter be as lengthy as my own, in the mean time believe me Affectionately yours Elmer."

Ellsworth said in this letter that one of his dearest wishes was that his brother Charley should become "an intelligent and honorable man, a brother to be proud of." What follows makes one suspect that Mrs. Ellsworth had written a worried report about Charley. For the elder brother on that same day, November 15, 1858, wrote the younger a long letter which is an earnest attempt to awaken a sense of responsibility in an eighteen-year-old youth. Evidently Charley had not developed any more serious purpose in life than he had had when he was nine.

Ellsworth's letter shows deep affection and concern. He began by saying it had been nearly four years since he left home "to do battle with the world . . . I have worked, studied and suffered," he continued, "and the experience and knowledge gained in those four years is worth thousands of dollars to me."

What had Charley been doing, he asked. "Are you prepared to go into the world alone, and pursue your course whatever it may be, with honor, and credit to yourself? . . . Have you realized that you are not always to remain a careless boy? . . . Are you a manly, honest straightforward boy?"

One suspects also that the mother had told of Charley's running around with the wrong crowd, as Ellsworth continued: ". . . are you permitting yourself to associate and mingle with that class, who lounge about with no aim or ambition, beyond keeping themselves supplied with segars and tobacco, and with opportunities for the indulgence of their low propensities? Charley, to find you the victim of the least of these vices, would cut me to the heart." (By Ellsworth's code, using tobacco was one of the lesser vices.) He dealt at length on the dangers of associating with this "fast" group.

Referring again to all he had learned in the past four years, he asked earnestly: "My brother, are you willing to accept my experience for your own? and to profit by it? Will you accept my views and be guided by me?" If Charley would do this, he would write to him regularly and "Your welfare hereafter shall be my care." Ellsworth went on to say that he hoped to come home before long and "I propose taking you with me, when I visit New York city where you will meet with a great many of the first people in the country.

They will all expect my brother to be a gentleman in habits and manner."

He explained that he would try to get Charley a position in New York among these fine people. Furthermore, "I have a very beautiful friend, a young lady in New York, who I am going to introduce you to." Meanwhile Charley must devote himself to his studies, especially arithmetic, grammar, and spelling.

Thus Ellsworth, in addition to his other problems, shouldered the responsibility of his brother. He saw clearly that Charley must be removed from Mechanicville, where there were bad associates and no opportunities. Before another twelve months had passed, he would bring Charley to Illinois where he could watch over him.

❖
❖

8

"For Your Sake, Dear Carrie"

After Ellsworth sent his letter of November 6 to Carrie, two weeks passed without any answer and he began to worry. Had his letter failed to reach her again? Or worse still, had Carrie's father objected to her answering? He seems not to have doubted Carrie's wish to answer him; all the indications are that he and Carrie understood very well that they were in love with each other. But Mr. Spafford plainly had not given his consent to their becoming engaged.

On Tuesday, November 23, the longed-for envelope addressed in the dainty handwriting arrived and brought welcome reassurance. There was no paternal barrier to their corresponding. "You cannot imagine how gratified I am, by this renewed evidence of your parents confidence," wrote Ellsworth in his reply two days later, "and it shall be my constant endeavor to merit it." He tried to put into words his feeling of happiness and wonder at their friendship: "This is the first time, that I have ever given way unreservedly to confidence in another friendship: and no words can express how implicidly I believe, in that of yourself and Mother at least, if I may not say your Father: and his friendship I am confident of possessing very soon." To have their affection, he said, "seems to me like a beautiful dream, from which at any moment I may awake, to find my life as blank and cheerless as before." He returns to this subject frequently in his letters.

The next topic was also one which was to recur in their correspondence. Ellsworth, handsome, magnetic, and splendidly uniformed, was inevitably attractive to women, young or otherwise. Not until one gets into the uninhibited pages of his diary can one realize what a problem this was to him. As an officer and a gentleman he had to be courteous and agreeable to the ladies he met socially and this in turn was likely to lead to further conquests. Carrie was not going to like it if he looked twice at another girl, and he was not going to take it well in a certain case where she was gracious to another man.

There are always gossips and busybodies who like to stir up trouble. "What friend (!) of mine," wrote Ellsworth, "has drawn so largely upon his (or her) imagination, for the materials of that precious story of the 'beautiful young Lady to whom I am paying such *devoted* attention,' And I assure you that this is an entire fabrication?" Protestingly, he gave a full account of all the ladies he had seen. The men he was training naturally brought their "lady friends" to meet him. He had also called twice on a girl who was a friend of a friend of his in Chicago, "in each instance, remaining just long enough to originate several brilliant remarks on the state of the weather — inquire when she last heard from Chicago — and bid her a good afternoon." Another lady at Madison, whom he had known in Chicago, invited him to call. He had done so three times but that was all right — she was "already engaged to another person." These incidents were the sole foundation of the story, he said, and added wisely, "I might spend half my time, in the society of the ladies here, without lessening my friendship for you, dear Carrie, you can never suffer by comparison with any of them."

He polished the subject off by telling her that the wife

of one of the professors at the University had invited him to her "literary conversaziones" but, he said, he would "*not* attend, less some one start a report, that I am desperately smitten with the charms of some antique blue." ("Blue" was often used then for "bluestocking.")

He was greatly interested in what Carrie had told him about her studies. She must use every hour to its fullest advantage. "Your future dear Carrie," he wrote, "is in your own hands, you can be one of the thousands of fine ladies who grace (!) this happy land of ours, or, you can make yourself an intelligent, high minded, noble hearted woman, as far above the mass, as the heavens, above the earth."

This letter reveals that Ellsworth's Mexican plans are flourishing at the moment. "Mexican affairs are fast approaching a climax," he wrote, "and if any reliance may be placed on the promises of men in high places, I may soon hold a position which will amply repay me for all that I have suffered from those large souled persons who seem influenced by some malignant spirit to throw every possible obstacle in the path of those who seek to rise above their own level." He was constantly irritated by malicious gossip. Possibly some of it arose from jealousy of his abilities and charm which enabled him to win prominence more easily than less gifted individuals.

In words seething with indignation he told Carrie about it: ". . . they called me, drunkard &c — it sickens me to think of the reports circulated so industriously to my discredit. Drunkard forsooth, I who never drank a glass of liquor in my life, an aimless boy! — *Wait*. If I cannot realize my ambition — if when the *trial comes* I am found wanting, I will acknowledge it, and *try again* in some other sphere. With the help of God I *can*, and *will* accomplish *some good, some where*. My name shall be spoken of *with honor*, or *not at all*."

Perhaps at this point he realized that he was telling his troubles and exasperations to a young, inexperienced girl. "Forgive me Carrie," he wrote penitently, "I tire without interesting you. But you are the only one to whom I can open my heart without danger of being misconstrued, and the privilege is so sweet, that I forget myself." This suggests Carrie's warm sympathy and understanding. The two had evidently talked over many things in those happy days at Rockford; he did not have to explain to her again, for example, what his Mexican plan was.

It occurred to Ellsworth also that his writing about his future achievement and honor might seem "egotistical" to Carrie. "I trust you will not do me the *injustice* to think this of me," he said. "I am quite conscious of my own deficiencies — my want of advantages, & my insignificant position; yet I *cannot* help these feelings, they were born with me, and must work out their own results."

He concluded circumspectly: "Remember me to your Parents, and believe me, Sincerely Yours, Ellsworth." Then he added a hopeful postscript, "May I not expect a letter from you very soon?"

Before his next letter to Carrie, there arose some sort of misunderstanding between him and her mother. He spoke of it in his letter to "Friend Parks" on December 12 and it was the cause of his writing to Mrs. Spafford herself on December 13. Henry Parks, editor of the *Rockford Democrat*, had become a good friend of Ellsworth's the previous summer. They were so close that, after he went to Madison, he had some of his mail sent in care of Parks at Rockford.

Apparently Parks let Mrs. Spafford read a certain letter concerning Ellsworth, possibly one which he himself had written or enclosed to Mr. Parks. One suspects (though this is conjecture) that the letter included accusations against Ellsworth which were part of that flood of slander about which he had complained to Carrie. Some special circumstance seems to have been involved.

Mrs. Spafford, knowing that Ellsworth and her daughter Carrie were in love, would have been deeply disturbed at seeing him spoken of as a "drunkard," "aimless boy," or in even more derogatory terms. Ellsworth in his letter to her wrote: "I cannot sufficiently express my regret, that this circumstance should have given you a moment's pain, and I blame myself as the cause of it, though I beg you to believe, that I had no thought of that letter being seen by you. You must not blame Mr. Parks."

Parks, learning that Mrs. Spafford had not taken the letter as he meant she should, hastened to Ellsworth's defense with the necessary explanation and set things right again. Ellsworth wrote to him, "Your *double* indiscretion has resulted very happily. Mrs. Spafford wrote me a long letter overflowing with kindness and completely restoring me to my former place in her esteem. I am fully sensible that I owe this to your prompt action and my gratitude is proportionate to the obligation."

In this letter to Parks, Ellsworth made a remark which incidentally throws more light on the state of his romance. After speaking of his plan to go to Mexico and acquire a fortune, he said he would thus "earn the right to come home & make *myself* and *another* happy." This is admitting that he and Carrie loved each other and wanted to be married. The barrier to their engagement was evidently Mr. Spafford's objection because Ellsworth had no profession or prospects for supporting a wife.

In replying to Mrs. Spafford's gracious letter Ellsworth said that when he first heard about her misunderstanding he "felt very much hurt," but he had no thought of blaming her. His letter overflows with appreciation of her friendship and he signs himself "Affectionately Yours," which was a liberty he had not yet taken with Carrie.

Thursday, December 2, 1858, was Carrie's sixteenth birthday, which was celebrated with a party by the Spaffords. Ellsworth wrote her a late birthday letter on December 13. He was very regretful he could not be at her party and gracefully offered his birthday wishes. "I will not wish you a life of unclouded happiness," he wrote, "for that I fear can hardly be realised by any of us. But I will wish, dear Carrie, what may, and I trust will be realised — that your life may be that of a true hearted, noble woman; unmarred by a thought, or deed to which in after years you cannot refer with pleasure — an ornament not only, but a blessing to society, and your friends."

Then he quoted for her one of the sweetly sentimental verses so popular in that Victorian era:

> *Angels attend thee! May their wings*
> *Fan every shadow from thy brow;*
> *For only bright and lovely beings,*
> *Should wait on one so pure as thou.*

Part of the letter is in less ethereal mood. Carrie had written him a sympathetic letter but a short one and he was disappointed. "Are you trying to cultivate that much to be admired virtue, brevity?" he asked, "if so, allow me to congratulate you upon your success." He was overworked in uncongenial surroundings; he had no leisure or privacy; he had to write his letters to her, as he said, "by detachments," and with men talking all around him. Her letters were the only bright events in his dismal existence. "If you only knew, how valuable, your letters become by the time they reach this dull settlement, you would write letters, of almost fabulous length, out of pure compassion for your unworthy correspondent."

He could hardly wait for his release from his Madison assignment. "Three weary weeks, and I am free from this place. I hope to arrange my affairs so as to visit Rockford,

the first week in January." He wanted desperately to see
Carrie and one suspects he wished to persuade Mr. Spafford
to agree to their being engaged. Then he must respond to
that pleading letter of his mother's which he had received
a month before. After his visit with the Spaffords, he continued, "I wish to visit my home and parents, perhaps for
the last time in many years." (This was likely to be the case
if he went to Mexico.) "I sometimes think I should never
again leave them, but I go, that I may sooner realise my
wishes for them, and others."

Toward the end of his letter he seemed to regret his
abrupt remark about the brevity of hers. "You must pardon me," he wrote, "for urging you to write longer letters.
In my momentary selfishness, I forgot how much your time
must be occupied with your studies — I would be content
with a line, rather than you should neglect them for me."
He signs himself "Sincerely and Truly Yours, Ellsworth."

Laboriously the three weeks went by. There was a parade
of the Governor's Guard on the day after Christmas in
which Ellsworth, seeing the result of his training, must have
taken some satisfaction. Then, with the coming of January,
1859, he wiped the hated mud of the Madison encampment
from his feet and turned his face southward, his heart no
doubt outspeeding the wheels which were carrying him to
Rockford.

One can imagine that meeting of Ellsworth and Carrie,
each finding the appearance of the other more wonderful
than remembered. Precious days in the Spafford home followed, in which their affection deepened more and more.
Friends in the Spafford circle, seeing the two together and
realizing how deeply in love they were, began to predict
the visit would end in a marriage, perhaps even an elope-
ment.

During the visit Ellsworth talked at length with Mr.
Spafford, telling him of his love for Carrie and of all his

circumstances and hopes. Would Mr. Spafford agree to their engagement? By this time the Spaffords had grown very fond of Ellsworth. They knew no one who would be personally more acceptable to them as a son-in-law, but how could he support a wife? He must have a trade or profession. Mr. Spafford had a suggestion. If Ellsworth would enter a lawyer's office and study until he could gain admittance to the bar, then he and Carrie could be married provided they were still of the same mind.

The suggestion must have floored Ellsworth at first. What would become of his military career and his dream of going to Mexico? He had not dreamed of becoming a lawyer. He loathed the four walls of an office. How could he tie himself to a desk? He was an outdoor man and a man of action. On the other hand there was Carrie, whom he loved with all a young man's ardor and who loved him in return. And the Spaffords, who had been so good to him and for whom he had so much affection thought the law was the best solution.

By January 20 he had been won over to the suggestion to the point of investigating its possibilities. On that day he drafted a letter which began, "Sir: — I am desirous of becoming a lawyer. I wish to study in the office of some person of extensive experience." The letter, which has no other address than the "Sir," goes on to explain that the writer must "work his way . . . with nothing to depend upon but his own resources."

When Ellsworth said a reluctant good-by and left Rockford, he and Carrie were engaged, though the engagement was somewhat conditional. He carried her picture with him, though it seems to have been only a loan. On April 20 he would write her that he had handed it back to her father after having it copied, adding wistfully, "but the copy does not do you justice. By and by, darling . . . you must get another picture for me." (He would carry her photograph with him continually and one day he would kiss it and slip it in his bosom as he prepared to go on a dangerous mission in the Civil War.)

He was going to Mechanicville now, but he stopped over in Chicago to look further into the question of studying law. The very morning he arrived, as he wrote Carrie, he met Judge Morgan, who had recently commenced the practice of law in Chicago, and asked him some general questions about the profession. That evening he called on his good friend General Swift and "remained with him nearly five hours listening to his advice and suggestions." General Swift advised him to devote himself to the real estate branch of the law.

The General asked Ellsworth (who had nearly starved two years before) whether he knew how to economize. "I experienced no great difficulty," wrote Ellsworth to Carrie, "in convincing the old gentleman that I had some slight idea of economical living, and immediately he became confidential and cordial." He told Ellsworth "how himself and wife had lived on seventy cents a week, and slept in a covered hand sled or cart, with heads sticking out of one end and feet from the other."

General Swift promised to help Ellsworth in his law work, especially with regard to real estate. "I returned to my hotel," he wrote Carrie, "went to my room — canvassed the whole matter over thoroughly — considered the chances, and contingencies — thought of you, dearest, and my determination was made." He did not try to conceal from her what a sacrifice it was: "God only knows what a struggle it cost me to forsake a profession for which I have prepared myself with so much labor, and in the face of so many difficulties — I have done this for your sake, dear Carrie, and I have now before me an ardous task, which will have to be pursued under *many disadvantages*, and I shall need all the *encouragement* which your rapid progress towards that *noble womanhood*, which I anticipate for you will afford me."

It was four o'clock in the morning when he made this decision and went to bed. Nevertheless, he rose early the next morning and began getting a start toward his law study. It seemed providential that he had met Judge Morgan the morning before; "decidedly he was the man for me," Ellsworth's letter continued, "and off I posted to his office and in a few moments astonished that excellent gentleman, by a proposition to enter his office as a student — he to give me the use of library — direct my studies, and — answer all my questions. In return for which, I would do all his writing and render him whatever assistance I could about the office." The proposition was accepted with pleasure by Judge Morgan and Ellsworth left Chicago, continuing his journey to Mechanicville "by Canada," with stops at Detroit and Albany. At Albany he called on the Adjutant General of New York who, after a pleasant afternoon's visit, "presented me," Ellsworth wrote, "with some very valuable *books*." He leaves unanswered the question whether they were military books to be devoured with eager interest or law books to be mastered distastefully by slow grinding study.

He was almost home now. On the night of Wednesday, January 26, he reached Mechanicville and was soon in the old familiar home embracing those two dear parents and his brother Charley, who seemed to have grown prodigiously since he last saw him. There was so much to talk about that he doubtless did not get to bed until the small hours of the morning.

9

❖
❖
❖

"WHAT SAY THE GOOD PEOPLE OF
ROCKFORD?"

WHEN a youth of seventeen leaves home and does not return until he is approaching twenty-two, he sees many changes. Some of the change is in himself; he is looking at things through different eyes. Ellsworth, by his own calculation, had had twenty "experience-years" since leaving and he had greatly matured. His father and mother, studying the handsome face, saw that it had lost the indefiniteness of the teens and become firm and grownup, though the straight figure remained very boyish.

The son, looking at them, noticed that they had aged somewhat and his heart was wrung to see his mother's hands shake with the palsy which had afflicted her the summer before. More than ever he must have realized that these dear people, defenseless in their limitations, needed him to make life easier for them. And there was Charley, grown taller than himself, affectionate and gay, but sadly in need of both guidance and opportunity.

Ellsworth wrote a long letter to Carrie the day after he reached Mechanicville, possibly in the evening, for he had had time to see a number of people. Perhaps he had dropped into that reliable meeting place, the general store. His letter gives a good description of the way many have felt on revisiting the old home town after a long absence. "Four years have worked a sad change in the society here," he said: "my old school-mates have dispersed in every direction. Several have died, and gone I hope to a happier and better world. A new society has grown up, composed of those who only four or five years since were children, they all know me, but the most of them have grown from my recollection." He had become accustomed to being called "Major Ellsworth" in general and "Ellsworth" by his closer friends, and he added, "It seems odd to be called Elmer by old and young." Doubtless it also seemed strange to be merely the son of Ephraim Ellsworth (the man who did various jobs), and difficult to fit himself into the shell he had outgrown.

His mother, he told Carrie, "is quite delighted with your picture, and my description of you. I trust you will love her Carrie," he continued, "all the good in my nature I owe to her."

This letter of January 27, 1859, is definitely the sort of letter a man writes the girl to whom he is engaged. He refers playfully to the disappointed gossips in her circle: "What say the good people of Rockford?" he asks, "now that we have neither married nor eloped." For the first time to her he signs himself "affectionately yours."

After telling Carrie in detail about his journey East, he gives his plans. He will remain in or around Mechanicville until February 20, when he intends to go to New York for a week before starting back West again.

There is little other record of what happened during his visit home, only one incident which Mrs. Ellsworth told later to a devoted friend of her son's. Elmer talked so much to her about his military activities, she reported, and with such glowing enthusiasm that she finally laughed and said he ought to be in Europe where wars were always going on. With his face suddenly grown sober, he told her he thought this country too was heading toward war and that he felt the North was wholly unprepared. That conviction doubtless made it more intolerable than ever to give up his military career to study law.

One can only imagine the renewing of his home ties, the talks and simple meals with his parents and Charley, with four at the table as when they were boys, the roaming over the farm. He would certainly have revisited his boyhood haunts, like the banks of the Hudson River, which may have changed somewhat too, in the manner of rivers. Perhaps the canal had remained much the same, though in the future it was destined to be the victim of the greatest change of all, when it would be filled in and become a street in Mechanicville.

It was after the middle of March when he started West again. He had evidently made the trip to New York, as he had planned, and this move had forced another difficult decision upon him. He told Mrs. Spafford later that he would have had "greater advantages" in New York if he had remained there "and nothing to discourage me." But Carrie was in Illinois. He wrote her on Wednesday, March 16, from Stillwater, near Mechanicville, where he had gone perhaps to look up some of the Black Plumed Riflemen who might still be around. "I start for the west Monday evening next," he said, "stop but a couple of hours in Chicago, then proceed at once to Rockford."

Since he expected soon to see her, it is a short letter but he does not fail to call her "my dearest one," and he makes one of his gay remarks. He had apparently seen something of a "Miss Warren" (probably a relative of Carrie's) in New York, and she had written Carrie that he had "absconded without biding her good bye." Ellsworth denied the allegation. "On the contrary," he wrote, "I called in 36th St. bid them *all* good-bye, and kissed *the* baby — for you."

Ellsworth evidently arrived in Rockford late in March.

The visit was good for him in more ways than one. To bask again in the warmth and love of the Spafford family and to spend happy hours with Carrie planning their future, as lovers do, had a pronounced effect upon him. He would write Mrs. Spafford after returning to Chicago: ". . . since my acquaintance with your family, and the assurance of your affection, I have begun to view life in a very different light, although I scarcely know why." Instead of "murmuring," he said, "against that power which caused me so much misery, I am content and happy to thank God for the blessings which I do enjoy." There was too much trouble ahead, however, for him to remain long in this mood.

One topic much talked of while he was in Rockford was Carrie's plan to go East to continue her studies. With strong roots in New England, the Spaffords selected a school there, the Tilden Seminary at West Lebanon, New Hampshire. Possibly there was another factor involved in sending her so far away, for one or two remarks in subsequent letters seem to indicate that Mr. Spafford wanted to separate these two young people for a time. Fond as he was of Ellsworth, he could hardly have considered him an ideal match for Carrie. To the practical banker the young man was a wanderer and dreamer, who had no profession and no income to support a wife, not to mention the fact he was to be burdened with the care of his parents.

Carrie started East early in April, stopping briefly in Chicago. Ellsworth saw her then, and there exists today a souvenir of this meeting. It is a rare little book in the Chicago Historical Society whose title page, adorned with a Sartain engraving, bears the words *Album of Love*. A girl would ask her dear friends to write some tender sentiment in an ornamental book like this and to sign their names.

It was evidently Ellsworth's going-away gift to Carrie when she was starting off to school and he had put much work in it. One page has an intricate pencil drawing of his in which a goddess-like figure sits upon a throne reading a large book. Beneath the throne, whose platform has the cupids and curlicues dear to the Victorian heart, is a scroll bearing the motto *Acquirit Qui Tuetur,* which has been loosely translated "He who cares for a thing acquires it." Perhaps the thing in this case was the knowledge Carrie would acquire from her studies.

On three pages of this *Album of Love* Ellsworth wrote careful, loving inscriptions. On the one which has Carrie's picture at the top he wrote in his artistic script: "When you look upon these lines, dear Carrie, may they remind you of the fond hearts, filled with high hopes and bright anticipations of your future, whose prayers 'that you may realize the glorious promise of your youth,' nightly ascend to Heaven. . . . Remember, dear Carrie, that your future usefulness, perhaps, happiness — depends entirely upon the disposal of your time during the insuing two years. As you dispose of this most precious time, so will you prove the extent of your affection for one whose whole happiness, is centered in the hope of your future excellence."

By present-day standards the emphasis Ellsworth continually put upon Carrie's studying hard for the improvement of herself seems pompous and somewhat amusing. After all, the implication that she stood so much in need of improvement was hardly flattering! But in considering this sentimental album and what Ellsworth wrote in it (and elsewhere too) it is necessary to shift back to the viewpoints of an earlier era. As a photographer adjusts his light meter to get a clear picture, so one must, to understand Elmer Ellsworth, adjust to the mental light of his time. Many people then had this attitude toward study. He himself had put every precious hour he could steal from necessary activities into study which had meant so much for him. He hungered for more.

Ellsworth was to continue to give Carrie a great deal of advice. With his instinct for leadership and his helpfulness toward others, he was quick to take over the guidance of those less mature than himself. He was paternal toward his brother Charley and to some extent toward Carrie. She was five years younger than he and infinitely younger in experience.

Carrie, after a sorrowful good-by in Chicago, sped eastward toward New Hampshire, and Ellsworth was left desolate. His inscription in the *Album of Love* is dated April 4, 1859. On April 10 he wrote to Carrie's mother, knowing that she, like himself, was lonely and homesick for the bright presence of Carrie. It comes as no surprise that he told Mrs. Spafford she must console herself, as he did, by picturing "how much she will change, and improve during her absence." He ends that paragraph, however, with deep feeling: "I sometimes think that God has decreed separation here on earth, that we may realize in its fullest extent, the glorious promise of an eternal reunion hereafter."

Ellsworth told Mrs. Spafford about a necessary change in his plan to study law. It had been arranged that he would study with Judge Morgan but now Judge Morgan had returned to Elgin, he wrote, "obliging me in consequence to find another person to study with. Yesterday I decided by and with (pardon my legal expressions, *we* of the *profession unconsciously* fall into the habit of using them) the advice of Gen Swift and Judge Higgins, to commence with J. E. Cone, Esq." Mr. Cone, he added was a "hard student" but did not, however, "possess the faculty of making himself acquainted with the public." One reads a trace of doubt between the lines. Such a succession of obstacles were to arise about Ellsworth's studying law that it was almost as if fate was signaling him that he was going in the wrong direction.

"Every thing is progressing nicely," he continued in his letter to Mrs. Spafford. He had, he said, "copying enough engaged to occupy three or four hours every evening for a long time." He did not mention that this copying of legal documents was his sole means of livelihood. "Tomorrow is my twenty second birth day," he went on, "I enter the second year of my manhood with my heart filled to over-flowing with gratitude for the many and undeserved mercies for which I am indebted to God." It was on that twenty-second birthday that he began his invaluable diary.

It happened that Ellsworth saw Mrs. Spafford four days after he wrote this letter to her. Carrie's parents came to Chicago on April 14 because Mr. Spafford had an offer to engage in business there. Ellsworth wrote Carrie about their coming several days later, saying he hoped Mr. Spafford would accept the offer as "it would be pleasant to have your mother in the City where I could see her occasionally." He added, "I am quite alone now, and do not go out of the office day or night except to go to the P.O."

He began this letter of April 17 by telling Carrie he had been feeling "low spirited" and "decidedly down-hearted." "Difficulties and obstacles seem to multiply at every step," he said in apology for having been so depressed. (Had Carrie known what one of the difficulties was she would have been frantic.) "Your sweet letter, dear Carrie," he continued, "came most opportunely and dispelled my sad thoughts, and in their stead, came sweet remembrances of happy hours passed in thy dear society."

Ellsworth had now reached the point where he could tell his love without reserve. The thought of Carrie's living presence beside him and of all the future held for them brought a surge of emotion. His words fairly poured out in a long passage which is a fervent expression, with mid-

Victorian overtones, of the feeling of a young lover in any age. Having these "bright anticipations of the future," he said, "when my thoughts reverted to my present difficulties, it was only to think of them as a means of proving my love for you, my darling, and rendering myself *more worthy* of that glorious embodiment, of *all* that is *noble* & *good* in woman who (God permitting) I may one day hold in my arms, and while heart beats to heart, feel the realization of those sweet lines —

> '*Two souls with but a single thought,*
> *Two hearts, that beat as one.*' "

Carrie had said in her letter that she was enjoying herself in the East and he told her how pleased he was about this. "And here Carrie, let me say to you, what perhaps I neglected to make you fully understand," he continued, "I refer to your going into society, and accepting the attention of gentlemen — I believe that an engagement is usually supposed, to place a certain amount of restraint upon a lady's actions, and debar her from receiving the attention of gentlemen as freely as she would under other circumstances."

Ellsworth went on to say that just because he had withdrawn from society was no reason why she should. "*On the contrary,* darling, I wish you to follow *your own inclinations entirely.*" It takes him about a page to tell her what "*implicid confidence*" he has in her never to "*do,* or *think* aught that . . . would *wrong my love,*" adding, "without *implicid confidence true* love cannot *exist.* Hence I say, Carrie, *act with perfect freedom.*" Broad-minded as this was, he would find in time that circumstances alter cases. These lovers, like most, were to have their misunderstandings.

Carrie had evidently said something in her letter about his going to Ann Arbor to study law. His reply was: "I would like to go to Ann Arbor very well, provided I *could be* among the first to graduate, but it will only be by the *greatest exertion*, that I shall be able to attend the Law School here." His going to law school at that moment consisted of his reading Blackstone while doing legal chores in Mr. Cone's law office. He was writing this letter on a Sunday, as he usually did, and the following Sunday, April 24, he told Carrie how this study was progressing.

He had read through the first book of Blackstone, he said, "read it very carefully, (as I imagined) averaged about fifty pages per day. When I had finished it, I attempted to review it and see if I had fixed the ideas in my mind." As his words flow on, one recalls him as a small boy making the rounds of the muskrat traps on the banks of the Hudson while the morning mists rose from the river: "Darling," he continued, "did you ever go out of a morning when the mist had just cleared sufficiently for you to distinguish a faint outline of surrounding objects, without any distinct idea of their location or character? If you have, you may know just my position and sensation, when I asked myself what I had learned of the law, in that first book of Blackstone."

He saw, he said, that he was wasting his time and decided to go back to the beginning and start all over again. Now he was averaging a page an hour. He went on to tell Carrie his method of study. "I read," he said, "a sentence, or paragraph that contains an idea or definition of the meaning of some part of the law, — then I read & re-read that portion aloud, then lay aside the book — repeat the ideas in my own language — apply it to some common ordinary occurrence of every day life — get it firmly fixed in my mind, — & then write it in a blotter or commonplace book — without any reference to the language used by Blackstone." This was the system of another man in Illinois who had had to educate himself in the law, Mr. Abraham Lincoln. It was the essence of his advice to young law students: ". . . get the books, and read, and study them carefully. . . . Work, work, work, is the main thing."

Ellsworth found that this method brought results: "Now the consequence is that I am conscious when I turn a leaf, that I am master of all contained on the preceeding page, & that I have not to refer to it again. And now that I am gaining a thorough knowledge of the elements & first principles of the science of law, the whole opens out into a grand and beautifully developed system."

It would seem then that everything was going well. Yet this letter tells of the dreadful headache that was almost blinding Ellsworth as he wrote; he could hardly distinguish the writing, he said. What has happened to this strong young man who was always tingling with health and energy? Why is there such pathos in the poetic ending of the letter? "Let me hear from you soon as possible, my darling. Your letters are the only stars, in my night of lonelyness and trouble."

It is time to go behind the scenes in Ellsworth's diary and find out why he was depressed and ill and what the "trouble" was.

$$\begin{array}{c} \diamond \\ \diamond \\ \diamond \end{array}$$

Secrets Confided to a Diary

Ellsworth began his diary, as he said in its first lines, on April 11, 1859, his twenty-second birthday. He was writing, he added, in the law office of J. E. Cone at 79 Dearborn Street, Chicago. "Have decided to keep a Diary in the future," he continued, "Shall write a sketch of my life up to the present time & place it in front of this book." Apparently he never got around to doing this and the pressure of work and events would force him to discontinue the diary itself after August 25.

Having stated when and where he was beginning the diary, he proceeded to tell why: "I do this because it seems very pleasant to be able to look upon our past lives — & note the gradual change in our sentiments & views of life & because my life has been & bids fair to be such a jumble of strange incidents that should I ever become any body or any thing, this will be usefull as a means of showing how much suffering and temptation a man may undergo and still keep clear of despair & vice." This purpose was in full accord with the moralizing spirit of the age; any upright mid-Victorian would have been delighted to point to him as an example of unimpeachable moral strength.

That passage is all of the record for April 11 except for a somewhat puzzling line at the end, "1 doz. Bists to day —

sleep on office floor to night." Each day's account usually concludes with a similar abbreviated statement. That of April 12 has "2 lb Crac." instead of "Bists." The entry two days later makes the meaning of these expressions all too clear.

Thursday, April 14, was the day that Mr. and Mrs. Spafford came to Chicago. Ellsworth wrote at the end of that day: "According to promise went for Mrs Smith & took her to Mrs Spafford at the Tremont House." A gallant gentleman who was acting as a lady's escort, of course, would never dream of letting her pay for her own transportation, no matter how impecunious he was. Ellsworth, escorting Mrs. Smith, was embarrassed because "The good woman insisted on paying her own fare in the Omnibus, she meant right & I could not take offence at it. I simply insisted upon her dropping the matter, & paid it myself (charged it to my dinner)."

The two ladies were determined that Ellsworth take dinner with them at the Tremont. He, with his firm resolution never to accept hospitality he could not return, refused and could not be persuaded to remain. As he recorded the incident in his diary, he commented, "Gentlemen who like myself live on Crackers & water seldom dine at Hotels (reason very obvious to inquiring mind)." This day's entry concludes, "1 lb Crackers—am living like a King sleep, on floor tonight."

The record of the first four days outlines the circumstances as definitely as stage directions in a play. Ellsworth, keeping up outward appearances, was living on bread and water and sleeping on the uncarpeted floor of Mr. Cone's law office. His one means of earning money was indicated in his account for April 12: "Called on Genl Swift last evening he gave me some copying to do for him & paid me in advance $7.00 which was very acceptable."

It might have been foreseen that he would be out of

funds. He had been, as far as one knows, without gainful occupation since the first of January, when he left the "advantageous" proposition at Madison. His traveling home had been expensive, especially as he was generous and delighted in doing pleasant things like giving presents. Carrie had received the *Album of Love* and it was possibly on this trip that he had given his mother the purse which, like the album, can be seen today at the Chicago Historical Society. Perhaps there were gifts for Charley, his father, and other relatives; at all events he had come back to Chicago with empty pockets. No wonder that seven dollars was acceptable. That would feed him adequately for a week at least.

Or so it would seem. Ellsworth, however, considered food the least important of his needs. With that seven dollars in pocket he went to an auction on April 12 and bought a forty-five-dollar desk for fourteen dollars, paying five dollars of his own money and borrowing the rest from James Clybourn. He promised "to return it next Tuesday." Ellsworth thought he could sell the desk any time for more than he paid for it and, he wrote, "I can indulge my idea of order in the arrangement of my papers etc to their fullest extent."

Ellsworth believed that using self-discipline to overcome hardship strengthened character. He seemed almost to take a pride in rising above his body's need for nourishment, to want to subjugate his physical comfort to psychological demands. It was a sort of triumph-of-mind-over-matter attitude which was much more prevalent a century ago than it is today. As a result of his application of this principle, the diary gives a clinical record of what semistarvation, as it progresses, can do to a healthy young man.

The diary reveals many other things. It is a remarkable document which, together with the letters which Ellsworth was writing to Carrie, presents his inner and outward life to a degree almost ideal for biography. It was a period in which it was quite the thing to keep a journal to which one confided without reserve one's private thoughts and feelings, and to write long letters of self-analysis. Dovetailing diary and letters almost enables one to live with Ellsworth for more than four months.

It is possible, for instance, to see what led to that blinding headache which he mentioned in his letter of April 24 to Carrie. On Saturday, April 16, he had spent twelve hours copying, had studied fifteen pages of Blackstone, and had had for food only one and a quarter pounds of crackers. On Monday he wrote in the diary: "Tried to read but could not — I am afraid that my strength will not hold out." He was more than hungry now; he was ill. "I have contracted a cold by sleeping on the floor, which has settled in my head & nearly drives me crazy with the catarrh. Then there is that terrible sensation which I begin to feel again which is a most effectual bar to long continued application."

He had heard some conversation in the law office that Monday to which it had been hard to listen in silence. A man in the office, he wrote, "is grumbling because he cannot be allowed to pay $7.00 per week for board through the summer. I like to board him about four weeks after which time I'll guarantee he will be satisfied with an allowance of 5 or 6 dollars."

Tuesday he recorded that he arose at six o'clock, copied for three hours, and then studied until half past three in the afternoon. "Severe sick headache prevented me from studying any longer," he continued, "a dull heavy sensation comes over me, while reading." To make matters worse a friend came in who, on learning that Ellsworth was reading law, asked him if he had given up his plans for going to Mexico. This was touching a sore spot, but Ellsworth replied briefly that he had given them up for the present. The gentleman told him emphatically, "You have done wrong," and spoke of the "bright future" he might have had, repeated, "Sir, you've done wrong," and departed, leaving him more miserable than ever. Wryly he commented in his diary, "encouraging that for a law student, very." He was in a constant state of frustration, being shut up as he was in an office away from all the activities he loved and forced to drudge over a subject in which he had no real interest. He mentioned that all who knew him were very much surprised at what he was doing.

By Thursday, April 21, he realized that he was not getting anywhere with his study of Blackstone, that his understanding of what he had been reading was as hazy as objects in a morning mist. Sick and starving as he was, he made the gritty decision to go back and start all over again. That day he spent his last eleven cents for crackers. He had been expecting some money to come by mail from the East, "but it does not arrive." Friday the 22nd he wrote in his diary, "My mind was so occupied today with the subject of getting money due tomorrow that I could not study." That day's record ends, "Nothing to eat today & I am very tired & hungry to night *Onward.*" Add to this the fact that on Saturday he recorded a severe emotional ordeal and it is quite obvious why he was depressed and had a sick headache when he wrote to Carrie on Sunday, April 24.

The ordeal was connected with what might be called Ellsworth's feminine complications. Handsome and magnetic as he was, he inevitably drew feminine interest. He regarded clothes as much more important than food and always dressed neatly — and as well as he could. He made it a point never to look woebegone but habitually wore a carefree countenance. He certainly must have grown thin on his diet of crackers and water but this did not diminish his romantic appearance; on the contrary, his eyes seemed all the larger and brighter in the lean face. In the middle of May he told in his diary of a sprightly exchange of remarks that touched upon the brilliance of his eyes.

He had been calling on his good friend General Swift, he wrote, and "As I came out from the Genls study I met Miss S." (presumably the General's daughter) "who had been attempting to light the gas in the back hall & by some accident had put out her taper. She came upon me very suddenly & exclaimed 'May I light this (the taper) by your eyes.' I replied I feared she would scarcely succeed as there was not enough of the Lucifer in my composition to make me a desirable Match."

Another feminine encounter was not so pleasant; in fact, it was an additional exasperating episode of April 19, the day on which the gentleman berated him for giving up his Mexican plans. After the visitor left, Ellsworth evidently felt that he had to get out of the office for a while. He had said in a letter to Carrie two days before, "Wouldn't you like to have my daguerreotype? If you really wish it you shall have *one*" Doubtless it was with this in mind that, as he wrote in his diary, he "Went into daguerreotype saloon to day." There "a young girl present" (he first wrote "lady," then crossed it out), "who has respectable parents but who is lost to all sense of shame was quite determined to establish an acquaintance but she did not succeed." He was indignant about it and about one or two similar cases involving young women also of respectable and well-established families.

The emotional ordeal of Saturday, April 23, was an episode in a poignant story which runs through the diary in April and May. It concerns a lovely woman who was a friend of his in Chicago. Being gallant, he used a long dash instead of her name to avoid the risk of her ever being identified. What happened was one of the troubles he could never tell anyone; it was an experience which almost tore him apart. She was a very beautiful married woman, somewhat older than he was, and she had known him when he was younger. He admired and liked her very much and called on her from time to time.

There are three passages in the diary which seem to be about this lady but, lacking the name, one cannot say so positively. What seems to be the first mention of her occurs on April 15. That day Ellsworth wrote in his diary, "Carried home the matter copied to night. When I returned I felt so tired sick & lonely I could not stay in the office, went out, saw Mrs —— stopped at the house a few moments. She acted very strangely. After a little she told me that she had inquired until she had found out very nearly how I was situated & then she said she wanted me to accept money that if I did not she would certainly find out all that transpired & perhaps place herself in a dangerous position for she was determined to aid me & force me to accept it."

Ellsworth was deeply moved. The diary continues, "I gently but firmly refused, she would not listen for a long time, at last I made her understand my scruples & she put up her money. God bless her for her kindness. I left her with a lighter heart. I had the sympathy of a true friend & had successfully resisted temptation."

The next passage which fits into this story was written on Saturday, April 23. Ellsworth told of talking with a friend about a lady whose husband, according to this gentleman, "was a brute." Ellsworth continued in his diary, "I asked him if he knew what caused her to throw herself away upon such a person . . . he professed to know nothing of her motives." The man with whom Ellsworth was talking was devoted to the lady and Ellsworth's great admiration for her was evident as he went on, "There are but few such women as she *was* living, the wildest description of beauty & fascination I ever read would not do her justice." Then comes the circumstance he could confide only to his diary: ". . . she lived to acknowledge that she who had reigned undisputed queen of the hearts of some of our noblest & most talented men in this country loved me, a poor unknown boy, who she had fondled, petted & told her hearts secrets, as she would a child. But when I was absent from her a year, a year of suffering which has shortened my life by many a bright year, I am afraid, & returned, I was no longer a boy but a man." He was evidently referring here to the year when he was "robbed" by the "infernal scoundrel." The diary continues, "I thank God that I came safe from the ordeal to which I was exposed without doing what would have brot unhappiness to more hearts than one — verily life is full of romance & reality is much more startling than fiction."

The last entry which rounds out this story was recorded May 28, over a month later. During that time Ellsworth had to fight the knowledge that the beautiful lady was in love with him and wanted to help him financially. He also had to contend with his own sincere affection and pity for her. Whether he took the risk of seeing her during that time is not stated. On May 28 he did the only thing he could in honor do.

He called on General Swift that day and the General had paid him five dollars which he intended should buy his food for two months. On the way back, as he said, "I could not resist the temptation to go into an eating saloon & get a plate of Buckwheat cakes — perhaps they were not good!" Then he stopped in to see the lady and, as he wrote, "told her that it was not right for me to see her & I would not call there again as I was convinced that it would only work us both harm, told her I loved a young lady & was engaged to be married to her."

The lady who had had so much experience in swaying men's hearts was not disposed to accept this. "She said," continued Ellsworth, "that [the engagement] could make no difference in her feeling toward me, she is most persevering in her love." He went on, "she had found out nearly the *extent* of my *resources* & insisted upon my accepting money. To do her justice she was as delicate about it as possible. I bid her good bye & came home in a perfect shower of rain." Ellsworth's deep emotion is evident in his concluding words: "I dared not stay longer. Heavens what a shame that such a magnificent woman should be bound to a man who appreciates her no more than he would a handsome horse or dog."

It looks as if he had been somewhat prophetic when he wrote in the preamble of his diary that it would show "how much suffering and temptation a man may undergo and still keep clear" of doing wrong.

❖
❖❖
❖

11

"The Gayest Captain in the Country"

Fate, in spite of all the trials she had been heaping upon Ellsworth, was at last getting ready to steer him into the path that would lead him to something in the way of success. It was a long, winding, rocky path that would in the end turn into a new, unsuspected highway and, as often happens with mortals, he could not recognize its final destination when it first opened before him. In fact, he very nearly refused to take it!

The story about this progresses through the diary and begins unpromisingly on April 16, 1859. That evening Ellsworth wrote in his journal, "Was visited by Secy of the Cadets with letter notifying me of my election as Captain. Told him I did not wish to accept it, as it would take to much time from my business & under my circumstances, I could give them but one night each week and as they were at present in a most deplorable condition this might not suffice to build them up." He added that in case this should happen, "my enemies would only be to glad of an opportunity to say that I ruined them, without considering that they were ruined before I became connected with them."

These were the Chicago National Guard Cadets who had come to Camp Sinnissippi at Rockford the previous September. They had become so disorganized that they were getting ready to disband and now suddenly they were confronted with an order to parade. Though some of them had been depreciating Ellsworth, they well knew that he had what it would take to pull them together again. Ellsworth did not quite close the door on their offer: "However I told him I would consider the matter & consult my friends & meet the company on Tuesday evening next for a final decision."

He did not even mention this matter in his Sunday letter to Carrie next day. He was in his usual situation of being pulled in two directions. The thought of getting out of the four walls of the office and drilling young men like himself had tremendous appeal; on the other hand he was studying law so that he could marry the girl he loved. Anyway, on Tuesday, April 19, when his aching head put a stop to his studying, he went to the evening meeting of the Cadets. Fate was baiting her trap well; just to get into the familiar atmosphere of soldiering with talk of arms and maneuvers instead of dealing with points of law was a relief and a pleasure.

He was called upon to speak on a question which was pending and, as he recorded in his diary, "made a few commonplace remarks." Then the captain arose and gave a spirited talk in which he urged the company to *"wake up.* It certainly woke me up," Ellsworth continued, "for I spoke nearly 20 minutes & roused the enthusiasm of the boys to a great pitch. They said they had not had such a spirited meeting in two years. They will attempt to parade in consequence although previous to this meeting it was considered impossible."

So wrote Ellsworth Tuesday evening. It is significant that the first thing he did Wednesday morning was copy the "pledge of Cadets (for parade)," have a conference with their captain, and write a subscription paper which they could pass around to raise some money. On Thursday he recorded that "several old members of the Cadets to day all say that they are coming back to the company if I will take command." That evening he attended a meeting of their "committee on Ways & Means," where every proposition he suggested was accepted. Ellsworth was being irresistibly pulled back into military affairs.

While he had friends among the Cadets, he also had enemies who had given him cause to be quite bitter, as his entry of Friday, April 22, indicates: "Had meeting & drill of Cadets to night. This is something of a triumph for me, a small one it is true, but nevertheless pleasant, after having taken from them every particle of their military prestige & reputation & in an honorable way to — met them on equal ground, now they come supplicating to me, the person of all others in the world who they left no stone unturned to wrong, whose reputation they have tried by evey means in their power to black. They come to me & ask me to command them. . . . It makes me laugh when I think of all they have said & done & then how matters are turning."

Throughout Ellsworth's story there runs frequent mention of malicious slanders and the trouble they caused him. He gave a specific example in his diary on May 6, which was after he had accepted the captaincy of the Cadets. One can almost see the scorn on his face as he began, "There is a race of curs without the generous nature of a genuine dog, who if you once tread upon their tails will ever after snap at your heels at every convenient opportunity." To this class, he continued, belonged "a certain Mr. B." who had been the leader in an ugly incident at Rockford the autumn before. Mr. B. had brought a "large crowd," a mob, to Camp Sinnissippi one night "with the avowed intention of breaking through the lines. It was late at night," wrote Ellsworth, "the men were asleep, tired & fatigued, & I being aroused by the noise at the lines went out to ascertain what caused the trouble — without calling up any who had not been already awakened. I found this man swearing that no power on earth should prevent his going into the camp — they had come prepared & were going to do it."

As commandant of the camp Ellsworth felt it was his duty, he wrote, "to see that they did nothing of the kind. I ordered the sentrys to load which they did." With fearless disregard of danger, he "then went out of the lines among the crowd & tried to reason with them." The hostile mob would not listen. "I then," Ellsworth continued, "simply ordered the sentries to keep their Posts & let no man pass without the '*Word*' if any attempted to do so they must not allow them to pass alive." Now it happened, he went on, "that the Sentries were men who had a constitutional tendency to obey orders. The crowd discovered this & were obliged to leave."

Ellsworth said that from the time of this incident Mr. B. had been his enemy "who now lets no opportunity pass at maligning me. . . . He told one of the Company yesterday that the Cadets would now run down immediately as they had for their Captain a *fool* & a rascal." In support of this assertion, Mr. B. went on to say, "that at Rockford I stole an officers gold watch. The officer found it out & challenged me to fight & I cowardly refused etc etc."

The cadet to whom Mr. B. was pouring out his scurrilous tale defended Ellsworth warmly and told how much he had built up the company. As to his stealing a watch, the cadet said, that was a lie. Mr. B., true to his type, began to back down at this and admitted that the officer afterwards "found his watch on another person." The story was evidently a much garbled version of the incident in which the farmer had accused Ellsworth of stealing his watch. Doubtless there were afloat equally twisted accounts of the embezzlement affair which had apparently left Ellsworth in an equivocal position.

It is possible that Mr. B. and his mob were incited to

move on the camp because many people thought the volunteer military companies were an evil influence, serving only to lead young men into bad habits. A New York newspaper later described them as organizations whose chief purpose was "getting into a gaudy uniform, parading a few of the streets and then having a grand 'spree.' The last thing thought of was learning the use of arms or the duties of a soldier." Drinking was so common in the companies that some took it for granted that Ellsworth was a drunkard merely because he was associated with them.

Even the Chicago *Railroad Gazette*, which was favorable to the Cadets (probably because its editor knew Ellsworth personally), admitted there were those who looked upon their training "as a fussy superfluity" or "an idle and foolish recreation" that had no real military value. And it is possible that the antagonism and abuse Ellsworth had received from the National Guard Cadets themselves came from those who had joined the organization merely to have a good time and resented both his discipline and moral standards.

The recurrent slanders about him, of course, got back to the Spaffords at Rockford, especially as "Mr. B." was evidently a Rockford man. Mr. Spafford could hardly have been pleased to hear that Ellsworth had gone back to drilling a military company. One can imagine how Carrie's father looked at the matter: he had given this impractical young man some good sound advice about settling down to getting himself a profession and now he was neglecting his law study to teach a group of men how to parade!

Ellsworth gave a full report about the Cadets to Carrie in his letter of April 24. After explaining that his head was aching so severely he could not write without making "a variety of mistakes," he went on: "I would like to tell you, how the Cadets had lost their Captain, and got in debt, and expected to be obliged to disband etc. — that they could get but eight or ten men in the armory to drill or meeting, and received an order to parade tomorrow and could not comply with it — when they came to me with a very flattering letter, begging my acceptance of the captaincy. — How I proposed to them to give them one evening in each week — got the men excited again — the old members who had left came back again, & tomorrow they expect to turn out with full ranks. If I dont stop I shall tell you all about it."

When Ellsworth wrote this to Carrie in New Hampshire, he undoubtedly already knew he was under her father's displeasure. The following Wednesday he wrote to Mrs. Spafford: "I regret exceedingly that Mr Spafford does not consider my explanation satisfactory. If you know what he wishes me to do, or what assurances he wishes from me you can do me no greater favor than by informing me, and I will most cheerfully do anything consistent with self respect, to prove my position in this matter to be what I represented." He said he would make "almost any sacrifice" rather than lose the confidence of Mr. Spafford and herself. With his pride hurt by the questioning of his veracity, he continued stiffly: "I like to have a perfectly frank & full understanding with all my friends, and when that ceases to exist, then all intercourse must cease untill they find whether I tell those for whom I profess regard, the truth and act honorably in all my intercourse with them, or whether I am two faced, saying one thing and meaning another."

The situation was a deep worry to him. He knew his engagement to Carrie was conditional upon his getting established in a profession and that he risked sidetracking his study of law in resuming his military activities. The fear hung constantly over him that Mr. Spafford might put an end to his engagement to Carrie.

The particular matter which had offended Mr. Spafford

at this time is not stated. A possible hint is given in a letter which Ellsworth wrote Carrie nearly a month later. He referred to her father's "misunderstanding about our matters at the time of your departure for school." Had Mr. Spafford objected to the meeting of Carrie and Ellsworth when she went through Chicago on her way East? This is pure conjecture, but there are several hints in the correspondence that Mr. Spafford may have requested the lovers not to see each other for a certain length of time. In his letter of April 24 Ellsworth had said: "My darling, how I long for the time to arrive when we shall meet again, our studies completed." Two months later he was to write her: ". . . we must not think of meeting yet awhile. Four months of the first year has already expired . . . never in all my experience have I known four drearier and to me more unpleasant months."

Carrie could not know as she read this what pain and hardship were covered by those words. The entries in the diary were continuing to end with such phrases as "lb bis today" and "1 lb cracs floor to night." Ellsworth's cold had evidently left him with what would now be called a sinus condition, a very painful one. He kept mentioning headache and neuralgia. A new trouble had developed by the last of the month. On April 30 he began the day's record: "One of my back teeth has decayed entirely & very suddenly — as it gave me no trouble until I commenced this mode of life — the consequence is I suffered all day with a toothache."

That evening three of "the boys" came in to see him and evidently brought some cigars along. Ellsworth disapproved of smoking as a weakness but there seems to have been a current theory that it had a medicinal effect as a sedative. He was desperate enough to experiment: "tried to smoke a cigar to cure the pain, of the two evils I con-

cluded to choose the least so stopped smoking and let the
tooth alone."

At least he had a more comfortable place to sleep — or
lie awake — that night. The day before he had had "an opportunity to buy a Lounge for $3.75," he wrote, and "I am
nicely fixed now I can sleep on the lounge & have my blanket
to cover me." He had probably rolled up in the blanket
when sleeping on the bare floor. He added, "I have an over-
coat for cold nights. Now if I could only be sure of something besides bread all the time, some meat or something
for a change I would ask nothing more."

He had another reason to be glad about his new sleeping
arrangements. "I was very lucky in getting my lounge just
as I did," he wrote, "for Mother would be put off no
longer & wanted to know in her letter today where I was
boarding so I could write back to her I had a good lounge
to sleep on — & the eating part I omitted saying that everything was going on nicely. There is no use of making
Father & Mother (God bless them) miserable by the
knowledge of my circumstances, I owe them already more
than I can ever repay."

The tooth, which had evidently abscessed, continued to
ache and the pain kept him awake at night. At times, he
wrote, it "nearly drove me frantic." "If I had money
enough," he said, on May 6, "I would get it filled."

He had, as a small boy, said to his mother that it was "too
bad" to have the toothache and to have to work too. Ellsworth was now forced to work very hard not only with the
toothache and cold infection but also with the constant
growing hunger of his starved body. He had taken on
the drilling of the Chicago Cadets while he continued his
copying and his determined reading of Blackstone. The
reading went more slowly than ever because he found it
difficult to concentrate. "It is no light task," he wrote on

May 5, "to confine your mind to your reading when your stomach is absolutely craving for food. If I get enough ahead by copying I will buy some dried meat of some kind, see if that will not produce a change."

Twice he tried to collect some money which a man owed him. On April 26 he wrote that he called on him and "asked him for the money due me which he has owed me nearly a year [he] plead hard times, could not pay it." Ellsworth thought the man was wealthy and was much disgusted. When he went back, however, on May 5 and the man said his creditors had almost ruined him and he had no money, Ellsworth believed him and had not the heart to press him. Like Abraham Lincoln, he had no defense against his own compassion.

He would give away his last few cents to help another. On May 26 he wrote that, when returning to the office, he was accosted by a stranger, an Englishman, "who inquired if I knew of a place where he could lodge for a shilling as that was all the money he had left." Talking with the man, Ellsworth learned that he had just come to the city in search of employment and that he had found a place where he could stay overnight for two shillings. The situation was that Ellsworth had just ten cents in his pocket which had to buy his food until Saturday (this happened on a Thursday). He handed the ten cents to the stranger and "told him to go to the place & they would not probably mind the two cents." The story ends, "I must trust to luck for something to eat."

On May 11, after a night rendered sleepless by toothache, Ellsworth arose with the grim determination to carry out his plans no matter what happened. He lettered and affixed to the door of his desk a card with this inscription: "So aim to spend your time, that at night when looking back upon the disposal of the day, you find no time *misspent* no *hour* no *moment even* that has not resulted in *some ben-*

efit no action that had not a purpose in it." He was giving himself the same advice he had given Carrie.

Below this resolution he outlined his rigid schedule. On Mondays, Thursdays, and Saturdays he would rise at five, study law until ten, do copying from ten to one, attend to business matters (perhaps tasks for Mr. Cone) from one to four, study again from four to seven and finish the day with an hour's exercises from seven to eight. There were no intervals between these various duties and significantly no time out for meals. On Tuesdays, Wednesdays, and Fridays he would rise at six, study until ten, devote himself to business until one, study and copy from one to seven and drill the Cadets from seven to eleven. The one night a week he had promised to give the Cadets had now grown to three.

On April 29 he had come to an understanding with them by a speech in which he had literally laid down the law. What he said strongly suggests that his rift with the Cadets had been over the question of rigid discipline both in military training and in moral conduct. Ellsworth wrote a full account in his diary: "I told the Cadets if they wanted a company of soldiers in every sense of the word & were anxious to make that company a source of improvement morally as well as physically then I would command them & commanding them would enforce the strictest discipline." He continued that unless their conduct satisfied him that they were willing to be governed by his wishes and work hard to place the company in a position second to none in the United States, he would have nothing to do with the organization. He wanted them to know, he said, that if they voted for him as captain they would do so "with their eyes open." It was quite a speech to make on a pound and a half of crackers which was all he had that day. His account ends triumphantly, "I was unanimously elected."

It seems astonishing that Ellsworth, weakened by starvation and pain, could keep up physically. How could he muster the vitality, the tact, the wit and magnetism which create that invisible but all-important force which draws an audience to a speaker? He had the innate quality possessed by certain powerful orators of being able to sway the emotions of others at will.

And he loved it, as a man always loves the fulfillment of his own creative talent. On June 4 he made another speech to the Cadets in favor of some question and they voted as he wished. He could always bring his men under his spell and fire them with his own enthusiasms. "What a glorious thing it is," he recorded that evening, "to feel that you control the minds of men."

Another inborn quality of Ellsworth's was brought out in an incident which happened eight days later, on June 12. By that time the company was in good shape and Ellsworth, speaking before the men, began to list the advantages they now possessed: "the best Armory, the finest uniform and —" when he was interrupted by an enthusiastic shout from one of the young Cadets. Instantly the others broke into loud, prolonged applause. Ellsworth stood still, his face suffused with surprise and pleasure. What the young Cadet had shouted was "And the gayest Captain in the Country."

12

"THANK GOD A TRIUMPH FOR ME"

THE fluctuations of Mr. Spafford's attitude toward the engagement of Ellsworth and Carrie can be traced in both the
Ellsworth letters and diary. Carrie's father continued to be
torn between his fondness for the young man and doubts
about his suitability as Carrie's husband. Whenever a fresh
installment of the current slanders about Ellsworth reached
Mr. Spafford's ears, he was likely to have a relapse into
doubt. This situation put Ellsworth in a delicate and painful position.

He could open his heart to Mrs. Spafford. It will be remembered that she had written him in this connection
about some matter which was troubling her husband and
he had replied with an explanation which Mr. Spafford did
not consider satisfactory. Ellsworth throws more light on
the subject in a letter to Carrie's mother on May 15, 1859.
He had felt, he said, that "Mr S. had the impression of
which you informed me, that out of consideration for
Carrie's feelings he would return an answer favorable to
my wishes, — when if he had not thought that Carrie
would have been seriously affected by it, the answer would
have been quite different." In other words Carrie was so
deeply in love with Ellsworth that her father did not have
the heart to hurt her by opposing the engagement. Ellsworth continued to Mrs. Spafford: "Under these circum-

stances as you will readily perceive, it appeared to me like taking a dishonorable advantage to ask what his affection for his daughter, would force him to grant even against his own wishes." Ellsworth then told how he, as a matter of honor, had been ready to give up Carrie's letters: "I was about to propose to make all the amend in my power to prove my regard for his wishes, by submitting to anything he might wish in regard to my relations with Carrie — though it were to cease corresponding with her."

Sympathetic Mrs. Spafford had smoothed matters over by writing Ellsworth that he was "not entirely right" in his supposition about her husband's attitude and advised him to talk with Mr. Spafford in person. She evidently realized that if the two came face to face, Ellsworth's complete sincerity and his personal charm would win her husband over. Ellsworth's letter continued, "I agree with you perfectly as to the propriety of this step, and will avail myself of the first opportunity to see Mr S." Both knew the gentleman was making frequent visits to Chicago, as the Spaffords were considering a business proposition which would involve their moving there.

This same letter of Ellsworth's to Mrs. Spafford has several passages which serve as bold brush strokes in the personality portrait drawn by his letters. His heart was moved by her understanding and sympathy and again he tried to tell her what "the priceless treasure" of her friendship meant to a young man situated as he was. "When the clouds of misfortune gather darkly about him," he wrote, speaking of himself rhetorically in the third person, "he turns to this, and feels in his heart this affection burning brightly, shedding a radiance over his pathway which no misfortune can obliterate, or machinations of enemies rob him of."

The word "enemies" brought up the subject of the repeated calumnies against him, and, as always, his resentment flared. Speaking of these "constantly recurring attempts" of his slanderers "to blacken my reputation," he wrote, "How they would hug themselves with very satisfaction, could they but see me begin a course of disipation, or commit *any act* which would *confirm their assertions.* I have never harmed these people, nor have I *willingly* given them offence."

All this leads up to a paragraph in which Ellsworth sizes up himself and his own shortcomings. He realized that to some he appeared overly strong-willed and proud. His pride, which had doubtless been intensified by his humiliations and frustrations, was both his vulnerability and his defense. It was what sustained him in his present difficult position. "I do not wish to make *any pretension* to being immaculate," he wrote Mrs. Spafford, ". . . I *have faults* — *very* many of them, that I am neither talented, nor educated, that I am doubtless haughty — possibly overbearing — poor, with no position nor any thing upon which to found any claim to one, all this I conceed." The next sentence suggests he was defending himself against some particular accusation: "*But* that I ever so far forgot myself, or the respect and obedience due a dear father and mother who I love more than life, so far as to commit any action unbecoming a man, or that there *exists* the *possibility* of my wronging the confidence of those who *love* and *trust* me, is FALSE."

He signs this letter "Truly and affectionately yours, Elmer," adding as a rather chilly postscript, "Present my respects to Mr Spafford."

Cordial relations with Carrie's father, however, were restored (at least temporarily) when Mr. Spafford was in Chicago on May 23. Ellsworth recorded their interview in his diary and wrote to Carrie, "I had a long conversation with your father in reference to it [the misunderstanding], and I am happy to say that it resulted most satisfactorily.

There is no longer any objection to our continuing our present relations to each other. I feared it was to be otherwise, but am most happily disappointed. Do you share my gratification? My own loved one."

The terrible thought that he might have had to give up her letters seems to have led him into telling her again how much these letters meant to him. "My dearest Carrie," he wrote, "with all due deference to your little Queenship, permit me to ask if you followed your *usual custom* in writing your last letter, that is, *did you reply to my* TWO LAST LETTERS." He continued pleadingly, "Darling, it is *very* lonely here, I take no relaxation whatever. I have dropped all my lady acquaintances without acception. My only pleasure is in receiving and perusing your letters." Then he added with that consideration which was natural to him: "If your time is all ocupied, do not fatigue yourself by writing me long letters. As *much as I prize them*, I would not have them cause *you trouble or loss of pleasure*. Good bye God bless and keep you. Darling — write soon. Elmer."

While he was writing to Carrie, struggling with delicate problems, reading law, copying documents, drilling and building up the morale of the Chicago Cadets, Ellsworth's physical condition was getting worse and worse. His diary, continuing the record of his crackers-and-water diet, shows all too well what was happening to him. On May 13 he wrote, "I am growing very weak & stupid I fall asleep while studying repeatedly." That day he was so driven by hunger and "so sick of crac" that he went to a market to buy "dried meat of some kind." He selected the smallest piece he could find and, after it was wrapped up, asked how much it was. The market man, perhaps seeing the hunger in the lean young face, said "that he would not accept any thing from me for so small an article." Uncompromisingly Ellsworth left the package lying on the table while he went out to a "segar store" and "bought a dozen segars which I judged came to a little more than the meat & went back took my meat thanked him, layed down the bundle of segars & started [out]." The man was thoroughly provoked but his protests fell on deaf ears. If he had not accepted the cigars, wrote Ellsworth, "I would not have touched the meat had I been starving. . . . What I eat I'll pay for," he continued, adding, however, with some realization that he had almost reached the limit of his endurance, "as long as *possible at least.*"

The torture of his toothache lasted well into May. He was naturally unable to throw off the infection left by his cold. On May 14 he recorded that he could not write on account of severe headache. The next day he wrote, "I find it impossible at present to rise at 5 & work through the day without sleeping two hours or more sometimes during the day I am very weak & troubled a good deal with my head. However I hope to get accustomed to it bye & bye."

On May 16 the diary reads, "My health has never been so bad as at present, my catarrh of which I thought myself completely cured has returned & when I study an hour steadily my head becomes like a furnace." He had gone that day to see General Swift, who was delighted with the excellence of his copying. Incidentally, the worthy general was also greatly pleased that Ellsworth was living "so regularly & economically."

On the way to the Swift house Ellsworth, feeling utterly miserable, noted: "How happy people looked as I passed down the Avenue, in their own homes with friends to love them." That day's record has a cry in it to which he could give utterance only in his diary: "Oh I do so long to go out, to be free again to exercise & live once more." Again on June 1 he wrote, "This confinement is just killing me by inches I cannot study more than 15 or 20 minutes before I am attacked by that terrible oppressive sensation about the head."

On June 12 he had something of a fainting spell which he recorded the next day. "I have not the slightest idea how or when I wrote the preceeding page," he began. He had stayed at the Cadets' armory to do his writing the evening before because it was so much more pleasant than at the office and "about 12 oclock a sensation similar to what one experiences, after taking Morphine came over me very suddenly. I was somewhat alarmed," he continued, "& immediately started for my room. I felt badly but did not suffer much pain." It was ten days before he wrote in his diary again. Between his physical depletion and some exciting new plans for the Cadets (which involved increased work for him), he had no time for diary writing.

How he mustered the physical vigor to drill the Cadets and the mental force to "control" their minds seems a mystery. Yet the diary reveals that during May Ellsworth went through a test which required even more physical fitness than the drilling. It will be remembered that he had taken fencing lessons from DeVilliers and then had taught fencing himself. The diary brings his skill in this art to life in an account of a fencing match.

John Hay, writing two years later about Ellsworth's mastery of swordplay, said that, superb as DeVilliers himself was, Ellsworth "could hold a rapier" with him. He "always had a hand as true as steel, and an eye like a gerfalcon." By the time Hay was writing this, Ellsworth had become famous and was a much-sought-after subject for photographers. Hay continued: "I have seen a photograph of his arm taken at this time. The knotted coil of thews and sinews looks like the magnificent exaggeration of antique sculpture."

The story of the fencing match begins in the diary on

May 14. "Have recd a partial challenge to trial of skill with a very expert fencer who is practicing daily," wrote Ellsworth on that day, "as I have not practiced with a master in nearly 18 months he will probably worster me the first time, after that I will trouble him. Nevertheless I shall foil with him as I must fence with some expert or lose my skill altogether."

On May 20 Ellsworth happened to pass "the place of that swordsman who I was challenged to fence with." He dropped in to meet the man and found him "an unassuming good natured fellow." The two "took the foils" briefly and Ellsworth noted that "my style of quick fencing rather annoyed him. . . . He said Mr O. taught him & he evidently thinks Mr O. a prodigy, he is going to bring him to the Armory some night where I shall undoubtedly get worstered, as O is in fine practice & I am entirely out."

The match took place on May 24 and doubtless had an interested audience of the Cadets, who were cheering for their young leader. It must have been an exciting scene and possibly excitement helped give Ellsworth the strength he so needed in the contest. He recorded it, however, rather matter-of-factly in the diary: "This evening the fencer of whom I have heard so much came up to the Armory to fence with me." Presumably this was Mr. O. "He said to his pupils & several others if I held to the low guard he would disarm me evry time. I raised my foil. He is a great gymnast & I fully expected to be beaten. The result was I disarmed him 4 times, hit him 30 times, he disarmed me once & hit me 5 times at the 'Touch à touch.' I touched him in two places at the same 'allonge' & threw his foil from him several feet." One can imagine the effect of this upon the watching Cadets and Ellsworth records the effect upon his opponent: "he was very angry although he tried to conceal it."

That fencing match was one of the last events in the old

armory of the Chicago Cadets on South Dearborn Street. This up-and-coming organization was preparing to move into new and better quarters three days later. Many improvements had been taking place since Ellsworth had accepted the captaincy less than a month before.

He naturally had to explain to Carrie why he was giving so much more time to military activities. She must have asked some questions about it, for on May 9 he wrote her, "Yes Carrie, I have changed my mind and have taken command of the Cadets for a limited time. . . . I have an object in view, which would justify me even in laying aside my studies entirely untill after the 4th of July, (the time for which I have accepted the command). . . . I have changed the company entirely and in every particular, uniform and all: they are now the Cadets of the 60th Regiment, instead of National Guards." Their new name was to be the United States Zouave Cadets.

When he had taken command on April 29, it had been on his own conditions: that the Cadets accept his strict discipline in moral conduct as well as in military training. Striking while the iron was hot, he had promptly written out resolutions embodying his ideals for the company which had to be signed by anyone joining it. These resolutions gave as purposes of the organization the physical and moral improvement of its members as well as learning the science of military tactics, the promotion of good feeling and gentlemanly conduct and the securing of the respect and confidence of the public. Ellsworth, fearing that his country was heading into war, would from this time on work toward increased efficiency for the militia and for the public's interest and confidence in it. The resolutions further stipulated that any member caught entering a drinking saloon in uniform or indulging in conduct unbecoming a gentleman would be promptly expelled.

The young leader astutely sent these resolutions to the

leading newspapers. In his diary on May 2, after telling about his writing another newspaper article for the Cadets, he said that the resolutions were published in all the papers and created a very favorable impression. He continued that four gentlemen, one of them editor of the *Railroad Gazette* and another a surgeon, had come to him that day to ask about joining the company. "If I had started an entire new organization," he added, "I could have filled the ranks immediately with just such men."

Ellsworth realized that to prevent young men from visiting places of dissipation it was well to provide a place of wholesome entertainment and companionship. He intended that their armory should have everything which would render it attractive to the Cadets — a reading room with plenty of books, a gymnasium, lunchroom, parlors, games, and facilities for social events like dances. The first step was to get an armory adequate for these requirements. On May 25, as recorded in the diary, the Cadets passed a resolution to rent the Light Guard Hall at the corner of State and Randolph Streets and undertook to raise fifty dollars for the first month's rent. To set an example, Ellsworth volunteered five dollars "& the boys came up handsomely & raised the money in a few minutes." He got the money from one of his fencing pupils who owed him that amount and, as a result of his generosity, when he helped the Cadets move two days later, he had nothing at all to eat that day.

When Ellsworth mentioned the Fourth of July in his letter to Carrie, he meant that he was planning a spectacular drill of the Cadets as a celebration. The occasion would be a testing of him and his company, an attempt to prove to the skeptical public that they were truly in earnest about their military training. One has already guessed, of course, that he was teaching the Zouave drill. Any young man who would go through the severe physical discipline necessary to master the Zouave drill would prove indubitably that he was no playboy.

Public interest was especially focused on the Zouaves that spring of 1859 because of the outbreak of the Italian-Austrian War. There the Chasseurs de Vincennes were distinguishing themselves in a spectacular way and were getting into the newspapers. Military men in the United States were keeping their eyes on what was happening abroad. On May 23 Ellsworth recorded, "Genl Buckner is going to europe to watch the progress of the war there." All of the young man's military longings rose to the surface at the thought: "What would I not give for his advantages now, what a career would be open for me, how tame this present life compared with it."

So the Cadets in June, with "the best Armory, the finest uniform" and "the gayest" (and most starved) "Captain in the Country," were in a fever of preparation for the glorious Fourth.

Ellsworth was skipping whole weeks now in his diary. There is a short entry for June 23, then nothing until June 30, when he wrote: "Have again been obliged to neglect my Journal. I have to work like a dog day & night, however it accomplishes something, this constant work." He had received quite a lift that day in a letter from General Swift expressing "a desire to have my company go through their evolutions before the Governor next Sept." Ellsworth was also receiving proposals to drill different companies.

Other organizations were clamoring to join the celebration of the Fourth which promised to be so brilliant. On July 3 Ellsworth wrote in his diary, "The officers of the Fire Brigade have solicited & recd permission from ME to parade with us tomorrow." The underscoring of "me" refers to the fact that early in June his name had been proposed as a member of the Fire Brigade and rejected. Four men were present who all had "some personal feeling against myself," he continued, this in spite of the fact that "I'm . . . well known as the getter up of the Fire Brigade."

Ellsworth recorded his solemn thoughts on the evening of July 3. "Tomorrow will be an eventful day to me," he began. "Tomorrow I have to appear in a conspicuous position before thousands of citizens an immense number of whom without knowing me except by sight are prejudiced against me. Tomorrow will demonstrate the truth or falsity of my assertions that the citizens would encourage military companies if they were worthy of respect. It is a trial I have courted let it come, tho' it is scarcely a pleasant thing to place yourself in a position where men who think you a devil or a fool are to decide upon your merit & make or mar your reputation." The "boys" slept at the Armory that night because "we must be on hand tomorrow A M at 4 oclock."

It was two o'clock on the morning of July 5 when he recorded what had happened on that glorious Fourth. The entry begins: *"Victory,* & thank God a triumph for me. This day has well nigh established my reputation." His pen fairly raced to tell each gratifying detail: the arrival of the Milwaukee Cadets at five A.M. to join them, the morning parade in which "our Boys looked very handsomely in their new uniforms & equipment & marched like old veterans," the crowded streets "wherever we passed." They stopped in front of the Tremont House, whose balconies and windows were as thick with people as the streets, and there they "went through a review before the Mayor & Council."

After the review and before the big exhibition drill Ellsworth had a chance to gather the boys around him and give them what would now be called a pep talk. "We commenced our movements first in quick time," he wrote, "then on the run." The crowd was silent at first, perhaps appraising, but soon that exhilaration which always quickens the blood at the color and beauty of a patriotic parade began to take hold of them. As the Cadets came down the street on the run, Ellsworth continued, a "chalk line could have been drawn across the front of the company & touched evry man alike, we cleared the crowd like chaff and such a cheer as we recd, I never heard given to a military Co before. From that time until the close of the drill, the crowd was absolutely enthusiastic applauding every new movement & cheering alternately the company & myself."

At the end of this brilliant exhibition the Milwaukee Cadets understandably declined to drill, "so," wrote Ellsworth, "we started for the Armory." The crowd, worked up to a high pitch, cheered them again as they left the grounds. Then came a feast. To one who has read the Ellsworth diary, with its record of exaggerated young pride and pitiful hunger, it is a genuine satisfaction to know that the company and leader were then served "a magnificent dinner."

Afterwards came welcome, exhilarating praise from all sides. Ellsworth recorded proudly: "An Army officer who had always scouted the idea of a military company drilling as well as Regulars, came to me of his own accord & said he wished to congratulate me, That he had been in the Army seven years, but he had never in the Army or out of it seen such drilling as our company performed that morning since he left the point." The habitual scorn of West Point men for the volunteer military companies had been another factor in their unpopularity.

Newspaper reading the next day was most pleasant. "The [Chicago] Tribune & Press which has hereto been decidedly down on all military companies," wrote Ellsworth on July 5, "after giving the company a long but flattering notice concluded by saying 'We but express the opinion of all who saw the drill yesterday morning when we say the company cannot be surpassed this side of West Point. The regulations in regard to liquor &c was rigidly enforced. The effect on the boys has been excellent, it has given them a name to be proud of & upheld & they will conduct themselves accordingly.' "

The morale of the Cadets was soaring. For them and for their leader it had been truly a day of triumph, an appetizer for the great feast of acclaim which would be theirs a year later.

13

"Buffetted Back into the Old Track"

Jᴜʟʏ 5 brought Ellsworth inevitable letdown and depression. He made a short entry in his diary beginning, "Am
not well for the last few days. I have been living in a
different style from what I have been accustomed to for
the past few months." How could he go back to crackers
and water after the delicious, satisfying food of the day before? How could he return to the tasteless drudgery of law
study after the glorious success of his military endeavors?
He tried, he wrote, to work but was unable to do so.

The next day was left blank in the diary. On July 7 he
wrote dismally, "Attempted to work but failed I can do
nothing with the same energy that I could bring to bear
when I was living like a human being." His mind was as
full of misery as his body. He had written Carrie he had
taken command of the Cadets for a limited time, only until
after July 4. How could he desert his boys after their marvelous performance and when he had such wonderful plans
for their future? They would think him almost a traitor if
he let them down now. It was not to be thought of. On the
other hand how could he explain to Carrie (and worse still,
her father) that he would continue his military activities
which would draw him away to some extent from his
law studies? He was grimly determined to go on with both
law and drills.

The Spaffords evidently decided they must talk things over with him. On July 11 he received, he said, a second letter "urging me to come to Rockford this week without fail. I shall make an attempt to go. I am still very weak & cannot reconcile myself to my food."

He arrived in Rockford on July 14 and went to that home on South Madison Street which had so many happy memories for him. It must have seemed strange that Carrie was not there. Mr. and Mrs. Spafford greeted him kindly, but there was a certain constraint in the atmosphere. Mr. Spafford was inevitably disapproving of the young man's return to military activities and on top of this there had been a fresh outburst of slanders about him. Ellsworth wrote in his diary that night: ". . . had some conversation with Mrs. S. in regard to my relations with the family, told her as long as people chose to listen to the stories of my enemies I felt that it must annoy her & Mr S. & I should release Mr S from his promises to me. & [they] need feel under no further obligation to treat me other than a stranger until time & my exertions had caused a change in the minds of those who now misunderstand & malign me. Mrs S. insisted that I should dismiss the matter from my mind & do nothing about it."

As they were talking thus someone entered and put an end to their confidences. Ellsworth then went to his room. "I felt," he wrote, "I had done & was about to do my duty, the highest and strictest sense of honor could demand nothing more, though in doing so I was about to dismiss so to speak my best almost my only friends." Weak from malnutrition, torn between two of the most powerful influences in a young man's life, his love for the girl he had chosen and his urge to follow unhindered the work for which his every instinct fitted him, Ellsworth for once gave way. He could tell this only to his diary: "Then a sense of my utter lonelyness, of my embarrassing position, of all that I have to contend with swept across my mind & for once I could not help it, I indulged in a real woman-ish cry."

He tried, he said, to pray but it was impossible for a while. The crying, however, seemed to give him a certain emotional release and "after it," he continued, "I was calmer & more resolute." He then took accurate stock of Mr. Spafford's attitude toward him. "I fancy," he wrote, "Mr S., although I believe he respects me, likes me when I am present, yet when he thinks of my position & that his daughter might have married some person of great wealth he must feel in his own mind that he would have been better pleased had I never met Carrie. This was what de-termined me to release him from his promises or per-mission rather."

That entry of July 14 ends on a note of physical com-fort. It seemed so luxurious to be in a real home, where meals were served regularly, and to sleep in a comfortable bedroom. "Had SOMETHING TO EAT TO DAY," he wrote with heavy underscoring, "& sleep on a BED TO NIGHT."

Rockford held many friends of his but he said nothing in his diary of renewing old ties. There was a "fencing academy" in the town now and he lost no time in getting acquainted with its "professor of the art of fencing." A fencing match with an audience was arranged in which he got the best of the professor in three bouts. Ellsworth com-mented in his diary that the man was "a better fencer than myself" but "I am rather quicker." After the contest he felt, he said, "as if I would faint, I had no strength left."

An exciting possibility, which incidentally showed how interest in the Zouave drill was spreading over the coun-try, was mentioned to him during his stay at the Spaffords. A former member of the Rockford Greys, who had re-cently visited California, said that the first question asked of him when he arrived there was "Can you teach the

Zouave Drill." The man said no, and then he was assured that anyone teaching the Zouave drill there could get eight to ten thousand dollars. He urged Ellsworth to go to California. The latter recorded in his diary: "I would not abandon my present course until its completion for twice ten thousand dollars. I will go after the completion of my studies & stay a year provided I can have a sure thing pecuniarily."

Ellsworth was to leave Rockford on July 22. His visit had been a tense, disturbed one, and on the night of the 20th he had an emotional experience which he recorded in his diary the next day. "Was awakened from a sound slumber last evening," he began, "by the music of the Cornet Band who were serenading Mrs S. The moon shone brightly & a barely perceptible breeze from the river seemed to waft the music to me with a softness indiscribable, under the influence of the spell I gave free rein to my imagination and it pictured to my mind such scenes of happiness as I fear I may never enjoy."

Worn out by conflict, he had turned his thoughts back for comfort to his happy boyhood at Mechanicville. He seemed to see the old home, the trees around it, the river and the hills, the farm animals he had loved. For a moment he rested drowsily contemplating the sweetness of this picture, then he remembered how his ailing parents had had to work beyond their strength on that farm and suddenly all his present responsibilities, frustrations, and problems came flocking back. Bitterness and a sense of the injustice of things overwhelmed him. "Looking back on the record of 10 long years," he wrote, ". . . every where I find trouble disappointment misery. Not one ray of happiness beams upon me from the past."

He felt apologetic about putting these thoughts into writing: "This is perhaps the first time I have ever given utterance to these feelings so plainly, it is wrong perhaps but to night I cannot help it, it is not the petulance of boy-hood or the still more unreasonable egotism of the man trying to shift the burden of his own faults, sins, omissions to other shoulders it is not this, I am to much in earnest."

He asked himself the age-old question, why had these misfortunes come to him? "I have tried to act right, have shuned dissipation of every kind as unworthy one who looked earnestly at life & its duties, have denied myself all pleasures . . . have worked, toiled, suffered."

Perhaps being in a comfortable home with proper food and normal living for the past week had made him feel more acutely the cruel existence he had had both after the embezzlement incident and more recently in Chicago. He burst out in an expression of utter misery: ". . . in the midst of plenty as God is my witness have I gone so long without food that in the solitude of my own room I have nearly choked myself in the extremity of agony, have walked the street night after night through the long winter, slept upon the hard boards, with no covering at all, this that I might succeed in that which was evry way worthy, all this have I endured not once but long months, years even rather than do aught unworthy of myself & what better am I to day, what have I received for it — sneers from those who fortune favors."

This led him to thinking again about the terrible disillusionment caused by the "infernal scoundrel" who had robbed him. Once more he recorded his feelings about that searing experience. Let others go through all he had had to take, he wrote: "Then they will understand my feelings & acc't for their existence in the mind of the *old* man of twenty two." It is a poignant expression of a young man's struggle and questioning to find himself.

It was nearing two o'clock in the morning in his quiet bedroom at the Spaffords when he finished unburdening himself to his diary. He concluded with a long passage: "I liken my fortune," he said, "to that of a traveler led or forced on by an invisible fervor who toils along a rough path beset with almost unsurmountable difficulties who anon sees on either side of him branching off in evry direction beautiful roads leading to most attractive spots which give promise of repose, but at evry succeeding attempt to exchange the one for the other is buffetted back into the old track to toil on, saluted at evry step by the jeers of all who seeing only the traveler know nothing of the influence which commands him."

Then comes a thoughtful self-analysis: "I almost think I have two natures separate & distinct, following the promptings of one. I would want my parents comfortably & happily situated, my brother an honest high minded man, a house adorned & beautified by the presence of such a woman as I could love with my whole soul, an honorable & respected name. This would constitute happiness, my ambition would extend no further although distinction at the hands of the public would give me pleasure, the absence of it would cause me no regret."

Ellsworth's letters have already given evidence that these were things he loved and prized. He continued with a description of the second half of his nature: "The other, freed from all care, giving free rein to an ambition as boundless as the air we breathe, not for personal advancement merely but to do good to my fellow man, making evry thing consistent with honor subservient to this. To estimate this latter or second peculiarity of my disposition I must have some powerful incentive." That was very much the same kind of ambition that was driving Mr. Abraham Lincoln at Springfield about this time. Ellsworth had described the humanitarian and the dedicated patriot. He, like Mr. Lincoln, was seeking prominence, not for personal gain, but to do good to his fellow men.

Fate, planning Ellsworth's destiny, had an eye for the

dramatic. In a little over a year he would wear upon his heart a gold circlet inscribed with the words *Non Solum Nobis sed Pro Patria* (not for ourselves alone but for country). And fate in the end would make dramatic use of that small circle of gold.

He left Rockford the evening of July 22 to return to Chicago. "There was a poor Irishman got on the train at the Junction & begged permission to ride to Chicago." The conductor "put him off at a little way station," Ellsworth said in his diary. "If I had had any money I would have paid his fare but my funds amounted to only 20 p so I was obliged to keep quiet."

There are several similar incidents in the diary showing his ready sympathy and generosity. Curiously, these incidents involve three different nationalities. His giving his last ten cents to a needy Englishman has already been mentioned; here he pities a poor Irishman; and on July 8, it had been a penniless old Italian patriot who had lost one leg fighting under Garibaldi. Ellsworth presented the Italian soldier's case to "the boys & they raised $5.50 to pay his board for a few days." It was Ellsworth who saw some influential people in the old man's behalf and made some arrangements to start him on his way back to Italy. The diary account ends characteristically: "I have undertaken to raise $8. to pay his bill at the Hotel."

Once back at Mr. Cone's office in Chicago, Ellsworth's existence reverted to the routine of bread-and-water diet, work, and study without recreation. His diary now begins to have brief entries and skips many days entirely until on August 25 it ceases altogether. It does round out the story of his near-starvation. He reached a point where his system would not tolerate the crackers; they caused nausea and illness that made it impossible for him to do mental work. Realizing at last that it takes more than valor and will-power to nourish one's body, he began of necessity to get some adequate food. In this connection, the very last diary entry is interesting: ". . . in order to get money for my expenses I have been obliged to sell my set of jewelry for $28. dollars which is just what it originally cost. This will with economy bear my expenses some months."

On the first day Ellsworth was back in Chicago from Rockford, he held a meeting of the Cadets. Since the Fourth of July drill people delighted to come to the armory to watch their maneuvers. On August 13 he wrote to Carrie about another satisfactory occasion: "The Cadets," he said, "gave an exhibition drill last Tuesday evening which was attended by a very large audience. We were *obliged* to *refuse admittance* to some two hundred ladies & gentlemen." Proudly he told her about their "magnificent Hall, and two parlors, fitted up with brussels carpet, handsome mirrors, Piano, and guitars &c ad libitum," and how every inch of space was filled with seated or standing spectators. Lover-like, he added, "HAD YOU only been *present*, my gratification would have been COMPLETE. I enclose an article from one of the newspapers."

The newspaper clipping mentions the "splendid audience, among whom were many of the F.F.'s of Chicago," the more remarkable because it was an evening of "intense heat." "The Cadets," said the friendly reporter, "appeared for the first time in the Zouave uniform, which is of course just the dress portrayed in the illustrated newspapers." (That last remark in itself shows the awakening interest of the public.) "In the picture," the article continued, "it looked awkward and baggy, but in reality it is unique, and is decidedly the loosest and lightest attire that any soldier wears. There is nothing to impede the movements as there is in the stiff dress of the British soldier, and the scarcely more convenient attire of our own regulars." The writer thought the cap "the jauntiest little scarlet head gear ever worn by a practical, fighting man," and he felt this new uniform might well "lead to important dress reforms."

The article commented on "the wonderful precision, rapidity and difficulty" of the Zouave drill and the prolonged cheers of the audience. "The boys," it continued, "exhibited the 'elephant' to their friends, 'a hannimile' that caused a general laugh." These lively young men with their fun-loving leader delighted to include in their programs some humorous drill or formation which was pure comedy. They had also organized a Glee Club and were inventing their own special yells. "The Cadets did something in the way of singing, and gave us a taste of their cheering, which is something new and startling." It ends: "We understand that during the State Fair they are going to do a Zouave feat — they intend to start from the Armory and run all the way to Cottage Grove. We think on that occasion we will take the horse cars but wish the boys 'a pleasant time.'"

The rollicking spirit of the Zouave Cadets romps through another newspaper article, written by one of their own members. He called it "The Progress of My Zouave Practice" and signed it "Doesticks P. B." He first paid his respects to the uniform. A Zouave, he said, was one who wore "two red bags" for trousers, "a cap like a red woolen saucepan," "yellow boots like the fourth robber in a stage-play," and "a sort of sword-gun, or gun-sword for a weapon." A Zouave must be able to "climb up an eighty-foot rope, hand over hand, with a barrel of flour hanging to his heels," or "walk up four flights of stairs holding a heavy man in each hand at arms length." He should consider it a mere trifle to "set up a forty-foot ladder on end, balance himself on top of it, and shoot wild pigeons on the wing, one at a time, just behind the eye, with a single-barreled Minie rifle, three hundred yards distance and never miss a shot."

Doesticks told something of his trials. Two other Zouaves

came to see him and "they Zouaved a little by way of setting me an example." They decided to measure his room athletically and found it was "three flip-flops long, and a handspring and two back-somersaults wide." Doesticks explained the use which he had learned for a handspring in war: "You reverse your position, and your bewildered enemy cuts off your foot instead of your head. Then you kill him, then you screw on a wooden leg and do it again."

He described his careful preparations for his first somersault and his assorted bumps and bruises when he woke up three-quarters of an hour later. But he triumphed in the end when he became a seasoned Zouave. He never thought of sleeping in a bed now, he said, and when he came down to breakfast in the mornings, "I generally walk on my hands around the table, and give each of the boarders a patronizing shake of my slipper."

It is clear the Zouaves were receiving much attention and so was their Major Ellsworth. Both, however, were having various ups and downs. With such strict rules of behavior for the Cadets, problems of discipline were inevitable and Ellsworth was an uncompromising disciplinarian. He recorded two cases in his diary. On July 26 after "our Glee Club serenaded," he wrote, "Some of the boys went into a saloon to get some beer & while there sang a song." Presumably they were in uniform and Ellsworth said he reprimanded them severely. He added that they "were quite ashamed of it."

The other incident occurred on August 22. One of the Cadets, Elmer wrote, "wanted to shirk a little" and came to him "to get excused. I told him he must ask the Co. as I had left such matters in their hands." The fellow became angry and said that if he were not excused, he would resign. Ellsworth continued, "the company had got almost down stairs but I immediately called them back, called a meeting & stated the circumstances, and told him to take

the floor and do what he so much wished. He got up &
apologised." John Hay was to say later that Ellsworth's
men "feared him as a Colonel should be feared, and loved
him as a brother should be loved."

August 16 was a day when several encouraging things
happened all at once. Ellsworth spent most of that day
with the state Adjutant General, who suggested that he
might be appointed on his staff, adding that "the work of
compiling a report for the Legislature must be attended
to" and he needed Ellsworth's assistance. People were finding out what an efficient young man Major Ellsworth was.
The Adjutant General also mentioned that the position of
Paymaster General of the State was vacant and that he
would speak to the Governor about giving Ellsworth that
appointment. On the same day the possibility of his becoming the Adjutant of the 60th Regiment or Brigade
Inspector was presented to him.

Nothing came of these matters immediately, and by
August 25 Ellsworth had received some upsetting news:
he had to move out of Mr. Cone's office. It was very dis-
couraging, but when he wrote to Carrie about it on August 29 it was with nonchalance. He was "in hot water,"
he said. Mr. Cone, through the rascality of a former partner, had been obliged to sell all his books and office furniture at public auction. In the office now there was "nothing to relieve the monotony of the four bare walls excepting 'your own correspondent,' who perched on his
desk in a corner surveyed his worldly possessions at his
feet, consisting of two trunks and a cavalry sabre, and
whistled, 'such is life,' to the tune of 'what's the odds, so
long's you're happy.' So you perceive my own darling I
am again thrown on my own resources."

He then takes Carrie playfully with him into a pleasing
daydream. "This is a very extensive world sweet one and
there are in it many people among them undoubtedly is

some aged and obese gentleman possessed of a fabulous fortune, in his own right, and a gold headed cane, who only awaits a convenient opportunity to pat me on the head and adopt me as his own. I expect to meet this individual about the same time my fortune changes and I can see in the future something else than *mis*-fortune and disappointment." He continues seriously: "Carrie darling, its a long lane etc you know the old saying, and if God only grants me health and strength I will yet surmount these difficulties and wring from old Dame Fortune her consent unwilling though it be to a change in the program of my existence."

He told her of something which he wanted very much. During the "U.S. Agricultural Fair," he said, "there is to be a prize of a handsome stand of colors given to the best drilled military company. We are to compete, but unfortunately, owing to the short notice and the fact of having a large number of new members who will not be fully posted in the drill, we shall not be able to take the Colors."

What a difference it would make if they could!

14

"To Love One Maiden Only, Cleave to Her"

In that summer of 1859 Alfred Tennyson, Poet Laureate in England, published the first series of his *Idylls of the King*. These poems became widely popular when they crossed the ocean and were read in the United States. Ellsworth, loving poetry as he did music and painting, one day came across a passage in *Guinevere* that spoke to his very heart. It seemed beautifully to express his own ideals about the most important things in his life. King Arthur, speaking of "the knighthood-errant of this realm" and "that fair order of the Table Round," was describing what Ellsworth himself (with allowance for the centuries between) dreamed of for the young soldiers under his command.

> *A glorious company, the flower of men,*
> *To serve as model for the mighty world,*
> *And be the fair beginning of a time.*
> *I made them lay their hands in mine and swear*
> *To reverence the King, as if he were*
> *Their conscience, and their conscience as their King,*
> *To break the heathen and uphold the Christ,*
> *To ride abroad redressing human wrongs,*
> *To speak no slander, no, nor listen to it,*
> *To lead sweet lives in purest chastity . . .*

John Hay, who felt that Ellsworth was like "a Paladin or Cavalier of the dead days of romance and beauty," told with what "exquisite appreciation" the young officer used to read this passage.

> *To love one maiden only, cleave to her,*
> *And worship her by years of noble deeds,*
> *Until they won her, for indeed I knew*
> *Of no more subtle master under heaven*
> *Than is the maiden passion for a maid,*
> *Not only to keep down the base in man,*
> *But teach high thought, and amiable words*
> *And courtliness, and the desire of fame,*
> *And love of truth, and all that makes a man.*

It is time to assay Ellsworth's portrait as a lover, to focus on the love story which unfolds in the stream of letters he was writing to Carrie. These letters have progressed a long way from his first hesitant epistle. "My Dearest Friend" has become "My darling Carrie." "Adieu, Ellsworth" has changed to "Accept a thousand kisses from your own Elmer." He himself said in a later letter, "I have come by degrees to use a *much warmer style of expression.*"

On June 26 in this year 1859 he wrote her, "Carrie, my love for you increases in depth and strength with every hour. Oh Carrie, how I *trust in you,* how *entirely* and *absolutely* I repose my *only hopes* of *happiness* in your love. You cannot, it *is not possible* for you to understand my feelings." He expressed the longing which all lovers have for the bright future when they do not have to be separated: "My own darling, what would I not give to be with you to day? but such wishes are fruitless, we can only look forward to the time when your studies concluded & you will return to go from home no more untill *we go together.*" Meanwhile, he could thank God for health, strength, and friends, "and, what *I value far more than all else, darling, your love.*"

Incidental items show how his thoughts were constantly on her. The artist in Ellsworth made him delight in doing ornamental lettering and among his papers is found the name "Carrie" worked into an elaborate design. She came into his dreams. "I dreamed last night," he wrote her, "that I met you. I thought we were both at the house in which I was born, which, by some edict from dreamland, had been changed to a seminary for young ladies. But alas, I awoke, just when I would have given worlds, had I been possessed of a supply of those articles, for a few moments more of sleep."

He wrote her in June of 1859 that he had always carried in his mind a "Beau ideal" of the woman he could love and how she fulfilled it, or rather how she would fulfill it after she had finished her studies. Carrie was only sixteen and Ellsworth was determined she should develop in the best possible way both physically and mentally. In his letters he continued to offer her advice on many subjects, some of them rather unexpected.

Carrie's full-length picture with its tiny waistline above wide-spreading skirts indicates she wore the tight corsets of the period. Ellsworth, convinced that squeezing in the waist was injurious, came straight to the point. "Carrie will you observe two things?" he wrote on May 8. "I request this observance, as an especial favor, and they are of vital importance to you: — to make it a rule, to take PLENTY of EXERCISE, and AVOID TIGHT LACING. Pardon me, for referring to this, you cannot appreciate its importance as I can, who have seen one of the most *lovely* and *fascinating women* the sun ever shown on, RUINED in *body*, *health* and *spirit*, by NOTHING ELSE than this *most pernicious habit*. Oh! most CONTEMPTIBLE VANITY."

Ellsworth, having conducted gymnasium classes, naturally was concerned with the proper development of the body and rules of wholesome living. He did not fail to give

Carrie directions for the exercise he requested her to take. By exercise, he wrote, "I mean something besides a demure little walk of an hour or so." "First thing you know," he continued in his next letter, "I shall send you a pair of Dumb Bells to exercise with if nothing better happens. I want you to feel that glorious exhilaration that only proceeds from a perfect state of health which can only be obtained by an abundance of exercise. . . . Why Carrie, when I have an opportunity I am going to make a perfect *woman* of you, I shall teach you to ride, skate, shoot, fence, and an endless variety of similar accomplishments not usually found in the list of studies embraced in the catalogues of our seminaries."

Ellsworth had firm convictions on the subject of ventilation, views that were not calculated to please any householder from whom he rented a room. Sleeping with closed windows was general at that time, and if he found the windows immovable, he knew what measures to take. "He used to amuse himself by shooting ventilation-holes through his window-panes," wrote John Hay. "Standing ten paces from the window, he could fire the seven shots from his revolver and not shiver the glass beyond the circumference of a half-dollar."

Carrie, of course, should have plenty of fresh air. Here are his directions to her on the subject: "Have a piece 4 x 6 inches cut out of the uper pane of glass, of the two oposite windows, and trust to good luck for the ventilation — or, have a piece taken from the uper door panel, if there is not a ventilator over the door, & cut a piece from only *one* window." His protective sense was reaching across the miles between them to care for her welfare in every way. ". . . promise me," he wrote, "that you will IN-VARIABLY RETIRE BEFORE 10 O'CLOCK. . . ."

Because the lovers were both young, deeply in love, and so far apart, there were occasional misunderstandings and

crises. Each frequently accused the other of not writing
often enough or of sending letters that were too short.
Sometimes Ellsworth used the playful approach, as when he
tells Carrie he "has to go about disconsolate, looking alas
for letters that do not come, and torturing the postmaster
into fits with frequent inquiries after the whereabouts of
expected letters, while you are reveling in the possession
of at least one letter per week." At other times he is very
direct: "You do not write me very long letters. I fear that
you forget that the most trivial matters interest me, when
written by you." He tells her that her letters "have already
degenerated into NOTES — and by & by I shall not be surprised if I receive nothing but a visiting card." It all adds
up to how much her letters meant to him.

Once, later, when he had begun to call her Kitty, he made
an interesting request. "Kitty darling," he wrote, "are you
far enough advanced in french, to write your next letter,
without any inconvenience, in that language. My object in
making this request is this, I want some incentive to famil-
iaring myself to a certain extent with French, & it strikes me
that if your letters were written in *Comanche*, I should not
rest untill I had made them out." He went on to say
that, as he could not ask any one to help him read her
letters, "it will *oblige me to study*."

Each of the two was in a position to recognize that the
other was extremely attractive to the opposite sex, and
young love is very susceptible to jealousy. If Ellsworth was
merely polite to another woman Carrie was sure to hear of it
and question him about it. He always wanted perfect frank-
ness between them; it was one of his ideals of their relationship.

When in the spring of 1859 Carrie wrote him fully
about a young man who was attempting to woo her and
what had happened in consequence, Ellsworth was so delighted that he replied almost rapturously: "Carrie, my

ELLSWORTH'S PARENTS

Mr. and Mrs. Ephraim D. Ellsworth. Their devoted son said of them: "I
nnot recollect of an instance where my father or mother have been guilty of
mean spirited or ungenerous action."

THE BOY AND THE MAN

Left, the boy Elmer undergoing the new experience of sitting for his picture.
ght, Colonel Ellsworth in an engraving from a popular photograph. Here the
cture is on a memorial envelope, as the curve of the postmark at the lower right
ows. Memorial envelopes with Ellsworth's picture were common in 1861.
his is a modern version; it was mailed from Mechanicville, New York, in 1932.

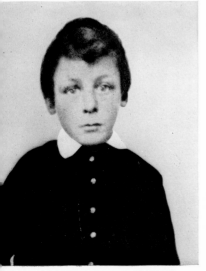 

Upper left, Ellsworth's birthplace, "the low-browed cottage" at Malta, N. Y. This picture was taken in the early nineteen-hundreds, after the porch had been added. *Upper right,* the Ellsworth home in Mechanicville, N. Y. Here Lincoln's friend spent his childhood years.

ELMER AND HER "LITTLE QUEENSHIP," CARRIE

ELLSWORTH AND MILITARY FRIENDS

Photograph taken in New York in July 1860 by Colonel E. L. Brand of the U. S. Zouave Cadets. In back is the Championship Flag. Ellsworth is second from the left.

THE PRIZE WHICH MEANT SO MUCH

The Champion Flag awarded the Cadets by the National Agricultural Society Ellsworth described it: "The silk . . . is six feet wide without being *pieced* . . On the white side is the Arms of the U. S. with the inscription 'Champion Flag awarded Sept. 15th 59.' On the reverse — is a large white Star — on the Centre of the Star, an American Shield with a *tiger head* in the Centre. . . ."

THE TRAGEDY

An engraving from a painting by Alonzo Chappel. The man in shirt sleeves, James W. Jackson, has just fired the fatal shot. Reading up, the men at the stairs are Corporal Francis E. Brownell, Colonel Ellsworth, and Edward H. House, correspondent of the *New York Tribune*. The two top figures are Lieutenant H. J. Winser and Chaplain E. W. Dodge.

Washington D.C.
May. 25. 1861

To the Father and Mother of Col.
Elmer E. Ellsworth:

My dear Sir and Madam,

In the untimely
loss of your noble son, our affliction
here, is scarcely less than your own.
So much of promised usefulness
to one's country, and of bright hopes
for one's self and friends, have rarely
been so suddenly dashed, as
in his fall. In size, in years, and
in youthful appearance, a boy
only, his power to command men,
was surpassingly great— This power,

to address you this tribute to the
memory of my young friend, and
your brave and early fallen child.

May God give you that consolation which is beyond all earthly
power—

Sincerely your friend
in a common af-
fliction—
A. Lincoln

Courtesy of the Huntington Library

LINCOLN WRITES ELLSWORTH'S PARENTS

The first part and the ending of President Lincoln's letter of sympathy to
Ellsworth's father and mother in the "common" sorrow which overwhelme
them all.

own beloved, you cannot conceive how much I am gratified by this renewed proof of your love, for so I consider it. The natural impulse of most women would have been to conceal such an affair, and perhaps, from a love of admiration and coquetry, to reply to the letter. But you my own noble Carrie, pursued just the course that I should have expected from one of truthfulness and purity of mind. May it *ever* be *thus*, may the *confidence* which is so *essential* to pure affection, govern and color all our intercourse."

Carrie had told the ardent gentleman that she was engaged but he had not taken that for an answer and had written her a letter which Ellsworth considered disrespectful, not to say insulting. She had evidently enclosed this letter, as he continued indignantly that what it said in effect was, "Miss Carrie, your a pretty nice girl, but dont know *your own mind* — true you told me once, that you were engaged, but, being a *woman*, you can easily forget *that*, and now that you have had time to come to a *full realization* of MY *attractions*, I have but to write you a letter no matter HOW INSULTING its tone, and you drop into my arms at once."

One suspects there would have been a fight if the two men had met. Ellsworth wrote furiously: "I would like the privilege of telling this *honorable* young man what I think of one who cooly insults a lady, and tries to wrong one who he knows nothing of . . . it sickens me."

Obviously Ellsworth could not tell Carrie about all his troubles with susceptible ladies, but he did write her about one. A woman who evidently found young Major Ellsworth a most charming figure "wrote saying she understood I wished to go to West Point, and through the influence of her relatives, she felt confident of being able to get me an appointment — as she took a great interest in me etc etc." (It is not hard to guess why he did not spell out the "etc." in writing to Carrie.) He wrote back saying briefly he did not want to go to West Point, "but," he continued, "a gentleman got hold of her letter and is carrying on quite a correspondence in *my name,* she evidently thinking, that she is receiving letters from me." (What if word came to Mr. Spafford's ears that Major Ellsworth was writing ardent letters to this unknown woman?)

An episode occurred in the fall of 1859 that made Ellsworth feel angry, hurt, and jealous. It appears that the city of Rockford, in addition to harboring a trouble-making Mr. B., had a similar character referred to as Mr. T. Ellsworth had reason to know that this Mr. T. was not a man to be trusted; he was, nevertheless, a friend of the Spaffords. When Carrie wrote her fiancé that she was corresponding with Mr. T., he answered with considerable vigor: "In reference to Mr T — I think you already have my opinion of that person, expressed on *several occasions,* in the most *emphatic manner.* I do not know that I have had any *good reason* to change it. I have also said, that I would never attempt to govern or control your action, when it was possible for you to understand what would give me pleasure or pain, by any word or act of mine." He expanded this theme and continued with a statement which one is a bit inclined to doubt: "You are very wrong in thinking that I am offended in consequence of your correspondence with this person, nothing of the kind can give me offence." But this correspondence *"might have this effect* — to convince me that you had not yet attained that degree of affection which would enable you to find pleasure in anticipating the wishes of the object of your love, and finding your highest enjoyment in their gratification. However this is a *kind* of *love* that we *read* of in *books* and *occasionally hear* of in some *remote* locality, I presume it is not to be looked for in *real life.* My absurd views of these matters must be attributed to ignorance. I shall become wiser by and by. In the meantime, dear Carrie, do just what pleases you without any reference to me and accept my thanks for your frank-ness in telling me of your correspondence."

The fear of losing Carrie's young affection flashes out in another passage in the same letter: "Oh Carrie! My own darling! . . . I look only in one direction for happiness on earth, to you, Carrie, loved one; for Godsake *be true* to *yourself and me.* I have borne with disappointment & trouble . . . but I *cannot* bear being disappointed *in you.* I dare not even contemplate the *possibility* of it."

Ellsworth's vigorous opinions about the correspondence with Mr. T. occupy only one page of a seven-page epistle which is entirely loverlike otherwise. This letter, written September 22, ends: "Accept ten thousand kisses, what would I not give to meet and converse with you. I could make you understand me so much better."

Carrie wrote back a "sweet letter" saying she was dis-turbed at what Ellsworth had told her about Mr. T. He re-plied on October 9: "I am sorry, darling, that any thing in my letter should have caused you any uneasiness. This, I trust, will be the last time that I shall have reason to refer to that matter: the *gentleman* has had a *little difficulty* at Rock-ford, and has gone to *Texas* in consequence."

The indications are that Mr. T. may have had designs of his own concerning the charming daughter of the wealthy Mr. Spafford. At least he had apparently tried to alienate Major Ellsworth from Carrie's parents. Ellsworth's letter continues: "I can say now, since the result has justified my estimate of the calibre and character of the individual, that it would pain me exceedingly to have *any young lady,* in whom I felt the slightest interest, carry on a correspondence with him unless she was *engaged* to him. His last *kind office* was to bring me a message from your mother, which evinced a feeling which *no act or omission* of mine has justi-fied."

Ellsworth, not trusting Mr. T.'s word, was disposed to

consider this message "a fabrication of his own" until he received a letter from Mrs. Spafford confirming it. What the implied accusation was is not stated, but it touched his pride sorely. He did not tell Carrie he had replied to her mother's letter on October 6 with the stiffest and coldest of notes. In it he briefly and formally acknowledged Mrs. Spafford's letter, expressed his regret that she "should have suffered so much inconvenience, for so trifling an article" and signed himself, "Respectfully your obt sevt E. E. Ellsworth." Now that Mr. T. had proved himself a rascal Ellsworth was sure the affair would be straightened out and he did not want Carrie to worry about it. He took occasion to say that he considered her mother, "next yourself, the *dearest friend I have on earth*."

One likes to imagine how these young lovers looked together. Ellsworth unconsciously painted such a picture in one of his letters. "Do you remember," he wrote Carrie, "when I tried to write on the dining room table and you lent me your valuable assistance?" Under circumstances so extremely satisfactory he had stretched out his writing as long as possible: "What work I made of it," he said happily. "I can fancy you now sitting in this chair just by my side with your dear little arm just resting — on my shoulder and 'me arm around yer waist.' " He explained that "this scrap of poetry is from the sentimental ballad of 'The Low backed Car' which having been hummed whistled & drummed in my presence for the last week has become quite familiar to me."

This was written after he had had the joy of seeing Carrie again. That seven-page letter of September 22, 1859, had contained wonderful news. In it Ellsworth expressed his delight that Carrie had unexpectedly decided to come home from school for a vacation.

Delightful plans for her coming went forward. He was invited to spend Thanksgiving with her and her family at

Rockford. Two letters of his on November 16, one to Carrie and one to her mother, express his intense disappointment that he could not arrive until after Thanksgiving. Perhaps they were able to celebrate Carrie's seventeenth birthday, December 2, 1859, together.

Something of the lovers' happiness at being together again is suggested by Ellsworth's letter written December 13, after the glory and uplift of the visit was ended. "With you, darling," he wrote, "my joy & sunlight departed, and I have returned to my 'slough of despond' infinitely happier for the brief release from care your dear society procured me." It develops in this letter that Carrie had also visited Chicago, where he had had the great pride and joy of introducing her to "the boys." He had received a letter from her since they parted and, girl-like, she had wanted to know whether she had made a good impression.

He answered, delighted: "So, Miss Curiosity, you would know *what* the Cadets say: in a word then, they are all *hugely pleased* with the future *Commandant-ta-ress* of the Corps." One of the boys, he continued, "has engaged me to be on the lookout for *just such another one for him*, & when found, he engages to fall in love *instanter*."

This letter answers the question all important to Ellsworth: was Carrie studying and blossoming into the woman he had hoped she would become? Emphatically she was. He felt that "a new era" had opened in their relationship. "You seem to me," he told her, "to have all at once developed new powers, and a determination of purpose which does you infinite credit. . . . You do not half appreciate, my darling, the power you possess for the accomplishment of great purposes. . . . Kitty, darling, I am proud of you."

King Arthur in Tennyson's quoted lines had expressed the thought that a young man's love for the woman he has chosen is a source of strength to him, a force to give him love of truth and other high ideals. How Ellsworth drew this kind of strength from his love for Carrie appears in a significant passage he wrote to her in this year 1859. "My own darling," he began, "without making any pretentions to christian conduct, and being sensible as I certainly am of my many imperfections, Yet I do trust in God, and whatever trials I may have during the day I know that the night brings me at least a few moments of perfect happiness when I kneel and pray that God will bless and keep you, I lie down to sleep my mind resting tranquilly in the belief of Gods mercy & your love, two thoughts inseparably connected in my mind."

15

JOURNEY TO SPRINGFIELD

Many developments along lines other than the romantic appear in Ellsworth's letters in the fall of 1859. Toward the end of August, it will be remembered, he had written Carrie about having to get out of Mr. Cone's office and had mentioned longingly the prize which the National Agricultural Society would offer the best-drilled military company at their fair in September. He had no expectation that his Zouave Cadets could win it because so many of them were new and untrained.

His omnibus letter to Carrie on September 22 gives the next installments of both stories. When he found himself *"kicked out* to look for an *opportunity,"* he wrote, "Having made up my mind to *try again,* and, if possible, find another opening, I started out and was met by an offer to go into the office of E. Van. Buren Esqr. a most excellent Lawyer, which offer I accepted and once more I'm duly installed and hard at work."

Being one to attempt the impossible, Ellsworth had also been hard at work drilling those new Zouaves from seven to twelve every night. The fair at which the contest for the "Prize stand of Champion Colors" was scheduled had occurred the week before he wrote this letter. There were seventy thousand people on the ground, he said, which made it very difficult for the Zouave Cadets to get sufficient room for their drill. Ellsworth's spirits had risen as he issued his commands and had seen his boys respond as one. They first went through the Hardee drill, then, after an intermission, their own spectacular Zouave drill. Only one competitor had appeared, the Highland Guards of Chicago, and their performance seemed tame beside this.

When the announcement was made that the Zouave Cadets had won the Champion Flag and the president of the society stepped forward to present it, Ellsworth suddenly realized that, not expecting it, he was not prepared with an acceptance speech. He mustered his courage, he told Carrie, "shut my Eyes, said a short '*exhortation*' and launched out, I managed to finish *somehow*, and the Colors were formally handed to me, & by me to the Company."

He gave Carrie an almost loving description of "the Colors." The incident must inevitably have reminded both of them of the occasion when she had presented the flag to the National Guard Cadets from the porch of her home. In fact, the "Principle flag," he told her, was "very much like the Rockford flag," and was made of silk six feet wide which was bought in New York. "One side is Blue, the other white. On the white side is the Arms of the U. S. with the inscription 'Champion Flag' " and the date September 15, 1859. The blue side, in addition to the names of the U. S. Agricultural Society and the Zouave Cadets, had "a large white star" and "on the centre of the star, an American Shield with a *tiger head* in the centre." The tiger head became the symbol of the Zouave Cadets.

The winning of this banner brought Ellsworth and his boys praise and congratulations from all sides. "*All at once*," he wrote Carrie, "I find myself surrounded by hosts of *friends*, of whose existence I *never dreamed* before — *friends*, who think they have discovered that *my stock*, is rising, and it *will pay to invest*."

One factor in this sudden attention may have been that

his appointment as Assistant Adjutant-General and Pay-master General of Illinois had come through. He had received, he told Carrie, "an immense envelop addressed to Gen E. E. Ellsworth, &c. containing my commission, requiring all under my command to *obey me* implicidly; which injunction Miss Carrie, you will please observe. So you perceive I'm no longer *the Major.*" What he was now being called was Colonel Ellsworth. He appreciated getting the appointment, he said; he had wanted it for three years but "there is no salary attached to it at present." It is to be hoped he was getting adequate food but he still mentions his severe headaches.

Ellsworth was constantly taking on more work and responsibilities. This same letter tells of a new undertaking. "There is an institution," he wrote, "called Linds University" (later the name was changed to Lake Forest University) "— situated at Lake Forest, about thirty miles from the city; which is controlled by a number of the wealthy men of this City, who have their sons there; and who are desirous of making military instruction & exercises, a feature of the institution. They propose to have the students adopt a uniform, and have me spend one day in each week with them, for the purpose of giving them instruction." Ellsworth continued that he did not know how the project would succeed, "I *trust* they will carry it through successfully, as it would be a very fortunate thing for me."

As it turned out, Ellsworth drilled the boys of Lake Forest Academy on Saturdays. He could have done this any time between September 29 and December 17, 1859. One of the boys he trained, Edward P. Bartlett, later gave his recollections of the drilling, and "the long hikes taken through the country surrounding Lake Forest; the miles of double quick marching; the bivouac and the camp," and most of all how they enjoyed their gay yet dignified young commander. They called themselves the Ellsworth Guards.

To Ellsworth himself these Saturdays must have been a glorious release from office and armory. His love of the outdoors and beautiful landscapes is evident in what he had written Mrs. Spafford in the spring of 1859. She had described to him some lovely country scene and he replied longingly: "Your description makes me almost sicken of the four walls of this office, which comprise all the scenery which enlivens my sight from one weeks end to another: If indeed, I except the top of a green tree which peers curiously at me from the *other side* of a large building in front of the windows. Would that at some price, I could purchase immunity from this heart-coroding, life-destroying care, and give myself up to all the enjoyment of the good & beautiful in nature of which the soul is capable."

Hiking along the shore of Lake Michigan and through the forest in the companionship of lively young lads, reveling in the autumn colors of the trees and the blue of the water, must have been pure joy to him. Lake Forest had all the qualifications Ellsworth had listed as a place where he would like to build his dream house.

The winning of the Champion Flag was destined to have far-reaching results. In his usual Sunday letter, on October 9, 1859, he brought Carrie up to date on what followed this triumph. "The Company (of Cadets)," he wrote, "have challenged any company in the U. S. or Canadas, to drill with them for the 'Champion Colors' which they won at the U. S. Fair." Fate in her design for Ellsworth had now put him in a position where he could not do otherwise than go ahead with his military work. When the Zouave Cadets had won a national award with only one competitor and that a Chicago company, an indignant outcry had arisen from the South and East that they had no right to call themselves the national champions when the contest had been merely local. The challenge, dated September 20, 1859, said that the Zouaves had entered the contest in good faith, had been disappointed that there had not been more competition, and "Having received the Colors, and not caring to wear honors until fairly and unquestionably our own, we determined . . . to give an opportunity to all . . . to contest our right to this honor." It was signed E. E. Ellsworth with his new rank "Col. Commanding Cadets."

Again Ellsworth had to explain to Carrie (and thus indirectly to her father, perhaps) why he was continuing his work with the Cadets. "It is a great task for me to remain in charge of them," he wrote, "but *policy* bids me do so. My connection with them thus far has *benefitted* me *beyond my most sanguine expectations.*"

The company of Zouaves was certainly more and more in demand. They had a delightful excursion in prospect for "Next Wednesday," Ellsworth told Carrie; they were invited to "go to Fon-du-Lac, Wisconsin, to attend the Celebration of the opening of the North Western R.R." This was the decade in which railroads were developing fast in the United States and people were thrilled with their emancipation from slow stagecoach and riverboat to this wonderful swift new means of transportation. The opening of each new line was usually celebrated with a gala excursion which included band music, parades, speeches, and all kinds of festivities. The trip to Fond du Lac, Ellsworth said, would occupy nearly three days.

They were days of enthusiastic, hilarious entertainment and the young Zouaves with their handsome leader, as usual, won all hearts. At the end of the holiday they were presented with a trophy which seems another age-of-chivalry idea transplanted into the Victorian era. Two hundred or more ladies among the excursionists each contributed a ribbon to be made into a rainbow-colored and perfumed bouquet which was ceremoniously presented to the commanding officer of the Zouaves. Ellsworth told Carrie about this "novel present" in his letter of October 23. He was used to receiving flags but not ribbons. "I was quite taken by surprise," he said, "I have the names of about two hundred ladies who *sacrificed* their ribbons."

Shortly after this "most delightful time," as he called it, Ellsworth learned of an incident which could not have failed to bring him chilling thoughts. On October 16 an abolitionist named John Brown had attempted to start a slave insurrection at Harpers Ferry, Virginia. It was quickly put down; on the 18th a force of United States soldiers, led by a handsome colonel named Robert E. Lee, had battered down the doors of the engine house in which the little group of insurgents had taken refuge and captured what was left of them. John Brown was hanged early in December.

It was relatively a small event in the numbers involved. Yet Ellsworth, deeply concerned with the threat of division and war in his country, must have realized along with thousands of others that this episode was a powerful factor in further dividing North and South. It had brought the conflict much closer. More than ever he must do what he could to build up the military strength of the Union.

He assumed another responsibility about the middle of October. It had been a constant worry to him that his brother Charley had no opportunity in Mechanicville and was not making anything of himself. Their parents were evidently worried about it too, and the older son saw only one solution. In his letter of October 9 he said to Carrie, "I expect my brother to arrive here next week, and I shall henceforth have the responsibility of his conduct added to my other cares. I assume it willingly as I hope to be able to make a man of him if a long residence & association in a country village has not spoiled him. I have the promise, for him, of a situation in a large Hardware Establishment here."

With so many responsibilities and tasks it is no wonder Ellsworth wrote Carrie on October 23, "You can form no idea, I can scarcely realize myself, how constantly my time is ocupied. . . . every moment . . . night and day, is taken up; it is now just six months since I have retired untill *after* 12 o'clock." He had before him, he said, "a stack of seventeen letters waiting replies, the authors of said epistles doubtless bless me abundantly, but I cannot help it."

On top of everything else another excursion in honor of the opening of the Northwestern Railroad was in prospect. Cities were having a fine time making calls on each other with this grand new means of transportation. About one thousand excursionists from Chicago had been royally entertained by Fond du Lac; now the citizens of Fond du Lac were coming to be entertained by Chicago. So were the good people of Oshkosh, Janesville, Watertown, Madison and other Wisconsin cities. Ellsworth, with the usual fate of those who get things done efficiently, had been appointed chairman of a committee on preparations for a festival in honor of the guests. He added rather unnecessarily, "it will give me quite an amount of work to discharge the duties."

His entire "disipation" for quite a while, he wrote, consisted of "*one* concert," "the theatre *once*," and "three or four calls." The concert was probably a treat, for Ellsworth's letters contain frequent passages showing his love of music. Once he described to Mrs. Spafford a concert he had attended: he pictured the Italian singer Piccolomini as "A girl with a pretty face, magnificent form — sprightly gracefull manner, voice like a gushing brook, (*very small brook*)." A portly male singer's appearance and manner suggested a "juvenile elephant" or a bear attempting "the german waltz," he said. "But his *voice* redeems all defects and leaves an incalculably large balance in his favor."

Ellsworth's letter of October 23 reported to Carrie how he felt about the progress he was making. "I am not generally inclined," he wrote, "to 'halloo before I'm out of the woods,' yet I think that I ocupy a far different position to day from that of a year since. I've barely a round in 'the

Ladder' yet — before I reach another I may fall to the ground."

Between Thanksgiving and Ellsworth's letter to Carrie of December 13 occurred the happy visit of the engaged couple already mentioned. There is a good chance that Colonel Ellsworth introduced his fiancée, Miss Spafford, to his company at one of their dances at the armory, for the Zouave Cadets had formed a Terpsichorean Club. Perhaps during that enchanted visit Miss Spafford, dressed in her hoop-skirted best and looking very lovely, carried to the armory the same quaint card, ornamented with flags and the American Eagle, which exists today. It was a "Ladies Honorary Membership Certificate" to the "Cadets Terpsichorean Club," of which Colonel E. E. Ellsworth was president.

Ellsworth's letter of December 13 casually mentioned a piece of news which would prove significant in his fortunes. Naturally, he did not recognize its importance at first. "By the way," he wrote Carrie, "I had nearly forgotten to say that I shall not go to New York before February. I am *very much disappointed*. I shall probably start for Springfield next Sunday evening." As they had so recently been together and had probably talked over his plans, he did not have to explain that his duties as Assistant Adjutant-General and Paymaster General of Illinois required his presence in the state capital.

So on Sunday, December 18, or thereabouts, Colonel Ellsworth took the train to Springfield, the sprawling town on the prairies which was to be a way station on the line of his destiny. For the first time he walked the four streets which enclose the public square, gazing at the domed capitol building which stood in the center of it. He evidently found out very quickly that his stay would be longer than he had anticipated, probably because he agreed to train the Springfield Greys for an exhibition drill. He made a trip to Chicago four days later to arrange matters there. Carrie was still at Rockford and he was desperately anxious to see her again before she returned to school in New Hampshire. "Write immediately & tell me when and where to meet you," he wrote her hastily on December 22. Still at Chicago five days later, he wrote again, "Your letter was handed me a few moments since, & you may imagine my disappointment to learn that you do not start for Lebanon, untill Jan 3d." He had to get back to Springfield by that time and it would be impossible for them to meet, he said, unless she could make a special trip to Chicago. Could she not come for a special party the Cadets were having "Thursday" (December 29) and return to Rockford the next morning? "I cannot be contented to have you go away without my seeing you," said his hasty note of December 27.

The New Year of 1860 had come in before Ellsworth was able to write a long, full letter to Carrie again. In the meantime they had evidently achieved the meeting, as he said in his letter of January 15: "I was pained to part with you darling in such an unpleasant manner & as I anticipated there was much omitted that I desired to say to you." There would have been little chance for the lovers to talk at that Cadets' party.

Ellsworth was writing from Springfield again. He was fast making friends there now, among them two young men whose names were destined to become well known in the future, John Hay and John George Nicolay. John Hay, who was studying law in one of the offices on the public square, was a dark-eyed, rosy-cheeked young fellow not unlike Ellsworth in size and coloring. Hay had a brilliant gift of phrasing and was witty, and charming except when overcome by one of his dark and cynical moods. He and Ellsworth were to become very dear to each other and exchange their intimate thoughts and hopes.

Nicolay, whom Ellsworth called "George," was taller and a bit older than the other two. He was a slender, blue-eyed, brown-haired man who was quietly efficient, a good listener, and had the charm of a slow, gentle smile. In his ultimate fondness for Ellsworth he said, "I felt almost a direct personal pride and interest in his success." The three were to share events which would be written into the nation's history.

Ellsworth was also getting acquainted with three of Springfield's very important persons. One was John Cook, Commandant of the Springfield Greys, at whose home Ellsworth wrote Carrie he was staying. "He resides about one mile out of the city and has a magnificent place." It is easy to understand why Ellsworth enjoyed that stately house (still standing) with its spacious two-decked porch on the south front and its pleasing cupola on top. It was set at this time in forty acres of ground, part of which was an orchard, and altogether it was just such a place as Ellsworth himself would have liked to live in with Carrie. He may have thought of this, especially as John Cook's wife, he wrote Carrie, "resembles you somewhat, & makes his home almost a paradise."

The Cooks were evidently warmhearted people who had taken their young guest into their full affection. Continuing his letter to Carrie, Ellsworth said, "I broke my watch a few days since jamd all the jewels out of place." This was evidently the watch given to him by the Rockford Greys. "Gen C— insisted upon taking it to a friend of his to be repaired when it was returned I found attached to it an elegant fob chain worth nearly fifty dollars a present from Gen Cook. I felt some hesitation about accepting it but he forced me to keep it."

It is plain that Ellsworth had given his heart to his host and hostess. In his letter to Carrie two weeks later he wrote, "My darling, you would be delighted with Mrs Cook, and by and by, one of these days, I propose to take you to pay them a visit, provided, you promise *not* to fall in love with *Mr* Cook."

A second important person with whom Ellsworth had formed a warm friendship was Governor William H. Bissell. Elmer told Carrie of two parties he had attended in Springfield, one at the Governor's stately mansion on the hill, the other at the home of ex-Governor Joel A. Matteson. With an evident twinkle he wrote Carrie later about an amusing incident which happened at the Matteson party.

Ellsworth, while frequently seeming like one of King Arthur's knights, also at times shows a mischievous humor which suggests Robin Hood. He liked the plucky Republican Governor Bissell, who at this time went around on crutches, and he did not like a certain politician he met at the Mattesons', a man named Don Morrison, who was the candidate for the Democratic nomination for governor and had recently made a violent attack on Governor Bissell. At this same party, Ellsworth wrote Carrie, "I met a lady from Mobile; a celebrated belle and a perfect queen of beauty." He noticed, he said, that Mr. Morrison seemed "exceedingly anxious to make the acquaintance of the said belle."

Deciding to frustrate the eager Mr. Morrison by monopolizing the beautiful lady himself, Ellsworth "obtained an introduction," he said to Carrie, and "remained in her society untill the party broke up. Outsiders were disposed to regard it as quite a flirtation." At this point in his letter it may have occurred to him that he better add an antidote to jealousy, and quickly, for he continued, "but in the course of the conversation I had discovered two things, which all the beauty in the world could not compensate for — a total want of regard for truth, and — must I say it? she betrayed *herself*, she was lazy, lazy beyond hope; of all things in this world, deliver *me* from a *lazy woman, perhaps* if I were wealthy, they would be my especial admiration: but they are not the women to enchant us poor men." There is no doubt of his strong sentiment on this subject. His next astutely chosen words should have made Carrie's reassurance complete: "When I went home that night I could not help drawing a contrast between this belle of the South, and my own sweet prairie flower. *You may rest assured*, darling, you *suffered nothing by the contrast.*"

It is not known on what occasion Colonel Ellsworth met a third important person of Springfield, the Honorable Abraham Lincoln. It is possible that at either the Bissell or Matteson crowded parties the young officer could have noticed a tall lean man with a plump, prettily dressed wife who looked amusingly short beside him. Ellsworth would probably have recognized him as Mr. Lincoln, whose speeches he had read and about whom he had heard so much. Conversation would have flowed after his introduction to the Lincolns; they were cordial people and in all likelihood had already learned about the guest of their friend General Cook who was drilling the Springfield Greys. They might have told him that their son Bob, now studying at Exeter Academy in New Hampshire, had been a fourth corporal in that company and that once Mr. Lincoln had served on a committee for arranging a "Grand Military Festival" of the Greys.

If not at a party, the meeting might have taken place on a downtown street, or perhaps General Cook, after learning that Ellsworth was studying law, had taken him up the stairs to Mr. Lincoln's office on the west side of the public square. John Cook, as Ellsworth told Carrie in his letter of January 15, wished him to come to Springfield and study law with Abraham Lincoln. Once he had met Ellsworth, Mr. Lincoln was eager for this too and wanted everything possible done to get this unusual young man in his office.

On some day whose date is not known, Ellsworth certainly walked out to the light brown Lincoln home at the corner of Eighth and Jackson Streets and called on the Lincolns. He romped with their two irrepressible little boys, Willie and Tad, and won the hearts of the whole family. Both Mr. and Mrs. Lincoln were incurably parental toward young people, and here was a young man they could love as if he were their own son.

The line of Ellsworth's life had reached that of Lincoln's.

✦
✦✦
✦

16

"No Telling What I Will Turn Out"

THE "exhibition drill" took place in Springfield on January 16, 1860, and Ellsworth returned to Chicago shortly there-after. He now had to give the Zouave Cadets intensive training in preparation for meeting the companies which might accept their challenge. "I look forward with no in-considerable dread to my winter's work," he wrote Carrie, "It will be a hard task to carry out the program." He was soon drilling the men four hours every evening except Sun-day besides attending to correspondence and hundreds of other details, financial and otherwise, connected with the competitive tour on which the company would start in June.

The U. S. Zouave Cadets received a highly prized honor late in January. On the 23rd, Governor Bissell appointed them the Governor's Guard of Illinois. More than ever now crowds flocked to the armory at the corner of State and Randolph Streets to watch these young citizen soldiers go through their spectacular drills. Sometimes they would give an exhibition drill with a parade to the music of the popular Light Guard Band, which had gone with them to Fond du Lac. The morale of the Zouaves was running high, but, un-known to them, that of their leader frequently sagged. "My darling you have no conception of the magnitude & diffi-culty of the project I've undertaken," he wrote Carrie on

February 14, "nor does any one of the company even, for it is policy, on my part, to keep them in ignorance of the real difficulties attending it: the contemplation of a tithe of them would discourage them. You can imagine how urgent must be the necessity, when at a distance of nearly six months, from the contest, I have found it impossible to get along without working (writing) for the last week untill five and six O'clock in the morning."

Some of this writing was on a document called the "Golden Resolutions." Ellsworth never lost sight of his objectives for the Zouave Cadets: not only to make them the best drilled company in the country but also young men of the highest character. The Golden Resolutions were an expansion and further definition of the resolutions he had demanded from the Cadets as the condition of his taking the captaincy the year before. The following acts were forbidden under penalty of expulsion and publication in the Chicago papers of the offender's name: entering drinking saloons at any time (except when compelled by imperative business which could not be transacted by proxy); entering houses of ill-fame under any pretext whatever; entering any gambling saloon under any circumstances. Even entering public billiard halls was forbidden, not because of any objections to billiards, but because the associations of the billiard saloon of that day naturally led to drinking. Any cadet who knew of any infraction of these rules was honor-bound to report it to the company.

Each member must wear on his vest or watch chain "the company badge, consisting of a gold star shield with a tiger's head in the center and name of the corps engraved on the star . . . that the public may know them as Cadets, and judge for themselves of the manner in which the foregoing resolutions are observed."

Mention was made again of the armory's need for recreational facilities. It had already become very much like a

pleasant club, a kind of home-away-from-home for the
young men. The document also stated that the company
should take care of its sick members and provide a sort of
unemployment insurance for those who lost their positions.
The resolutions were to go into effect on March 9, 1860,
and of course, they were widely published in the newspapers. Colonel Ellsworth knew the value of publicity.

The provisions for the sick and jobless show something of
the fraternal relationship which existed among the Cadets.
A glimpse of their loyalty to each other is given in an incident which Ellsworth related to Carrie in his letter of February 14. When their Quartermaster Sergeant Alfred S. Cobb
left Chicago, the Cadets gave him a gold medal as a farewell
gift. Ellsworth made the speech of presentation and copied
part of it into his letter to Carrie. "Friend Alfred," he began, ". . . For you, the 'Tide, which taken at the flood,
leads on to fortune,' is now at hand." Continuing in this vein
in such phrases as "let *conscience* be your compass . . . as
you sail down the 'stream of life,'" he worked his way
through Alfred's future career with like metaphors until he
reached his lofty climax: "When at last, the time arrives to
'up anchor,' & sail for the world beyond, may your *'clear-
ance be regular,'* & the experiences of this life have been
such, that you will set out with the *joyous certainty* of making port, in the regions of eternal happiness."

When Ellsworth finished writing this in his letter to Carrie, he brought himself quickly down to earth in a whimsi-
cal comment, "Quite white-neck-clothish for me, isn't it?"

There is a special quality to the companionship of young
men in their early twenties, and the Zouave Cadets would
always have fond memories of those scenes in the armory.
Ellsworth was evidently staying there at night now, which
was much pleasanter than sleeping in a law office but presented certain drawbacks for letter writing. "Let me give an
idea of the surroundings which aid me to write a *coherent*

letter," he wrote to Carrie on January 29, ". . . on my right hand, sits a young gentleman, deeply immersed in the fascinating mysteries of Frank Leslie's Magazine, next him, gent no 2, playing 'Silver Shower' on the Piano with an impromptu accompaniment on the back of chairs, floor &c. Another enterprizing youth, is balancing a short sword on his chin. You may fill up the room with a dozen or more, excentric individuals, each following the bent of his particular inclination, and you can then account for the appearance of this letter."

It was a lively scene. Some of the individuals, however, must have been quite cold, as Ellsworth, beginning his letter with an apology for using red ink, explained that "my black ink has frozen, which will, I trust, satisfactorily account for the warm complexion of this letter."

The letter with the warm complexion went to Carrie in the East again. It had been a question whether she should return to her studies at the Tilden seminary and Ellsworth, of course, was extremely anxious for her to do so. He wrote her on January 15, "You do not know how glad I am that you decided upon going to school this winter instead of remaining at home. Had circumstances compelled you to remain at home I should have felt dear Carrie that your time had been quite thrown away." The "circumstances" were that Mrs. Spafford was expecting a belated baby in April.

While Ellsworth perforce was giving less attention to his law study at this time, he intended to go back to it after the competitive tour of the Zouaves was finished. "I don't know what I shall decide in reference to Mr Lincolns proposition," he wrote Carrie, ". . . Mr Cook told me that Mr L— *especially desired him* to *leave no means unturned* to induce me to come to Springfield. I cannot but regard this as a very great compliment." There was a special appeal to Ellsworth because Mr. Lincoln, like himself, had come up the hard way. "I believe that the influence of Mr L— would do me great service," he continued, "I mean the influence of his early example. He earned his subsistence, while studying law, by spliting rails, and it is said that at the age of 20 he could neither read nor write, so you percieve, Carrie, I have a *greater advantage than he* possessed, I can *read*." (What Ellsworth had heard was not accurate; Lincoln could read and write, in a limited fashion, at twenty, but, as he said, ". . . when I came of age I did not know much.")

The decision about going to Springfield was much on Ellsworth's mind. He was drawn toward Mr. Lincoln and others there but, on the other hand, he had deep-rooted ties in Chicago and Chicago was nearer Rockford. He wrote Mrs. Spafford about the matter on the last day of January, revealing incidentally that the people at Springfield had tried to keep him from returning to Chicago at all. "I was offered very great inducements to *remain* at Springfield," he said, "and still stronger ones, to go there in the spring & complete my studies, with Hon Abram Lincoln. . . . What think you?" (The name Abraham was often abbreviated to Abram.)

Overwork, loss of sleep, the responsibilities of the Zouave Cadets and of his brother Charley, who had joined the company, not to mention his worry about his father and mother, were all pulling Ellsworth down. Then he received a letter from Carrie which plunged him into gloom. "Your letter — *reproaches* and all came duly to hand," he wrote her on February 5. Though he does not state for what she reproached him, certain conjectures may be made from what follows. "Sweet one your interest in my changing my mode of life does you infinite credit and I am deeply gratefull to you." Was Carrie raising the old objection that he was giving his work and attention to military matters to the detriment of his law study? "Hope and pray for me darling I am truly a graceless wretch. . . . I will try and live more in accordance with duty but I cannot force my feelings." Carrie had evidently said that perhaps she had not exerted her influence in the proper manner, for he answered, "be assured dearest that as far as I am concerned you have nothing to reproach yourself with." He then told her what can hardly be doubted: if she had "put on a sanctimonious demeanor its tendency would have been rather to repel than attract me in the direction you desire."

He let himself give way to his deep depression. "I am half sick and disgusted, there is no telling what I will turn out. God bless you as you deserve darling. . . . I sometimes think I am not worthy of anyones love I am such a butt for ill luck that I almost fear to connect any one with me." He then apologized for telling her how "blue" he was, adding, "but as a young frind of mine once said 'the future is so far off.' "

"The future" was nearer than he thought; nationwide acclaim was to be his in about six months, though a heavy sorrow was to come to him before then. Between worrying over his problems and constantly overtaxing his strength, he could hardly keep going in February. On Sunday, February 19, he wrote Carrie, "No letter from *me* to day. I am *compelled* to defer writing as I am completely exhausted, & have to make all the preparations for our *first grand parade* which takes place Wednesday." He ended this note, ". . . am trying to gain strength *& will* for tomorrow & next day by lying still."

He reported again to Carrie a week later. "The long anticipated parade has taken place, the grand agony is over, and it was a success." He felt no exultation, however; he had reached the point of overwork where he was momentarily fed up with the whole business. "I am *driving* by sheer force of will all the machinery of the company," he continued, "and it would be exceedingly pleasant if I could occasionally turn from all this work to something more pleasant. This job *once done with*, I am free of the thing forever untill driven to it for means of subsistence." Perhaps Carrie was glad to read that last sentence. It was followed by an expression of utter discouragement: "Oh my god how tired of this existence I become." He felt he was not getting anywhere, "my parents still toiling & slaving for existence, & I rendering them no aid — doing nothing. I dont no *what I am*, I *may be* a miserable vagabond." His next sentence shows that Carrie's "reproaches" and the fear of disappointing her were playing a large part in his distress of mind; "And then if I do not realise your expectations what will be your regret to think that you have thrown away two or three years of love upon such a worthless wretch as I. God only knows to what purpose I am living. May he grant it *will be to some* purpose, that my life may not be quite fruitless."

Ellsworth, however, was in his usual fine spirits by March 11, if one may judge from his letter to Carrie on that date. He began it cozily: "Now for a good long letter. Its twelve o'clock, every body has gone from the armory, Chicago's abed." Having therefore no fear of interruption "except from some mid-night prowler or ghostly visitant neither of which I expect," he continued, "I give myself up to the pleasure of communing with my darling." He had an exciting episode to tell her about his company.

"We were ordered to hold ourselves in readiness to quell a riot which was expected to occur on election day," he wrote. Election day was March 6 and the Cadets had to go on the alert the evening before. "We had been under arms all night and during the day untill about 5 o'clock in the afternoon and thinking the day would pass off without any serious disturbance were singing & carrying on as gay as larks." Then word came that they must "be in instant readiness to go to the tenth ward as there was over three thousand Irishmen there all under the influence of the greatest excitement — swearing that if the polls were closed at 6 o'clock they would destroy the ballot boxes." The polls were going to be closed at six and trouble seemed inevitable. "The company formed at once," said Ellsworth, "& placed themselves in line at the door ready to spring into the Omnibuses (we had 5 with 4 horses each) waiting at the lower entrance."

"I knew," he went on, "that there was imminent danger of a riot and that it was my duty to prepare for all immergencies accordingly I caused the men to load their pieces with ball cartridges; as the balls struck the bottom of the musket bore the boys seemed for the first time to awake to the fearful responsibility of our positions if we went out." This was no matter of drill or parade; those balls were meant to tear living flesh. "The hour of the expected disturbance was near at hand," continued Colonel Ellsworth, "and that no time might be lost I brought the men to attention and commenced to march them slowly about the room, when they started, with one accord they commenced Annie Laurie and shaded in the expression by the sober feeling at that moment pervading the company I never heard any thing sound so inexpressibly sweet."

Two hours of suspense went by before word came at eight o'clock that everything had quieted down and "so ended our tour of duty," concluded Ellsworth, "without giving any of us a chance to distinguish ourselves . . . by extinguishing a '*w*ow, a *w*umpus or a *w*isit' . . . 'sich is life.' "

In the same letter he spoke further about Mr. Lincoln's proposition. He had just received a letter from John Cook, emphasizing again Lincoln's extraordinary interest in him and the lawyer's earnest wish that Ellsworth would come to Springfield. John Cook added, "My conviction that this is the place for you to commence life as a public man is un-

changed." The words "public man" opened up new possibilities. Ellsworth asked Carrie's advice about it: "Now little
one what is your Majesty's sage opinion?"

While Ellsworth was thus considering settling in Springfield, bad news came from that town. His good and influential friend Governor Bissell died of pneumonia on March 18.
This meant that the Zouave Cadets, as the Governor's
Guard of Illinois, must go to Springfield for the funeral. His
brother Charley, now connected with the company, went
along.

In the funeral procession, according to the *Chicago Daily
Journal,* was the "Hon. Abram Lincoln." He had recently
returned from a trip East where, on February 27, he had
made a memorable speech at the Cooper Union in New
York. People all over the country, reading that speech, were
beginning to wonder if this Illinois lawyer and politician
might not be presidential timber. Ellsworth had a chance to
talk with Mr. Lincoln on this visit to Springfield; again he
looked into the kind gray eyes of this magnetic man and felt
the warmth and power of his personality.

A former member of the Chicago Zouaves, J. C. Barclay,
said many years later that Ellsworth told him the circumstances of his meeting with Mr. Lincoln. According to this
account Ellsworth and his brother Charley were walking
along a Springfield street when Lincoln met and stopped
them. He invited them to come up to his office, where he
talked with Ellsworth about coming to Springfield and
studying law with him. Ellsworth told Lincoln about his
deep interest in military matters and how he wanted to
prove that the Zouave Cadets were the best-trained company in the country. That was his immediate undertaking,
but it will be remembered that he had already told Carrie he
intended to leave the Cadets after the summer's competitive
tour. Just when the decision and arrangements between
Ellsworth and Lincoln were made is not known; it is known,

however, that at the end of the tour Ellsworth was prepared to go to Springfield to study law with him.

Ellsworth had made many friends in the town during the preceding December and January. When these good people found he was there with his talked-of Zouaves, they requested an exhibition drill from them after the Governor's funeral. Later a hundred leading citizens signed a testimonial of their admiration and appreciation of this exhibition. When this gratifying document reached Ellsworth, his heart was heavy with anxiety. His brother Charley had been taken ill in Springfield.

Ellsworth had said very little of Charley in his letters to Carrie, merely that he had arrived the middle of October, 1859, and that no position was open to him at that time. What to do about this lovable brother who had little education, training, or ambition was one of his many problems. The disease which Charley had developed in Springfield was typhoid fever, and the course of the illness can be traced vividly in Ellsworth's letters.

Somehow he got the sick youth back to Chicago and the armory, where he nursed him night and day. In his note to Carrie of March 25 telling her of Charley's illness, he said he thought the patient was "a little easier this morning," then hastily ended his letter because "Charley is calling me." On Sunday night, April 1, he wrote, "I am watching by the bedside of my brother . . . it is now nearly 12 o'clock." Two pages later he wrote, "You must not look very closely at the remainder of this letter as I have just been compelled to turn the gas down untill I can scarcely distinguish the lines, in order to allow Charley to get asleep." On April 7: "Charley was suddenly taken much worse last night. . . . he is delirious to night."

The words create a picture of the devoted care Ellsworth was giving this younger brother for whom he had had a deep and fostering love since he had "bought" him for six shillings when he was a baby. It is said that at the hours of greatest crisis Ellsworth, in his grief and anxiety, prayed for Charley in the presence of his men. It was not only his own affection for Charley; he felt responsible for him to their father and mother, who loved him so dearly too.

The illness dragged on, and it was not until Ellsworth's letter to Carrie on April 16 that the good report appeared: "My brother, I am happy to say, is convalescent, & gaining strength rapidly." This letter of April 16 was headed "Chicago, I mean Rockford." Ellsworth was visiting Carrie's parents at the time, even though she was away in the East. It is one of the gayest and most humorous of all his letters. The main topic of it is "Babies," with emphasis on the amusing upheaval and new centering of attention which the arrival of a baby brings to any affectionate household. Carrie's little sister, whose name — Eugenia — Ellsworth was permitted to select, had been born on April 9, 1860, and was thus one week old when he wrote.

" 'Baby in the house,' " he began, "it completely unnerved me. It was equivalent to a *cry* — of fire, murder, thieves etc. etc." After hearing the news, he said, he wandered around in a semi-lethargic state in which these incidents occurred: "Lady friend of mine came along looking radiantly happy — spoke to me & I unconsciously asked if she had a baby? she flew of[f] in a passion and a symphathetic friend asked what was the disturbance? I replied a baby. Friend came up with Theatre bill in his hand; asked me if I'd seen 'The Object of Interest?' told him no, but was going to, [he] immediately handed me two Theatre tickets & asked who I would take. I answered the baby. Gentleman said he would like to join my company — asked what were the qualifications? I answered — a baby. He said something about — babies, & I strolled into an eating house, being hungry, meek looking waiter inquired what would I have? told him, a dozen fried; waiter impudently asked, 'fried what?' and I replied *babies*."

He told Carrie, "When you return you will be quite an important personage, Miss Spafford — a reflected importance." For all his fun-making, he evidently had something of the same absorbing interest in this new member of the family which he had once felt for his baby brother Charley. His letter continued: "I do hereby solemnly retract, all remarks of whatsoever kind, shape or nature to which I've ever given utterance calculated, or having a tendency to prejudice or bias the minds of the people against babies." Later he wrote Carrie that little Eugenia "has the prettiest deep blue eyes imaginable." Carrie could hardly have failed to reflect how much Ellsworth would enjoy a baby of his own.

His letters continue with their passages of love and concern for her. He sent her his photograph even though he did not consider it a good one. He had given his picture, he said, to two young ladies, adding hastily, "I think both of them are engaged." He was still anxious about her getting plenty of exercise and ventilation, which suggests that Carrie had been a bit noncommittal about having a hole cut in her windowpane. However, he recognized a limit to ventilation; he reminded her that spring was a time when one was "in constant danger of contracting serious colds" and she must not sit by an open window when the air was damp.

He even cautioned her not to get her feet wet!

17

"HI-HI-HI" AND "TIG-A-R! ZOUAVE!"

ELLSWORTH's letter to Carrie of April 29, 1860, was from the Chicago Armory again. As he sat writing, he was surrounded by his men "talking of that (to us) all absorbing topic our trip east." After the challenge of the U. S. Zouave Cadets had been published over the country the fall before, there had been little response except newspaper ridicule. The view of the military companies in the East was that they were not interested in taking a trip to the Western wilds to compete with some upstart company. Ellsworth that spring even published an offer from the Zouaves to pay the expenses of any company which would come. (He would have to raise the money but that did not daunt him.) This offer also failed to bring results. If the competitors would not come to the Zouaves, the Zouaves would have to go to the competitors.

What Ellsworth had to accomplish to bring this trip about he summed up in a letter to Carrie on May 27: "I have to make arrangements for passes or reduction of fare over three thousand miles of Rail Road, & raise for the company, seven thousand dollars, a part of this is to be done by writing nearly two hundred letters" (the money was being raised by subscription, and seven thousand would not prove enough), "besides this I have to finish & superintend the publication of our Manual of arms."

The last undertaking presented great difficulties. He had studied enough French to learn the Zouave tactics and had introduced them into this country. By this time the use of the Zouave system was growing so that it was necessary to have a Zouave manual of arms, and he was the only one who could write it. It becomes clear now why, about this time, he asked Carrie to write him a letter in French so that he would be forced to study the language further. The *Manual of Arms* was printed before June 11, 1860, as on that date the author wrote Carrie, "I have mailed one hundred & seventy letters & over Seventeen hundred books within the last eight days."

Studying this now rare little book, *Manual of Arms for Light Infantry Arranged for the U. S. Zouave Cadets* by E. E. Ellsworth, makes one realize the great intricacy and physical demands of the Zouave drill. (A revised edition would be published the following year.) To describe the movements involved in merely stacking arms takes more than a page, yet it was done so swiftly and smoothly that it seemed like sleight of hand. A newspaper account stated that this method of stacking arms was "discovered" by Colonel Ellsworth. The book contains details about the coming tour: there would be a band of fifteen pieces and sixty-one Zouaves with an average age of twenty-two, each of them taking three uniforms: one full dress of blue and buff, one Chasseur de Vincennes uniform of blue and red, and one of the brilliant, loose Zouave drill uniforms.

At the same time Ellsworth was working night and day to make all the arrangements, he had to keep the Zouaves at the peak of perfection by constant drilling and gymnastic exercises. Knapsacks of service weight (over twenty pounds) were worn at the drills. Those who were unable to keep up physically were weeded out; those who were able but complained of fatigue were told to sit on a bench and watch the other boys do it. The occupants of the bench were dubbed "the sore toes," which promptly reduced their number.

It is no wonder that Ellsworth's letters to Carrie at this time became less frequent and more hurried in style. She evidently mentioned this in one of her letters, for he said, "My birdie, how, when & where did that idea gain admission into your mind? that my letters are not the same, in tone." He explained to her about all his tasks and that "eight in ten" of all his letters had to be written in the midst of a talking, singing crowd. He also assured her in unmistakable terms that the longer he knew her the more he loved her.

Perhaps because of this reproach he made this letter of April 29 more chatty and gay. He teased Carrie about her curiosity. She had evidently written inquiring who those girls were to whom he had given his picture. "The names of those young ladies," he wrote with a twinkle, "are — By the by, I remember that you are doubtless ocupied with young Mr — what *is* the gentleman's name? & will not care so much about those young ladies." (At the end of the letter he gave her the names.) He spoke of a "Second Lieutenant" whom he liked very much and continued, "Now dont get your curiosity cap on, for *he is* married, is twenty eight years old & his *name* is Laflin. There Oh Woman! have I not anticipated?"

Between his letters of April 29 and May 27 a tremendous event occurred. On May 18, 1860, in the huge building in Chicago called the Wigwam, Abraham Lincoln was nominated as the Republican candidate for President of the United States. Ellsworth was so filled with enthusiasm that he almost lost his life celebrating the event. He and several of the Zouaves decided to take a howitzer to the roof of the Tremont Hotel and fire it off in proper celebration. (The story was told later by one of the group, James M. DeWitt, whose name is on the roster of the Zouaves who made the tour that summer.)

The celebrators had to make a blank cartridge. To avoid

accident, they took their boots off while working with the powder: "we were all in our stocking feet around the powder," wrote DeWitt. After the cartridge was completed Ellsworth put on his boots again and this fact probably saved his life. In moving the howitzer into position "he jumped on the copeing stone his foot sliped and only the heel of his boot kept him from falling off the roof."

Needless to say, Carrie heard nothing of this. Ellsworth, in his letter of May 27, apologized for his "long neglect" in not answering her last letter and stated essential facts briefly. He told what he planned to do after the summer's tour was ended: "if we succeed I promise myself one week of unadulterated enjoyment in your dear society." If they failed, he would not visit her but would go at once to Springfield & commence work." He wrote the reason for omitting the visit to her in case of failure, then crossed it out, leaving it legible: "if we fail why it will not be quite so pleasant for you to have me with you." His plan for studying law in Springfield with Lincoln thus seems definite by this time.

On June 11 Ellsworth sent Carrie a brief note in which he said he was "overwhelmed with care and anxiety." Nine days later he wrote her from Mechanicville of the tragedy that had come to him: "My darling — My cup of affliction is nearly full. My brother died in Chicago, Saturday morning of the Small Pox." He had brought the body back home for the funeral "but shall leave here as soon as possible." Having nursed Charley during his illness, Ellsworth was thinking of the ominous fact that he himself was extremely likely to develop the disease. He would not expose his father and mother, so he was going to the Astor House in New York to wait and see. "I would have informed you before but I did not wish to trouble you unnecessarily."

"If I do not become sick," he continued, "shall go back to Chicago as soon as possible. This is a terrible blow for all of us." He had not only lost a dearly loved brother; he had lost the one person who might have shared the care of his father and mother. They were almost crushed with sorrow over Charley's death. "I can write no more now," he said.

Yet there was one thing that he must, in conscience, tell Carrie at once. Fresh from looking on the loathsome aspects of the disease and knowing the disfigurement which followed it, he said that if he did have the smallpox and recovered, she must no longer consider herself "under obligations to act other than your own pleasure" in regard to their relationship. "God bless you, dearest," ended the letter.

Ellsworth's anguish as he waited in New York for the dreaded symptoms to appear can be imagined. He had staked his heart's desire on this tour, whose underlying purpose was to awaken the country (drifting, as he believed, toward civil war) to military consciousness and the need for militia reform. Charley had died on June 16, just before the date the Zouaves had set for the beginning of their trip. Now the days of waiting out the smallpox incubation period must have been almost intolerable to him. When he knew at last that he had not caught the disease, he returned to Chicago and plunged into feverish preparations for the departure of the Zouaves on July 2.

As usual, Ellsworth had to operate financially on a shoestring. He had raised some money but not enough to carry them through. According to an account in the *Troy Whig* that summer, just before their departure the Zouaves' goods and chattels were seized to pay their debts and the loyal people of Chicago hurriedly raised funds to get them out of this embarrassing situation. This disagreeable incident was instigated out of spite by some members of the company who had been expelled. Perplexities of discipline and finances were to accompany Colonel Ellsworth continuously on those three thousand miles of travel.

They would give their Zouave drill in twenty cities.

They would cross the states of Michigan, Ohio, and New York, with exhibitions in eight places before reaching New York City. After the performance there, they would visit Boston and Salem, Massachusetts, then turn back westward to have their shining hour at West Point. Leaving New York, the Zouaves would then bend southward, visiting Philadelphia, Baltimore and Washington. The return route would take them through Pittsburgh, Cincinnati, St. Louis and Springfield, and so back to Chicago.

There was a general tightening up of appearance and discipline before the departure. The men had their hair cut alike and many grew mustache and goatee. A certain uniformity of appearance was desirable in the pictorial effect of the drill and it was observed that very tall men were not in evidence. The Zouaves tended to be under rather than over medium height, which may have been a matter of satisfaction to the proud young leader who was only five feet six.

In regard to discipline Ellsworth, knowing that his men would be subject to extra temptations while away from home, stressed the keeping of the Golden Resolutions in his final talk to them. "By the Eternal," he told them, "the first man who violates his pledge shall be stripped of his uniform and sent back to Chicago in disgrace, so help me God."

On July 2, Chicago gave its prize company a proper send-off. The Zouave Cadets with the Light Guard Band were escorted to the railway station by two other companies, the Light Guards and the Highland Guards. Their first engagement was at Adrian, Michigan, where they were to take part in a Fourth of July celebration.

They were going to be rained on considerably during this tour, and they received a thorough initiation in wetness when they arrived at four o'clock in the morning in a torrential downpour. They were met by the Adrian Guards, who conducted them to a camp in a grove which (while it honored their leader by having the name Camp Ellsworth) was soaking wet. The Zouaves, however, delighted to prove their hardihood by ignoring physical discomforts; in fact, they courted hardship. According to the *Troy Times* of July 12, there was a rule on the tour that the men could not sleep in beds except by order of their surgeon, who, incidentally, was that old friend of Ellsworth's, Dr. Charles A. DeVilliers.

There were several other visiting military companies quartered at Camp Ellsworth. These, with the Adrian Guards, and led by the honor guests, the Zouave Cadets, had a grand parade and then marched through the streets of the city on the morning of the Fourth. Stirring martial music, the glitter of band instruments, waving flags and soldiers in colorful uniforms are always irresistible. In addition, everyone was curious about the Zouaves. People had flocked into Adrian to see them; the sidewalks, windows, and housetops were crowded with delighted spectators as the companies marched by.

It was three in the afternoon when a great throng assembled to witness the Grand Exhibition Drill. Colonel Ellsworth was always an expert showman: his men made a dramatic entrance on the field marching to the music of their own band. The maneuvers began. The people had doubtless seen the drills of the local companies but never anything to equal this. The huge crowd sat enthralled by the intricacy, skill, and beauty of the swiftly changing spectacle. Their eyes were held by the young officer who issued the commands. They were lifted and carried away by their interest and excitement. Like the Zouaves themselves they had come under the spell of Ellsworth's magnetism.

To describe this quality, one must borrow the words of John Hay, who knew him so well, and who recognized that only those who had felt it themselves could ever understand the effect of this magnetism. "No man," wrote Hay, "ever possessed in a more eminent degree the power of personal fascination. That faculty . . . 'of winning, fettering, moving and commanding the souls of thousands till they move as one,' he enjoyed, in a measure, of which the world will forever remain ignorant. He exercised an influence almost mesmeric, upon bodies of organized individuals with whom he was brought in contact." Hay continued that he had seen Ellsworth enter an armory "where a score of awkward youths were going sleepily through their manual, and his first order, sharply and crisply given, would open every eye and straighten every spine. No matter how severe the drill, his men never thought of fatigue. His own indomitable spirit sustained them all."

It takes a passage like this to prepare one for what was going to happen on this tour — and later. The Zouave system itself combined the great popular appeal of the military with spectacular elements calculated to seize upon the imagination of the public. In addition, the Zouave Cadets were a company built up around Ellsworth's personality and ideals. He captured the admiration and trust of the many who met and dealt with him. Here was a young leader and company the people could take to their hearts. When Colonel Ellsworth and his men departed a city, they left behind enthusiastic thousands to sing their praises.

The stay at Adrian set the general pattern of the Cadets' visits to the various cities. On their arrival by train or steamboat, they would be met ceremonially by the local military company and conducted to their quarters. Prominent citizens would make speeches of welcome and Colonel Ellsworth would make graceful speeches in reply. The program invariably had a parade through the principal streets and the big event, of course, was the exhibition drill. In between times the Zouaves would stroll around the city in their striking red, blue, and gold outfits, being flatteringly stared at by the inhabitants.

They carried along with them the Champion Flag of their

challenge but actually the tour was an exhibition, not a competition. Any local military company would concede the superiority of the Zouave Cadets' drill rather than put on a performance that would make them a colorless anticlimax. Always the Cadets were honored guests to be feasted and entertained. The hosts did not suspect what an important part of the program those bountiful dinners and banquets were to the hungry company whose treasury was in a very precarious state.

At Adrian on the evening of July Fourth they had a fine supper at the residence of a prominent citizen. With gorgeous uniforms, high young spirits, feasting, and the gay music of the Light Guard Band, the Colonel and his men had a wonderful time. In return they thrilled their hosts by giving their own special salutation and the company yell which would become famous, the "Tig-a-r" cheer. The first was a full-throated "Hi-hi-hi" and the yell was an accelerating roar of "One-two-three-four-five-six-seven! Tig-a-r! Zouave!" Each man kept time by doffing his cap and jerking it up and down before him. (The number varies somewhat in different accounts.)

At Detroit, the next engagement after Adrian, Colonel Ellsworth had to deal with the first case of discipline on the tour. A cadet broke one of the rules of the Golden Resolutions. He was promptly stripped of his uniform, given a cheap suit of clothes and a ticket, and sent back to Chicago in disgrace. There was little or no disciplinary trouble after that. An amusing incident, however, occurred several stops farther on.

It was when the Cadets were giving their exhibition at the fair grounds in Syracuse. In the "skirmish drill" two of the men who were some distance away from Colonel Ellsworth failed to hear his order. Their lack of response, of course, resulted in a blunder for the drill. Ellsworth, tense, disappointed, and angry, reprimanded them sharply and said something about their being "stripped and sent home." Perhaps he said that they deserved to be stripped and sent home.

After the performance was over and Colonel Ellsworth was receiving congratulations from an admiring crowd in the armory, the two who had been reprimanded appeared before him clad only in their underwear. Ellsworth, surprised and taken aback, asked, "What does this mean?"

"We report for clothes and transportation."

"Clothes and transportation?"

"Yes, sir."

"Oh yes, now I remember. Well boys, put on your uniforms. You need not go back to Chicago to-day."

Cleveland, Ohio, was their next stop after Detroit. On Sunday, July 8, 1860, Ellsworth wrote "My dear Colonel" (otherwise unidentified) some close-up details of the tour. At Cleveland "the Citizens took hold of the entertainment & overloaded our boys with kind attention," he said. "The moment parade was ended a dozen carriages belonging to the Citizens were placed at our deposal. A dinner was given & attended by the common council &c &c, in a word all of the Citizens seemed to vie with each other in endeavoring to render our stay pleasant."

Here too the drill had been completely successful, he told the Colonel. "We left on Saturday Evening escorted by the military who in turn were surrounded by an escort of Hosemen bearing torches & loaded with fire works with which they kept the street blazing along the line of march." Torchlight and flare of fireworks on the bright-colored Zouave figures must have created an unforgettable scene. "By the time we reached the Depot," Ellsworth continued, "at least half of our men had boquets." It was quite the custom in that day to present gentlemen with bouquets of flowers. With his ever-present problem of expenses Ellsworth added gratefully that in Cleveland "as before we were not allowed to pay anything."

How completely the Zouave Cadets captured Cleveland is clear in the account of their visit which appeared in the *Cleveland Morning Leader* on July 9, 1860, the Monday after they left. The article ends: "We heartily bid the Zouaves good-speed. . . . And if these two columns do not convince our readers that we go for the Zouaves . . . then let them call on us and ask what we think of the United States Zouave Cadets of Chicago. One, two, three, four, five, six, seven, tiger! Zouave!"

❖

18

"MOST TALKED-OF MAN"

ELLSWORTH's letter to "My dear Colonel" was written from Rochester, New York, which seems to have been an unscheduled stop. A special committee had come to Cleveland, he said, and "urged us very hard to go to Rochester at once as they had made all the arrangements. The whole Regt would parade to receive us, one company were coming 40 miles to see the drill, and in addition to all this they had expended $500. on fire works."

As Buffalo was on their route the Zouaves seized the opportunity to visit Niagara Falls, which happened to be in the public mind more than usual that summer. The year before a Frenchman called Blondin had crossed the fearful gorge of the Niagara River about a mile below the Falls on a tightrope, crossed it several times with breath-taking variations: blindfold, trundling a wheelbarrow, carrying a man on his shoulders, and even sitting down midway to eat an omelet. Such exploits were after the hearts of all true Zouaves, who doubtless gazed curiously at the scene, picturing it in their minds, while other onlookers, like as not, gazed at them as a spectacle of equal interest.

At Rochester not only the military had received the Cadets; citizens also were assembled at the depot and lined the streets as they passed. "I can give you no idea of our reception here," Ellsworth wrote the Colonel. "It was particularly noticeable along the route that the older & in fact the best class of Citizens are the men who take the Company in hand. They seem to look upon the Company with real respect & feel that they cannot do enough to convince them of their friendship & admiration of their principles."

It was becoming clear to the mature citizens of the nation that the high ideals of the Golden Resolutions were not mere talk, but that the Zouaves were living up to them. Fathers and mothers, anxious about their sons in a world of temptations, were looking eagerly at these fine examples of young American manhood. Drunkenness was an especial worry to parents in that day because it was so widespread. Mrs. Abraham Lincoln who, like her husband, did not touch alcoholic drink, was to be anxious (needlessly) about her son Robert on this matter.

What Colonel Ellsworth came to mean to these parents is expressed with deep feeling in a letter which the mother of five sons wrote him on August 26, 1860, after the tour was over. (This letter was so treasured that it was copied into Mrs. Ellsworth's recollections.) The lady wrote, she said, to thank him as all mothers ought to do, "for the noble example you have set to young men, in forming and *keeping up* a military company under such strict temperance rules. How anxiously," she continued, "did I watch your movements through all your journey, fearing you might fall through temptation, but you marched boldly on — and when you arrived safely at home in all your glory — I felt as if my old voice and hands would have given you 'three cheers' had I been there to welcome you. . . .

"What an achievement!! Had such a thing been told us two years ago, we should not have believed it. . . . God bless you and your men for ever and ever." She had seen so many young men's lives ruined by drunkenness, and had so longed "for some one to help, and none came till 'Ellsworth' rose like another David, to destroy the Goliath."

The "admiration of their principles" which Ellsworth mentioned was a powerful element in the fast-growing popularity of the Zouaves. The tour was proving a moral campaign as well as a military one. When the great appeal of soldiers, defenders of the nation, is joined to a strong moral force, the result can be tremendous. Ellsworth's personality completed the conquest of popular interest and sympathy.

Ellsworth's letters to Carrie during the tour were few and brief. There is no lack of information about the tour, however; he himself wrote her on July 21, "You can easily keep track of our movements by the papers. See the New York Herald, Times, Tribune & World. . . ." And, it might be added, many smaller newspapers anywhere near their route. The U. S. Zouave Cadets and their leader had become headline news.

The company had its usual success and acclaim at Utica, New York. Ellsworth was getting into his home territory now; the next stop was Troy, where in his mid-teens he had worked in the linen store for a year. What joy it would have been to that daydreaming boy if he could have known that one day he would return to this city in a handsome military uniform, the famous leader of a famous company! With his naturally happy response to living (a quality which still retained its boyishness), he inevitably had many thrills at Troy and the next stop, Albany. Yet there was the sadness of Charley's recent death, the knowledge that his mother was ill and that neither of his parents was able to rise above the grief of losing their younger son.

At Troy Ellsworth and his company called to pay their respects to General John E. Wool, a hero of the Mexican War. Perhaps this call had something to do with an important service which General Wool would do for Ellsworth and his men at a critical moment in the following year. At Albany, after their visit, a new company called the Albany Zouave Cadets was formed. John Hay would say of Ellsworth's tour: "In its wake sprang up hundreds of new military companies like phosphorescent sparks in the track of a ship."

The snobbishness which had been so apparent when the Zouaves gave their challenge had disappeared. Praises were being showered on them by the very men who a short time before had sneered at those green boys in the rowdy West who wanted to drill in competition with companies that had "Revolutionary ancestry." American people like to give nicknames to their favorites, so now the Zouaves were being called the "Red Breeches," or "Zous." (In a private letter one finds the term "suvays," which becomes more understandable if spelled "Zouvies.")

Songs were being composed about the company and hummed in homes and on the streets. Among Ellsworth's papers in the Godfrey Collection is a penciled copy of the "Song of the Tiger Zouaves." According to a notation it was sung to the "Air Viva la companie!" meaning "Vive la Compagnie," a phrase which occurs in the chorus of "Vive l'Amour." There are six verses in all of which this is the first:

> *Here's luck to the boys who never say die,*
> *The boys of the Tiger Zouaves;*
> *The world, the flesh and the devil at once*
> *they defie*
> *The boys of the Tiger Zouaves.*
> *The Tiger Zouaves, the Tiger Zouaves,*
> *The boys of the Tiger Zouaves.*

By the time the Zouaves reached New York City on July 14 they had become all the rage. Vast crowds greeted them with a roaring "Welcome Zouaves" and even gave their own tiger cheer for them. They remained in New York about a week giving exhibitions, and the only element which did not cooperate with them was the weather. When a drenching rain interrupted one of their drills, the Zouaves took their red blankets from their shoulders, wrapped up in them and stood motionless until the rain was over, looking like a group of statuesque Indians.

It was in New York that the Zouaves' finances reached a crisis. They had found they could count on receiving two meals a day, but young men going through such strenuous exercises had appetites which demanded three. Ellsworth was used to ignoring hunger; his men, however, were not. The situation had become acute when help came from an unexpected quarter.

Some prominent citizens invited the company to drill in the Academy of Music with admission to be charged and the proceeds given to them. Ellsworth's first impulse was to refuse, but his hungry men soon won him over. The proposition no doubt appealed to his sense of showmanship.

The *New York Tribune* of July 20, 1860, gave an almost rapturous account of the first night's performance. In spite of terribly hot weather, every seat was filled and people were turned away in droves. The stage was set with a simple scene with the arms of the Zouaves stacked in the center. The Zouaves made a dramatic entrance to thunders of applause. The spectacular drill, done to tap of drum, had the usual electric effect upon the audience.

Comedy movements were introduced. The Zouaves, using the "lock step," formed a line which was like a brilliant serpent coiling around the stage. Then came an order to halt. The head and tail of the creature came together. At another order, it doubled up, an effect produced by the men sitting down on each other's knees. The crowd went wild. As the *Tribune* said, "Spontaneous combustion was the fate of every individual."

Of course the audience wanted a speech from Colonel Ellsworth and he turned comedian in giving it. He apologized for the imperfections of the drill and offered atonement for the dissatisfaction of the audience "as indignantly indicated by rousing shouts, vociferous cheers and such tokens of displeasure." He explained that they were not used to the "slippery boards of a theater, and it was not their custom to do their work in the glare of gas." The crowd was delighted. At the conclusion of the performance, the men dashed down to the footlights, gave their tiger cheer, tossing their caps in the air as they did so. This show made the Zouave treasury richer by about two thousand dollars.

Being in New York on Sunday, July 15, the Zouaves with their leader attended services at Trinity Church just as they would go to the Church of the Unity in Boston one week later. The company took Boston by storm as it had New York. There too they were asked to give a performance at one of the opera houses, which was not nearly large enough to accommodate the crowd. One of the Red Breeches remarked, "It is a great pity they do not build larger theaters in Boston." Once during the show the Zouaves rushed to the front of the stage with such impetuosity that the startled spectators on the front seats were about to flee for their lives.

From Boston, Ellsworth wrote Carrie, "I have only time to express my intense disappointment at not meeting you at Buffalo." Apparently she had been traveling West to Rockford as he came East and they had hoped to see each other. Now they would have to wait until the tour was over.

As the company approached their next stop, Salem, Massachusetts, Ellsworth's heart was warm with the knowledge that he would see an old friend. The Zouaves were met by the Salem Light Infantry, whose captain was Arthur F. Devereux. He had returned to his home town of Salem after the Devereux-Ellsworth business in Chicago had been ruined by the dishonesty of the "infernal scoundrel." The two friends had gone through a bitter experience together. Now it was good to meet again on a festive occasion. The stopover and drill at Salem had a personal flavor for some of the company too, as Arthur Devereux had been a leading member of the National Guard Cadets of Chicago. When the Zouaves were entertained at breakfast by Arthur's father, General George H. Devereux, there was an air of reunion. It comes as no surprise that after this visit the Salem Light Infantry became the Salem Zouaves.

Perhaps the peak of triumph for Colonel Ellsworth was the visit to West Point. He could remember how, as a half-grown boy, he had pored over Scott's *Rules and Regulations for the Field Exercise and Manoeuvers of Infantry* and Hardee's *Tactics* until he knew them by heart. Now he was to appear before these well-known officers and put his company through the Zouave drill which he had introduced to the country and made famous; now he was himself the author of a *Manual of Arms* which was just then in great demand. Never did the Zouaves go through their intricate maneuvers more brilliantly than at West Point. It is not clear how many features of their drill they gave in their exhibitions (the complete Zouave drill would take about four and a half hours and involve more than five hundred movements), but it is certain that they did their best before the West Point military experts.

After the performance, Hardee, "old Tactics Himself," remarked of the Zouave drill, "It is only showy and not at all practical." This was reported to Ellsworth, so the Zouaves promptly went through Hardee's own drill. He warmed up a bit at this and said the loading and firing drill was well done but that the men kept watch on each other to keep perfect time. Ellsworth issued his orders, whereupon the Zouaves shut their eyes and gave the Hardee drill equally well! Won over, Hardee pronounced this feat "most wonderful." Finally the Zouaves honored General Scott by going through his drill. It was a supremely satisfying occasion.

Triumph followed triumph in the tour. The newspapers printed long detailed accounts of each stopover but the general pattern was the same. By now the newspaper articles included the stately speeches of welcome by the mayor or other prominent citizen and Colonel Ellsworth's replies. This exchange of courtesies at Philadelphia took place at Independence Hall, where Ellsworth, out of his heartfelt patriotism, paid an eloquent tribute to that beloved building.

He was receiving many gifts and tokens now. At Baltimore the Baltimore City Guard, perhaps realizing its appropriateness, gave him one of their company badges. It was a gold circle with the inscription *Non Solum Nobis, sed Pro Patria.*

The visit to Washington was another brilliant highlight in the triumphant tour. The Zouaves marched along historic Pennsylvania Avenue. By special invitation they gave their drill on the White House grounds before President Buchanan, his niece Miss Harriet Lane, and various members of Washington officialdom. President Buchanan in his speech of welcome to them as "Citizen Soldiers" and "benefactors of the country" made it clear he understood the larger purpose of the tour: to increase military awareness and to improve the efficiency of the nation's militia, especially as that nation was now in the shadow of war.

"The regular Army of the United States is comparatively small," he said. "It never can be very large, except in time of war. What we have is admirable. Nothing can be better. But the people of this country must be prepared, themselves, to defend their own rights and liberties, and their own firesides and their altars. And whatever tends to induce a military spirit among the people, and render them capable of standing erect against a world in arms, that is surely patriotic, that is surely beneficial to the nation."

Colonel Ellsworth made a fitting reply. "Having just returned from a visit to the tomb of our beloved Washington," he said (he and his company had just visited Mount Vernon), "with all our patriotism and love of country awakened by the reflections incident to the visit — the recollection and contemplation of the glorious deeds and sacrifices made by that noble band of Revolutionary martyrs that gained for us the liberties we enjoy — we thought it particularly appropriate that we should call upon you, the representative of these principles . . . we consider it a high honor to be addressed as citizen soldiers."

A well-known journalist in Washington, Ben: Perley Poore, having watched them march, noted that "The step of the Zouaves was in itself a peculiarity." It had, he wrote, along with its perfect precision, "something of a steady *loping* movement, but yet so firm and springy that its effect was most animated." There are frequent suggestions from those who saw the Zouaves in action that their motions were not only skillful and precise but full of rhythm.

Poore must have viewed with special interest the Championship flag which the Zouaves carried. He had good reason to know all about that contest which had taken place at the Agricultural Fair in Chicago the September before. A yellow card in the Ellsworth papers is a membership card of the "United States Agricultural Society" which bears the name of the Society's secretary: Ben: Perley Poore.

At Pittsburgh, after the usual round of speechmaking, parade, and exhibition drill, a hollow square was formed for a special ceremony. The Duquesne Greys presented to Colonel Ellsworth in personal tribute a magnificent sword of Damascus steel etched with a beautiful design. On the blade near the hilt was an appreciative inscription to Colonel E. E. Ellsworth. According to the *Pittsburgh Post* of August 8, 1860, this sword had been shown at the exhibition in London in 1851.

All this glory had an effect upon the doubting Mr. Spafford at Rockford. All evidence of dissatisfaction has now disappeared from the record. The Spaffords had loved Ellsworth from the first; now they could be tremendously proud of him. Among the presents he received that August was a handsome Bible from Mrs. Spafford. Carrie's thrills and pride that her lover had become the nation's idol must be imagined. One would give much to read the letters, now lost, which she was writing to him at this time.

The Zouaves captured Cincinnati and St. Louis in their usual fashion and then came Springfield. For Ellsworth it was like a homecoming. When the Cadets jumped off the train, there stood the Springfield Greys with their commander, his loved friend John Cook. In his speech of welcome and congratulation Adjutant General Thomas S. Mather said among other things: "The curse of a standing army will never be ours if, by wise legislation and proper encouragements, the volunteer service is maintained as it should be. The force of your example is being felt throughout the length and breadth of the whole country." People now realized Ellsworth's underlying purpose in the tour.

The exhibition drill was given in Springfield on the hot afternoon of August 13 before a huge crowd, and Mr. Lincoln stood in the shade of a cottonwood tree in a yard to watch it. Since the Zouaves spent that night at the Springfield armory, perhaps there was time for Ellsworth to talk with him about reporting to his office the next month.

On the train from Springfield to Chicago hilarity in the company ran high. The Zouaves were going home now, triumphant heroes to their proud families and friends. For once Colonel Ellsworth relaxed discipline so that they might have an outlet for their high spirits. During the tour the men had been given all kinds of souvenirs and presents, and now they began to decorate themselves with these "trophies of war" — caps, epaulets, pistols, plumes, badges, ladies' gloves, lace handkerchiefs, and even dried and faded bouquets. When they arrived in Chicago on the evening of August 14 and got off the train thus comically adorned, the waiting crowd went into convulsions of laughter.

The ridiculous decorations had to be disposed of quickly, however. The Zouaves must parade through the streets to the place where Mr. Lincoln had been nominated for President three months before. Chicago's welcome to her heroes was to take place in the Wigwam.

Bands played as the Zouaves moved with a great procession: the fire department in its splendor, the mayor and other city officials, military groups, and long lines of dark figures holding aloft their flaring torches against the blackness of the night. Buildings were illuminated as they passed; bonfires blazed on the streets. Mayor John Wentworth said in his address to the Zouaves at the Wigwam, "We all claim you as our own; and as our own, we have rallied tonight as Chicago people never rallied before."

The vast crowd at the Wigwam heard the mayor say other things very much to the point. He spoke of the unique nature of this celebration. "Politicians have done honor to their idols here," he said, "and office seekers have made their ovations to successful candidates; but on no occasion has there been an assemblage like this, which, irrespective of sect, party, or condition, spontaneously rallies in testimony of its high appreciation of the success which has attended all your efforts."

He praised the "fresh impetus" which the Zouaves had given the volunteer military system. "But you have won plaudits from other than those who have a taste for military tactics; you have a moral as well as a military discipline." Just what an evil drunkenness was at the time stands out in the words that followed: ". . . you have resisted a foe within that has desolated a wider expanse of country, captured more towns, rendered miserable more firesides, made more widows and orphans, than the sword. Well did you provide yourselves at the start against this common enemy. . . . That a company of our Chicago young men should travel the distance you have, amid so many exposures, without once partaking of the intoxicating cup, is a source of greater pleasure to us, your fellow-citizens than the unexampled honors you have received for your perfection in the military arts."

Colonel Ellsworth had become the man of the hour. "His pictures sold like wildfire in every city of the land," wrote John Hay. "School-girls dreamed over the graceful wave of his curls." People hopefully named their boy babies after this young man who embodied the ideal of what parents wished their sons to be. At the end of the tour Americans were talking about him in somewhat the same way that, in the following century, they would speak of a young aviator named Lindbergh who had just flown across the Atlantic. What each achieved was an event unique in history. Elmer Ellsworth in August, 1860, was, as John Hay said, "the most talked-of man in the country."

◇
◇
◇

19

"It Is No Part Of Religion to Be Gloomy"

IMMEDIATELY after the tour Ellsworth discovered what all Americans do who get into the public eye — that people not only talk about them but also write letters to them. He was receiving scores of fan letters and many of them included questions and requests which called for replies. By the middle of September, 1860, he wrote: "I have within the past eleven days received one hundred & seven applications for descriptions of our uniforms, & copies of our manual." It was an "absolute impossibility," he said, for him to answer all these requests.

He was delighted, at this juncture, to receive a proposition which offered him a way out. "Ed. Mendel's Lithographing Engraving" firm in Chicago wished to reprint his *Manual of Arms* with colored illustrations and directions for the Zouave uniforms. Ellsworth promptly gave the firm permission to do this and agreed to supply the illustrations and directions.

On September 15 he wrote Mr. Mendel from Springfield: "I have hastened to complete the drawings & patterns of a uniform upon which I have been experimenting for the past five years." He had found out on the tour, he said, that the Zouave uniforms, while basically good, had some objectionable features. After this experience and much consultation with "Army Officers," he had designed a new one "for active service," he continued, adding, "I have also designed a second uniform for dress occasions." Incidentally, one finds much variation in Zouave uniforms, not only because of different styles for various occasions but also because companies had their own individual features.

The letter to Mr. Mendel proves beyond doubt John Hay's assertion that Ellsworth was too generous for his own good. He admitted he had worked long and carefully on the designs and instructions, then continued: "I have no desire to make anything by the transaction, but present them to you with pleasure, on condition that you publish them as soon as possible. I have distributed gratuitously the first edition (1250) of our manual."

According to his plan, Ellsworth left the U. S. Zouave Cadets late in August. Without his personality to inspire and unite it, the organization at once dwindled and in October formally disbanded. The Cadets could well rest on their laurels.

Ellsworth's letters show that between August 25 and September 15 he visited Rockford. It will be recalled that he had promised himself "one week of unadulterated enjoyment" in Carrie's society, if the tour was a success. The joy of that reunion to the lovers, Carrie's pride in the acclaim which had come to him, the warm affection of the Spaffords, even his interest in baby Eugenia, must all be imagined, because the only mention of the visit to Rockford in his letters is a casual reference in a letter to Carrie written at Springfield on September 23.

He told Carrie he was greatly pleased at his new situation, but otherwise this is a depressed letter. He had exhausted himself again by overwork and had constant toothache besides. A letter from home the day before had told him his father and mother were failing fast and he was wrestling with the problem of getting a suitable person to take care of them.

When he wrote Carrie fifteen days later, however, he was his usual self again. He was settling down in Springfield now and had just moved into a room which would serve both as office and a place to live. At present its furniture consisted, he said, of "two desks, a camp chest & several trunks two broad swords & a revolver." The letter began: "I send my loyal greeting & inform your most gracious Majesty that I am enthroned 'Monarch of all I survey' not to mention a box in the post office & a cord of wood which being piled in the hall can't be surveyed at the same moment with my other possessions." A stove was being set up in the room while he was writing, he said, with somewhat nerve-racking effect.

He was ready to finish his study of law in the Lincoln office. This same letter of October 8 gave a close-up picture of the presidential candidate. "I had the distinguished honor of quite a chat with Mr. Lincoln yesterday," Ellsworth wrote, "he is as unconcerned & calm as if he had nothing at stake in the coming contest." Then followed a remarkably comprehensive description of Abraham Lincoln: "He is a glorious good man."

Whenever Ellsworth settled down to intensive law study, fate immediately went to work to divert him. What happened next was made almost inevitable by two circumstances. First, the air of Springfield that fall was charged with the excitement of Mr. Lincoln's campaign; political speeches and parades were the order of the day. Second, here was a brilliant young man, devoted to Mr. Lincoln and a popular idol, who had unique power as a speaker. Who conceived the idea of Ellsworth's making campaign speeches is not known; it could easily have been that astute judge of men and events, Mr. Lincoln himself. He was watching Ellsworth with great interest and getting fonder of him every day.

It is not surprising then to read in Ellsworth's letter to Carrie of October 20: "Yesterday I launched my *bark* on the troubled sea of politics. That means, in plain English that I made my maiden speech, (on political topics I mean)." He had, he continued, addressed a crowd the day before on the "all absorbing issues of the present campaign."

"I had," he explained, "no intention of engaging in this campaign as I thought it would require at least two months hard application to the study of political matters to fit myself for speaking. But . . . I sat down to work, studied very closely eight days & made my debut yesterday." It was now arranged, he added, "that I am to speak every day, untill the election, in the county precincts. Hurrah for the next President." It turned out that he often spoke twice a day.

Knowing Ellsworth's talents for speaking — his powerful voice which could reach great crowds, his command of words, his humor, which he used, like Mr. Lincoln, as a lubricant in his dealing with people — one can readily see how he captivated his country audiences. He was, said John Hay, "one of the most popular speakers known to the school-houses and barns of Central Illinois." Many who heard him were reminded of the young Stephen A. Douglas. In the remaining days before the election Ellsworth threw himself completely into strenuous campaigning for Mr. Lincoln.

He took time out on Sunday, October 28, to write a long letter to Carrie, finishing it on October 29. The girl had gone back East again to attend a school in Brooklyn, and had written that she was lonely and homesick. He answered her letter from the friendly home where he apparently spent many Sundays and weekends. The letter is headed: "Evening, at John Cooks house. All gone to church except the writer hereof, who remains *at home* to indite an epistle to a young lady supposed to be in the *goolie* [goodly] city of Brooklyn."

The school was in charge of Carrie's uncle, Edward Warren, and she was living with his family. For some reason, perhaps because rules in girls' schools then were unreasonably strict, Carrie felt rebellious toward her Uncle Edward and had written Ellsworth about it. Apprehensive that she was getting off on the wrong foot at the beginning of two years' study, he gave her in this letter four pages of sound advice about how to win friends and influence people, especially uncles. He told her that her feeling of antagonism would ruin her relationship with Mr. Warren. "Never let your uncle think *for a moment*," he said, "that you do not respect his experience, desire to profit by it, & rely upon him to guide & direct you in all things." Ellsworth was anxious that nothing should interfere with Carrie's further studies.

Of course he told her about his campaigning. He had made speeches "every night last week — having to drive on an average twelve miles after my speech was concluded. . . . Although quite confident of the result of the election," he continued, "I am prepared for defeat. I take good care when going into a yard to hold an argument with a strange mastif to leave the gate open behind me."

One finds no account of Election Day in Ellsworth's letters to Carrie. Possibly some letters to her around that time were lost, as the next one at hand is dated November 17. Yet there is every reason to think that on that memorable evening of November 6, 1860, Ellsworth was one of the huge, excited crowd who gathered at the public square in Springfield, while Lincoln with a small group of friends sat listening to the election returns in the telegraph office upstairs across the street. From time to time the returns were shouted to the people outside, and soon it was clear that if Lincoln carried New York, he would be elected.

Tension mounted as the hour grew late. Suddenly the little group of men in the telegraph office rushed down the stairs and out into the street, the one in the lead holding aloft a paper and yelling breathlessly, "Spatch! spatch!" The dispatch said that Lincoln had won New York.

The crowd went wild, shouting, throwing up their hats, singing, yelling, dancing — old men, young men, everybody. Springfield was delirious with joy. Ellsworth can be pictured in that rejoicing crowd, perhaps with John Hay and George Nicolay (both, like himself, had worked heart and soul for Mr. Lincoln's election), the three sharing in that high moment in our history as they were destined to share other historic moments in the months ahead.

Ellsworth's success at campaigning had opened up new possibilities. In his letter of November 17 he said to Carrie: "There is a prospect of my plans for the future undergoing a material change." She was not unprepared for this statement, as he had written her on October 29, "the result of this winter will decide whether I am to be a Lawyer, Soldier or Politician or a good for naught." It had become clear that he was tremendously interested in politics and had extraordinary qualifications for public office. He further told Carrie on November 17, "I am working in the office of the State Auditor every day at the desk & studying & writing nights." He added that he would explain his possible new plans in his next letter.

As opportunities were opening up before him, his obligation to his parents was becoming more urgent than ever. With Charley gone, the whole responsibility for their care was his. Now their grief and increased ill health were bringing matters to a point where some decision must be made. If he had to take them to live with him on limited means, what would that do to his marriage with Carrie? Ellsworth was unhappy over the same problem which had made Mr. Lincoln so miserable nearly twenty years before when he fell in love with Mary Todd and wanted to marry her. Was it right to ask a girl who was used to every luxury to share his hardship and poverty? Ellsworth wrote Carrie on December 2: "I realize that to you, with life opening so brightly before you, there can be no inducement to turn aside from the flowery path in which God has placed you, to labor with me over the rocks and through the thorns that beset mine, in the barren prospect of sharing a life which I now realize must be one [of] sacrifice and severest self-abnegation."

He added that he was submitting to this increased responsibility "cheerfully," for "I do believe that an Almighty and just God has a purpose in all the burdens imposed upon man." He prefaced this declaration of faith with a surprising statement: "I am not a christian." How could a man who lived the principles of Christianity so conscientiously not be a Christian?

It throws some light on the matter to remember that Mr. Lincoln was also said not to be a Christian. A word in a past generation may have a usage different from that of today. Mr. Lincoln too lived a remarkably Christian life but he never joined a church. He could not accept the narrow orthodoxy of his time, and to join would have implied acceptance of doctrines that he could not believe in. It would have been acting an untruth.

No evidence appears that Ellsworth joined any church, though he — and Mr. Lincoln — both attended church. Apparently not being a "Christian" or "technical Christian" was then used at times in the sense of not being a church member.

There is quite a bit about churchgoing in Ellsworth's letters to Carrie. That fall of 1860 she asked him to promise her he would go to church regularly. He answered, "I will make the promise you desire very cheerfully. . . . I have always intended to be regular in my attendance at church as soon as I became a little more settled & acquainted."

What was Ellsworth's religion? His reason for not joining a church was doubtless the same as Mr. Lincoln's: because to join involved saying he believed in certain doctrines that he could not accept. Both men were scrupulously careful always to speak the truth. Both gave ample evidence of their religious faith in what they said and did. Each expressed his trust in God and his reverence for Christianity.

Ellsworth's attitude toward Christianity was shown indirectly in an incident which he recorded in his diary. A friend called on him to invite him to join the Masonic Order. This gentleman, wrote Ellsworth, told him that "Masonry in its true sense & christianity were synonymous terms, a member of the order who lived up to the requirements could not be otherwise than a christian. I intend to join the moment I have money enough."

Ellsworth speaks more fully and directly of his religion in a letter which he wrote his father and mother from Springfield on December 7, 1860. The letter as it exists today is in Carrie's handwriting. She, appreciating the rare quality of it, copied it from the original held by his parents.

Ellsworth's father and mother in this fall of 1860 had found it almost impossible to rally from their grief over Charley's death. They were living in an age which emphasized mourning and made almost a ceremony of it, a fact that gives additional point to what Ellsworth said to them in this letter.

He began by telling them how he prayed daily for help for them in their sorrow. "The last words uttered at night are prayers that you . . . may both experience the joy of faith in God . . . I mean light hearted, ever present peace and contentment of spirit, as faith and love of God. It is no part of religion to be gloomy, cast down, and regretful. Our

God is one of *love not fear*, and the nearer we come to feeling that every thing that occurs is by his hand and for some good purpose, and that the true way to worship is with a *light heart* the better christians are we."

Ellsworth told his father and mother of a deep, comforting belief which had come to him since Charley's death: ". . . as I kneel down at night, the thought comes over my mind that I once had a brother who I would gladly have share my happiness — a feeling of sorrow may fill my heart, and tears rush to my eyes as they do now — yet — a moments thought tells me that I am not, *cannot* be weeping for *him* — these are selfish tears, they are for ourselves, he is far happier than we, he is beyond care — knows no care or sorrow, and for every joy we feel he enjoys a thousand fold — he can see us and *know our thoughts*. However great may be the seperation it is only *on one side*, *we* seperated from *him*, and our mourning is for ourselves. These thoughts pass through my mind, and I am content to thank God for his mercy and go to sleep with a perfectly happy heart."

A basic part of Ellsworth's religion is shown in a passage in his diary already quoted: that his great ambition was "not for personal advancement merely but to do good to my fellow man." Lincoln could have said the same thing. One finds the religious outlook of these two very similar. Once Abraham Lincoln told a friend that when he found a church whose sole qualification for membership was the injunction "Thou shalt love the Lord thy God with all thy heart, and with all thy soul . . . and with all thy mind; and thy neighbour as thyself," he would join that church. Love and trust of God and good will toward men likewise formed the essence of Ellsworth's religion.

20

✧

On to Washington with Mr. Lincoln

Darling Kitty, It is ten oclock I have finished my task this evening sooner than I expected . . . have drawn up an easy chair & am sitting by the fire — thinking — of the past — of the future of my parents — of what I *would* do — of the possibilities of success in my present undertaking, and of you my dear child, and the part *you* play in my thoughts plans and aspirations." So began Ellsworth's letter to Carrie from Springfield on December 20, 1860. It is a letter notable both for length and content.

The cozy atmosphere created by this beginning is misleading; he was deeply troubled. He had not wanted to take up the matter with Carrie in a letter at all; he had so hoped they could meet and talk it over face to face. Now, however, she had written despondently, saying she feared he did not love her as he did formerly and he had to lay bare "the stern realities of life, to one who had seen only its brightest pictures. Events that will tinge & color *my* future, are crowding thick and fast upon me," he said. "let us look at them together, Kitty, and see if I am wrong in my views."

Once more he felt, he continued, "*compelled to sacrifice myself to my duty.*" He told Carrie his parents were now physically unable to carry on at the home in Mechanicville. This new situation coupled with the death of Charley made it necessary "after this winter" for him either to go live with them or bring them to live with him, becoming their sole support in either case. "They are almost heart broken," he said, "they have only me to love . . . *my ambition for advancement must be laid aside.*"

"*A permanent location*" and "*an immediate income sufficient for my increased expenses*" must be secured as soon as possible, he wrote. "And in brief, these are my plans — first to obtain the position of clerk in the War Department, for which I am a candidate." (His close friendship with President-elect Lincoln would be helpful in this matter.) "In the event of obtaining this I should be compelled to *reside in Washington for four years, the salery being just sufficient to support a family in the most economical manner*. At the expiration of the term I should go to New York City and commence the practice of law."

If they were to marry at "the end of two years," Carrie "would be the wife of a *clerk on a salery*," he went on. "We should at once commence housekeeping because my parents would be with me. It would be necessary for me to rent as small a house as would accomodate us." At this point he recalled to her the happy Sunday when they had planned, as lovers do, how they would furnish the home which they would have together in the bright future. This humble abode in Washington would not be anything like their daydream; it would be fitted out, he said, "according to my means." He continued that "it would be utterly impossible for us to go into society, general society, at all . . . in consequence of the enormous expense."

Ellsworth put the question directly to Carrie, would she exchange her carefree girlhood and "all the pleasures you now delight in" for a plain home, hard work, "*the presence of two strangers to you and resignation of society, and the companionship of a working man*"? "Could you expect happiness with me under such circumstances? And would *you* be able to *bear the change* and *become the woman with whom I could be contented & happy?"* He could not be happy unless she was; furthermore, he could not be content unless she measured up to the changed situation with the full development and maturity which he had constantly hoped would be hers. He said with rather terrifying frankness: "I *could not live with* a woman who did not *command* my *entire devotion* a single day."

He was careful to look at her side of the matter. She had been "*the petted child, the careless School girl,* and *the young lady of society*" and she would have to "*undergo a change of circumstances that would try the philosophy of any woman.*"

It was on page fifteen near the close of the letter that he gave a passionate answer to her doubts about the state of his affection. "Do I love YOU?" he wrote. "*God knows I do — better than any woman on earth* . . . and every night I pray oh! how fervently — that *notwithstanding this change,* YOU WILL *become the woman that* I *will* DARE *to* MARRY and *lavish upon a wealth of love — now held in check.* . . ."

In closing, he asked her to reflect carefully upon what he had said "for an *entire* day," then write her answer "IMMEDIATELY." "Let me have a full reply and for GODS SAKE be PERFECTLY FRANK HONEST & EXPLICIT. Sincerely Yours, God bless you, Elmer."

The date of this letter, December 20, 1860, was the day of a far-reaching decision in the nation's history. On that day South Carolina seceded from the United States. This move was like the first narrow arc which bites into the circle of the sun at the beginning of an eclipse. Other Southern states would follow this lead until the Civil War, which was indeed like a great eclipse, would spread over the land, darkening the light of peaceful living into a twilight of fear and hate.

To Ellsworth, already aware of the danger of war, the

secession of South Carolina was fearful news. It was the beginning of that division of the country which Mr. Lincoln had said would lead to its fall. It brought civil war much closer. And then, as John Hay remembered from the talks they had in Springfield and later, there was a special factor which troubled Ellsworth. He had never lost his Mexican dream, the plan which would ultimately lead to the annexation of Mexico to the United States. The secession of the Southern states with the setting up of their own government would prevent this.

With the war threat so much nearer, Ellsworth, knowing the Union was not adequately prepared for war, was working more than ever to improve the efficiency of the militia. The tour had been a dramatization toward that purpose; now he was trying a legal method. On January 6, 1861, he wrote Carrie from Springfield: "The Legislature have been assembling this week and I have been preparing a law — have had to work night & day." This "law" was a nineteen-page bill entitled "An Act for the Reorganization of the Militia of Illinois," and it presented his carefully thought out plan for reform. One item specified that no liquor should be allowed in any armory or on parade or camp grounds. He was throwing himself wholeheartedly into this undertaking.

This same letter of January 6 gives in its opening lines the answer to that all-important question: what did Carrie say about getting married on a small income and living with her parents-in-law? Carrie, who had just had her eighteenth birthday, proved herself the woman Ellsworth wanted her to be; she would cheerfully do so. She shared his strong sense of duty to parents, and the magic of his love and presence outweighed any other consideration.

"My dear dear Kitty," he began in answer, ". . . your *good* letter is received and how happy it made me. You can never know how great my anxiety is that you *should fulfill* what I desire of you. My whole happiness rests upon it. Your letter was *very noble* my darling, and afforded me *great satisfaction*."

It was hard to put all he felt into words. If only she was with him! "I would give anything for an hours conversation with you," he went on, "I can embrace you only in imagination, accept an unlimited number of kisses. There Kitty mine, that will do for me I guess, its about as near the lover as I ever come but I shall — well never mind."

He told Carrie he had visited Rockford briefly and spent a day at her home. Mrs. Spafford had shown him a letter from Carrie's uncle, Edward Warren, which praised the girl highly. Apparently she had taken Ellsworth's good advice on how to win an uncle and it had worked.

It seems that each of the lovers had the idea of visiting the other's parental home. Carrie had evidently decided to go from Brooklyn up to Mechanicville to get acquainted with Ellsworth's parents, with whom she expected to live in about two years. Then they would not be "strangers" to her. Ellsworth's letter continued, "Give my love to *mother* and make my excuses for not writing." It is said that while on this visit she copied the letter of faith and hope which he had written them several weeks before on December 7, 1860. One can picture the parents proudly bringing out their son's letter to show to the beautiful young woman who was to be his wife.

His excuse for not writing his parents was that he was too busy trying to get his law passed. "I'm just now engaged in the highly interesting occupation of *lobbying*," he wrote Carrie on January 18, 1861, "trying to get a bill through the Legislature — for the Militia. I want to do them a favor before I *leave* the State *forever*." He was forced, he said to "dance attendance" upon the legislature constantly and was even writing this letter "near the Speakers desk and half compelled to listen to a *Large talk* about *Disunion* and its results." The letter has the appearance of hasty jottings.

For all his strenuous efforts, he foresaw that the bill would not pass "on account of the great party feeling." Time would prove him right in this prediction: after various ups and downs in two sessions of the legislature the measure would meet ultimate defeat early in May. The Illinois militia was the loser.

Ellsworth evidently expected then that the question of its passing would be decided within a few days. "If the bill fails to pass," he wrote, ". . . I shall go at once to Chicago, & I presume from there to New York City. From there? *probably* to Washington. . . . I have *decided* upon devoting myself to military matters hereafter to the Exclusion of every thing else — until my ability fails, or I find I must adopt some other means of gaining a livelihood. . . . In ten days I shall be *en route* for some where — *again* a wanderer." But, as with so many young men, his plans were overshadowed by the threat of war. "Heaven only knows how it can be averted," he wrote.

"You ask," continued Ellsworth, "what shall I do if I fail, I dont know." Just what is meant here would not be clear if Carrie herself had not written later on the margin, "This *fail* was in relation to his entering the Bar." He had at last reached the stage in his study of law when he was ready to take the bar examination.

The *Washington Chronicle* of May 26, 1861, stated that Ellsworth was admitted to the bar in Springfield in February. This statement requires some explanation. Being admitted to the bar in Illinois then required certain formalities in addition to passing the law examination. The final step was the filing of a record with the Clerk of the Illinois Supreme Court. No such record regarding Ellsworth is found in the records of the Illinois Supreme Court, nor is there any such record in the Circuit Clerk's office. Evidently he did not complete all the requirements. Yet, after all his close study, he could easily have passed the law examination, which was a very informal matter is those days. The explanation may be that Ellsworth did pass this examination (thus giving rise to the impression he had been admitted to the bar), but that he did not complete the process necessary to practice law in Illinois.

During these days in Springfield from September, 1860, to February, 1861, Ellsworth was seeing Lincoln constantly and their friendship had become, to use Lincoln's own word, "intimate." After his nomination Lincoln spent a large part of his time in a room on the second floor of the State House receiving visitors from everywhere. He and Ellsworth (who was working in the State Auditor's office on the first floor) were under the same roof, and the neighbors could sometimes see Ellsworth entering the little gate in front of the Lincoln home, where he had become a familiar visitor. No one could know better than he did how to manage those two little irrepressibles, Willie and Tad, and enter with gusto into their pranks. Mrs. Lincoln's warm motherly affection went out to him completely. As a cousin of hers would say shortly, he had become "a great pet in the family."

Naturally Mr. Lincoln had taken an interest in Ellsworth's enthusiastic and successful campaigning in his behalf. The lawyer had found out, as he wrote later, that this boyish-looking young man had a "power to command men" which "was surpassingly great." Mr. Lincoln also said that he considered Ellsworth's military aptitude "the best natural talent, in that department, I ever knew." He not only gave Ellsworth great affection (a love which John Hay compared to that of a father for his son), but he was tremendously interested in this military talent at a time when it seemed very likely that the Union would need all the military strength

and astuteness it could muster. Mr. Lincoln knew and approved of Ellsworth's ideas for the reform of the militia.

When Ellsworth wrote to Carrie on January 18, he was
very uncertain what his next move would be. All Springfield was now keyed up by the approaching departure of
Mr. Lincoln for Washington, where he was to be inaugurated President. He and his party would leave on February
11, 1861, and make a roundabout trip which would last
nearly two weeks, stopping at various cities where Mr.
Lincoln would speak. Ellsworth's closest friends John and
George (Hay and Nicolay) were going on that special train
as Mr. Lincoln's secretaries; how he must have longed to
go too.

His pleasure when Mr. Lincoln invited him to be one of
the party can be imagined. The invitation must have come
shortly after Ellsworth wrote a certain letter to Mrs. Spafford late in January. In this letter it seems evident that he
knew nothing yet about his trip to Washington, but he does
say, "I shall be in Chicago very soon."

This chance remark incidentally gives a clue about the
time and place of an undated letter which Ellsworth wrote
Nicolay. It begins, "Dear George, Your measure came to
hand this P.M. and I placed it in the hands of the tailor with
orders to proceed to manufacture Coat Pants & Vest forth-
with." Ellsworth had evidently gone to Chicago as he
planned and Nicolay wanted him to order a new suit of
clothes from a city tailor. Ellsworth's letter continued, "I
am getting a pair of pants & vest from the same style of
goods which I think for traveling & morning wear would
suit you admirably."

He went into details which describe what the well-
dressed young man of 1861 wore: "Understand me I have
now ordered for you a business style of frock of black
cloth & a dress Vest of black velvet and do pants of doe-
skin." His gaiety cropped out in his next lines: "Now 'In

Re.' Shirts, as *we* lawyers say — I find upon close inquiry among those who wear the article that a good quality of shirt costs $24 pr Doz — I will however extend my re-shirtses — (dont let John see this) and may do better." Apropos of costs he added, "I find that this matter of accompanying the President Elect involves an expense which, if I were not a (prospective) million-air would make my pocket-book exceedingly easy of transportation." This letter was evidently written in Chicago late in January or early in February, 1861.

Ellsworth mentioned that "People here are in a huge sweat about secession matters" and there was a belief "among the better informed" that some attempt on "Mr L—s life will surely be made." This threat was a matter of deep concern to Ellsworth, not only because of his entire devotion to Mr. Lincoln but also because he was to have official security duties on that trip East.

Elaborate precautions had to be taken for the personal safety of the President-elect. A circular of instructions was sent to all the reception committees of the various towns where stops were scheduled. This circular contained the following paragraph: "*First:* the President elect will under *no circumstances* attempt to pass through any crowd until such arrangements are made as will meet the approval of Col. Ellsworth, who is charged with the responsibility of all matters of this character, and to facilitate this, you will confer a favor by placing Col. Ellsworth in communication with the chief of your escort, immediately upon the arrival of the train."

It was a fearful responsibility in the inflamed state of the nation. The seceding South was infuriated because this small-town lawyer from the West had secured the Presidency. Shortly after the election in November, Mr. Lincoln learned that he had been hanged in effigy in Florida. In early January, Mrs. Lincoln had received from South Carolina what was evidently intended as a ghastly Christmas present: a painting showing her husband with a rope around his neck, his feet chained, and his body covered with tar and feathers.

There were so many rumors of intended attack upon the President-elect on his way East that Mrs. Lincoln was told she and their two little sons, Willie and Tad, had better not accompany him on this trip but should join him later. (Like any plucky and devoted wife, she declared with spirit that she would see Mr. Lincoln on to Washington, danger or no danger, but in the end she did not leave Springfield with him.) Now Ellsworth must make certain that no hate-filled assassin got near Lincoln when he went into crowds on that journey.

Colonel Ellsworth doubtless scanned anxiously the flock of people who came to the Great Western Railroad depot that rainy morning of February 11, 1861, when Mr. Lincoln said good-by to Springfield. This crowd was made up of the old friends and neighbors who loved him and had come to see him off — but who could say whether some would-be assassin had not slipped in among them? Mr. Lincoln as he stood on the train platform would have made a perfect target to one with murderous intentions.

The train engine, with funnel-shaped smokestack and pointed cowcatcher, was festive with brightly colored flags. But the old friends stood wiping their eyes as they listened to Mr. Lincoln's deeply moving words from the platform: "I now leave, not knowing when, or whether ever, I may return. . . . trusting in Him, who can go with me, and remain with you and be every where for good, let us confidently hope that all will yet be well. To His care commending you, as I hope in your prayers you will commend me, I bid you an affectionate farewell." The train moved down the track, its banners stirring into life as its speed increased.

There were many exciting things for Ellsworth to share

on that long journey. With his love of richness and color he doubtless luxuriated in the interior of the Presidential car which was the latest thing in railroad elegance. Crimson plush covered the side walls beneath the windows while between the windows hung heavy blue silk studded with thirty-four silver stars. Two national flags of fine silk were crossed at each end of the car. The assorted personalities of the presidential party were equally colorful. For Ellsworth the camaraderie with John Hay and George Nicolay was especially welcome.

At Indianapolis came the first test of the young Colonel's responsibility for the President-elect's safety; he had to approve the arrangements of the local committee for taking Mr. Lincoln through the crowds to the Bates House where he was to spend the night. The circular of instructions specified the order of the carriages. The President-elect and prominent officials went in the first two carriages, Ellsworth himself with Nicolay rode in the third, while John Hay with the Lincolns' seventeen-year-old son Robert came in the fourth.

The Colonel must have breathed a sigh of relief when Mr. Lincoln safely boarded the train again the next morning and shortly thereafter he undoubtedly witnessed a merry scene. Just before the train started who should come aboard but Mrs. Lincoln with Willie and Tad. The train had left all three standing at the station in Springfield when it pulled out the day before, the shrill hurrahs of the little boys being one of the last sounds they heard. The explanation was that Mrs. Lincoln had not wanted to be left behind because of danger and when word came from General Scott at Washington that Mr. Lincoln would be safer if he had his family with him, she promptly made up her mind to go to Indianapolis by another route and overtake the presidential party. Her appearance with the children was a birthday surprise for Mr. Lincoln, who was fifty-two on that February 12, 1861.

At Indianapolis, Ellsworth had dashed off a hasty note to Carrie at Brooklyn. He told her the President-elect's party was scheduled to arrive in New York at three o'clock on Tuesday, February 19. She could get the name of the hotel from the newspapers. "As matters look now," he continued, "it will be absolutely impossible for me to leave the party for an hour. Can you not arrange with some proper escort to be at the Hotel in the Ladies part when we arrive?" She could drop him a line at Albany and she might ask her uncle to come to the hotel with her.

Albany, in Ellsworth's home territory, was one of the stopovers on the tour. In fact a number of the stops were in cities where the U. S. Zouave Cadets had drilled the summer before. Possibly as the procession of carriages drove through the streets to the cheers of the crowd, some may have recognized the familiar figure in the third carriage and given a special cheer for him.

The party reached New York on schedule and went at once to the Astor House. One trusts that there Colonel Ellsworth found waiting "in the Ladies' part," properly escorted, a small hoop-skirted figure with eager, radiant face. Carrie's uncle, Edward Warren, may well have been with her and possibly told Ellsworth of some kind of government appointment he wanted. At least, Ellsworth wrote Carrie about two weeks later, "Tell your Uncle I am making the strongest kind of effort for him."

The train was now within four days of its destination. Because it was believed that in Baltimore a plot had been made to assassinate Lincoln, he was taken secretly through that city the night of February 22 ahead of his schedule. Ellsworth came through the hostile city with the party the next day, arriving in Washington in the late afternoon of

February 23. Conspicuous on the skyline as they drove to Willard's Hotel was the unfinished dome of the United States Capitol, its top part missing just as the seceded states were missing from the Union. It was a striking symbol of the divided country of which Mr. Lincoln was about to become President.

"I Would Do Nothing to Cause
Ill Feeling Toward Mr L."

ELLSWORTH wrote to Carrie from Washington two days later. "Ive only time to say that we arrived safely and I received your letter yesterday," began his letter of February 25. "You must not expect a letter from me untill after the Inaugeration. . . . send love to mother in your next letter." Carrie, now affectionately acquainted with his parents after her visit, was, at Elmer's request, writing to them to relay the news she received from him.

One has no description from Ellsworth's pen of that momentous March 4, 1861, when Abraham Lincoln was inaugurated President of the United States. Staying at the Willard Hotel as one of the presidential party, he certainly attended the Inauguration, which took place on the great platform which had been erected on the east front of the Capitol. Ellsworth with his literary instinct, his zeal for the Union, and his awareness that the country was on the edge of civil war, could appreciate the eloquence of Lincoln's closing lines addressed to the seceding South: "We are not enemies, but friends. We must not be enemies. Though passion may have strained, it must not break our bonds of affection. The mystic chords of memory, stretching from every battle-field, and patriot grave, to every living heart and hearthstone, all over this broad land, will yet swell the chorus of the Union, when again touched, as surely they will be, by the better angels of our nature."

The *New York Times* of March 5, 1861, mentions three interesting young men who entered the brilliant scene of the Inaugural Ball together on the evening of March 4. They were John Hay, Robert Lincoln, and Colonel E. E. Ellsworth. In the color and magnificence of that grand dress parade, Ellsworth could have seen Mrs. Lincoln on the arm of Stephen A. Douglas, whose power in speaking was said to resemble his own.

From the time the Lincolns moved into the White House, Ellsworth was a constant, welcome visitor. Mrs. Lincoln's cousin, Elizabeth Grimsley (who had come to stay with her for her first months in the Executive Mansion), said later of the young Colonel: "He had been a member of the family ever since we went to Washington . . . and was much beloved." She added her own description of him: "a magnetic, brilliant young fellow, overflowing with dash and spirit." Ellsworth's two best friends, Hay and Nicolay, slept on the second floor of the White House and their "secretary's room" was opposite the President's office on the same floor. Ellsworth was in constant touch with the President, who was concerning himself much with certain plans for this young friend's future career.

Ellsworth himself was taking prompt steps to get the position he wanted. Before he had left Springfield he had written his old friend of Chicago days, General Simon B. Buckner, about the matter, asking him for a letter of recommendation to the Secretary of War.

General Buckner, then commandant of the Kentucky State Guard at Louisville, replied to Ellsworth's letter on February 18. He had a genuine interest in the younger man and wanted to help, but he was in an unhappy position. He foresaw that civil war was coming and that his conscience in the end would make him fight for the South. Yet he was a West Point man and had fought valiantly for the United States in the Mexican War. Few letters bring closer the painful conflict in the minds of Southern men on the eve of the Civil War or give a more striking expression to a Southerner's way of looking at the dreadful possibility of dividing the country.

General Buckner enclosed with his letter a splendid recommendation of Ellsworth for a second lieutenancy in the United States Army. It was addressed to the Secretary of War at Washington. His accompanying letter to Ellsworth explained why he did not recommend him for a clerkship: "If you wish to follow a soldier's life, the position of Clerk in the War Department will not suit. . . . If you wish to be a soldier I advise you to apply for an appointment as Lieutenant in the Army. Such a place is in the gift of Mr. Lincoln, and he will doubtless give it to you." He added that if Ellsworth obtained a second lieutenancy "in a regiment in which there were many Southern men you will probably advance rapidly in rank." Many vacancies were being created by Southerners leaving the Union Army to join the Confederacy.

The general was especially bitter at the moment because Mr. Lincoln in his speech at Indianapolis six days before had used the word "coercion" in regard to the United States holding its own forts in the South. "I have recently come to the conclusion," Buckner said, "that the northern people are conscious they will be doing God a service to cut southern throats; in other words they believe their position is right and in so believing they have no compunctions in waging what they regard a righteous war against traitors! . . . The indications are that in six months' time we will be in hostile Camps."

There is pain in his next sentence, the same regret which saddened the heart of Robert E. Lee when he made his decision to fight with the South. General Buckner continued: ". . . strong indeed must be the cause which will induce me to oppose the colors under which I have fought with true loyalty to my country. But we are as staunch in our faith as you in yours." He believed, he continued, that the Republican platform on which Lincoln had been elected was "revolutionary"; that the Northern people "are the real traitors; and we believe that our position is but the counter-revolution bringing back the Republic to the days of its purity."

General Buckner was expressing his ideal of loyalty to the forefathers who fought for independence in the American Revolution. Lincoln at Gettysburg would say that the North was fighting to preserve the government of the people which these same forefathers "brought forth upon this continent," that the war was a testing of their great experiment of democracy. These two living viewpoints, both involving loyalty to the founders of the nation, epitomize the tragedy of the Civil War.

Ellsworth did not transmit General Buckner's recommendation to the Secretary of War. He would not have wanted to use it after what the General said; besides, by the time he received it, he was undoubtedly in a situation where events had moved rapidly beyond his need for the General's recommendation.

He had come to Washington wanting a clerkship in the War Department. Before appealing directly to the President, he wished to canvass the situation and see certain persons, and the result was that he found himself in a tangle of what he called "hard wire pulling." He used this expression in an undated letter to Carrie's mother (around March 22), in which he told what had happened to him since his arrival a month before, asking her to send the letter to Carrie.

"As soon as it was known that Cameron, was to be Sec of War, I had Thurlow Weed, Judge Davis, & another person of great influence with him go & urge my claims, & obtain from him a promise 'to do nothing', untill he heard from me." Ellsworth had chosen two influential advocates in Weed and Judge David Davis. "I then went to Mr Lincoln & told him I would like a note to Mr Cameron, he immediately wrote a request to C. to appt me Chf Clerk."

This note exists today in the Cameron Papers at the Library of Congress. Its date, March 5, 1861, shows it was written on Lincoln's second day as President. One can picture the scene: Ellsworth watching the President write at his desk in his office on the second floor of the White House. After he finished and laid down his pen, "he swung round in his chair," Ellsworth reported later, "and said in a peculiarly deliberate manner, 'I've been thinking on the way, & since we have been here, a long while in fact, that by & by, when things all get straightened out & I can see how the *land lays,* that I'd put you in the Army, somewhere.' " Ellsworth said he thanked the President but at present his purposes could be best accomplished out of the Army. He explained to Mrs. Spafford that his plan was "to get into the War Dpt in order [to] pave the way for & secure the establishment of a Bureau of Militia . . . & secure the control of it myself." This Bureau of Militia objective is something added since he wrote about the clerkship to Carrie in December.

In Lincoln's note, addressed to the Secretary of War, he introduced Ellsworth as "my friend" and requested that he be appointed chief clerk of the War Department, "If the public service admits of a change, without injury." This note being delivered to Cameron, Ellsworth, as he said, "discovered from his manner & a remark that, '*that note,* & my own reputation would be sufficient if he wasn't so peculiarly situated,' that he was compromised. I made up my mind in a moment that there was a promise somewhere, however, I said nothing untill I met him again."

Meanwhile Ellsworth busied himself finding out what steps would be necessary to create a Bureau of Militia. He learned, he continued in his account to Mrs. Spafford, that "the President could select any officer from the Army & order him to do the duty of Adj't & Insor [Inspector] Genl. of Militia for the U. S. & station him at Washington." Furthermore, Ellsworth discovered "that there was a vacancy in the Pay Department (the only one in which the President can appoint with a higher rank than Lieut) with the rank of Major and pay of $3000. pr year."

Armed with this information, Ellsworth said he "posted off to our friend Cameron" and very soon found his suspicions were correct, that the Secretary had promised the chief clerkship to someone else. Ellsworth then presented the case for establishing a Bureau of Militia of which he would be in charge. Cameron "agreed to recommend it, & we arranged a meeting with Mr Lincoln at 8 o'clock the same eve."

When Ellsworth "went up" to the President's office that evening he took with him two army officers, Major David Hunter and Captain John Pope. "When we were all in the room together," continued his letter, "I explained what brought us there, & when I had concluded Mr Lincoln, said Well gentlemen, with all proper regard for the rights of Mr Cameron, or any body else i want Col Ellsworth to have a good place & more to the same effect. Said I, Mr L— here are two old Army officers to tell you what can be done in this matter. Maj Hunter then explained that Mr L, could appoint me to the Pay Dept & then make me Chief of a Bureau of Militia &c."

"Well said Mr L. again, I am pressed to death for time — and dont pretend to know any thing of military matters — fix the thing up so that I shant be treading on any bodies' toes, or carrying anybody across lots, & then come to me &

Ill finish it." Secretary Cameron said he would arrange everything to Colonel Ellsworth's satisfaction.

An interesting bit of additional pressure was brought to bear upon the Secretary of War. "*Mrs.* Lincoln," continued Ellsworth, "sent for Cameron & made him *promise* that I should have the Majority." It is an indication of how much she cared for the young colonel that she did this, though her taking a hand in the matter might be open to criticism.

The progress of events can be traced in Ellsworth's other letters and in President Lincoln's official correspondence. Ellsworth wrote Mr. Spafford late in March: "I have the *positive* promise of both Mr. Lincoln & Cameron to create the Bureau of Militia and make me chief of it. I had to take a commission first as they could only assign Army officers to such duty."

What the commission was appears in the document addressed to the Secretary of War which Mr. Lincoln wrote on March 18, 1861, beginning: "You will favor me by issuing an order detailing Lieut. Ephraim E. Ellsworth, of the First Dragoons, for special duty as Adjutant and Inspector General of Militia for the United States, and in so far as existing laws will admit, charge him with the transaction, under your direction, of all business pertaining to the Militia, to be conducted as a separate bureau, of which Lieut. Ellsworth will be chief." This document further directed that the Secretary of War should provide Lieutenant Ellsworth with all facilities that "he may desire for the successful prosecution of his duties; and also provide . . . for a monthly payment to Lieut Ellsworth, for this extra duty, sufficient to make his pay equal that of a Major of Cavalry."

Lincoln sent this draft to Attorney General Bates asking him to give his opinion whether the Executive had "any lawful authority" to make such an order. In other words he wanted to know if any action by Congress would be necessary (which proved to be the case).

Why was Ellsworth's commission only that of a lieutenant after all the talk about making him a major? The answer to this question is one of the most interesting episodes in the Ellsworth story. He told it in full detail in his letter to Mrs. Spafford. The incidents involved evidently took place before Lincoln wrote his draft on March 18.

Ellsworth said that matters reached a point where the papers were ready to be signed. These papers would have made him a major. "I started to get the papers signed, on the following morning," he wrote, "& met Gen Sumner, who, learning that I was to be appointed Major, made the following representations — 1st that the position was so desirable that half the Captains in the army were, & had been seeking it for years: 2ndly that it would arouse the ill will of these men against Mr Lincoln — &c &c"

Such an appointment did not take into consideration the prestige of West Point men, the rivalry between officers in the regular army and the rule of seniority. Ellsworth was all too familiar with the army attitude that he was a mere upstart. If Lincoln made him a major the act would create antagonism and enemies just when the new, untried President needed to win confidence and friends.

Ellsworth knew what, in conscience, he must do. He went on, he said, to Mr. Cameron and asked him if he was ready to sign the papers. Cameron said he was. "Then," wrote Ellsworth, "I related the conversation which had just occurred — & told him that I would do nothing to cause ill feeling toward Mr L. or himself & I would not therefore take the Majority." He continued: "thats the manner in which I kicked myself out of a three-thousand dollar *life* position, into the Cold!"

Cameron assured Ellsworth that he and the President could "take care of" him. Ellsworth's letter to Mrs. Spafford continued: "The next best thing was to take a Lieutenancy — about $1,850 a year (Cameron has *positively* promised to make it up to $3000.) & be ordered to duty at Washington & placed in charge of my Bureau."

Lincoln's draft of March 18 shows that he had given Ellsworth his commission (2nd Lieutenant) by that date and was making arrangements for him to receive the salary ordinarily given a major, when he should be placed in charge of the Bureau. The President was one to appreciate Ellsworth's scruples in not accepting the majority under the circumstances; he had the same kind of conscience himself.

Ellsworth concluded his account of this chain of events to Mrs. Spafford: "All the papers are drawn up & undergoing examination in the hands of the Atty Genl & if *promises* are not *freely broken* I shall be — *all right* again. The next step will be to ask Congress to create the Bureau by Law."

In this same letter he mentioned a subject which was causing him great indignation at the moment. It will be recalled that he had already been a favorite target for abusive gossip. Now the fact that he was so obviously a favorite of the President's was bringing him additional unfriendly attention. In the bitter politics of that critical period, individuals and newspapers opposed to Mr. Lincoln seized eagerly on any excuse to belittle him directly or indirectly. Ellsworth said in his letter to Mrs. Spafford, "Now a word about that Times & Post Trash. I had received read & preserved it all; in addition to it there is an immense amount of malicious lies circulated by individuals." He had explained to Carrie that these individuals were men who had been expelled from the company.

Among Ellsworth's papers is an undated clipping marked "Chicago Times."

> *Zouave, Oh! The Telegraph announces that Mr. Lincoln has requested Gen. Cameron to appoint Col. Ellsworth, of Chicago Zouave notoriety, to the fat office of Chief Clerk of the War Department. Oh, my! calico Colonels are in the*

ascendant. And who is it, pray, that Mr. Lincoln is so anxious to put into a twenty-two-hundred dollars a year office? A mere adventurer; formerly the pompous Captain of the Chicago Zouave Cadets, who went into the show business and traveled on free passes all over the Union last Summer; a second edition of "fuss and feathers". . . . Vive la humbug! Won't he make a roaring chief clerk of the War Department.

There seem to have been more than one of these articles. John Hay thought that the weeks following his arrival in Washington "were the least pleasant of Ellsworth's life. They were brightened only by the society of those he trusted most," continued Hay, "and by the unvarying friendship and confidence of the President and his family."

In Washington Ellsworth had been suddenly plunged into a turmoil of rumors, slanders, jealous office seekers, political intrigue and political mud-slinging. Hay said he "was placed in a false position. He never wished office for its honor or its profit, but you can never get office seekers or office dispensers to believe any such story." Hay knew from talking with him that Ellsworth's efforts to be appointed chief of a Bureau of Militia were based on a patriotic desire to carry out his plan of militia reform and thus strengthen the military forces of the country.

In the midst of these complications he experienced a severe ordeal. It must have been not long after the Inauguration that he felt he was developing a very bad cold. He had fever and was feeling wretched, but he was never one to give in to physical distress.

What was his horror several days later to discover himself broken out with red spots. After his experience nursing Charley he could think of only one thing — smallpox. Ellsworth in his room at the Willard Hotel was utterly miserable. He told the story of this fearful experience on "Thursday" (March 21) in a note to Carrie which he wrote with shaky hands and eyes too weak to "look steadily at the paper."

"I have strength enough to write a letter for the first time since my illness," he began. "I have been confined to my bed by the measles and inflamation of the chest. . . . I would have let you known but when I was taken & untill I became so ill that I could not write I supposed I had the Small Pox & of course I wrote to no one."

It is possible Ellsworth remembered that when he had recently dropped in at the White House, Willie and Tad, who always welcomed him with delight, seemed to be "coming down" with colds too. At all events, he said in a brief note to Carrie's father written around this time, "Both Mr Lincolns children have the measles I took it from them." All three cases were severe. Ellsworth's, with the complication of pneumonia, was critical.

He was still extremely weak when he wrote to Carrie again on March 24. "Why dont *you* write to *me* — ?" he began. "Here I've been sick unable to leave my bed for a long while every day longing for a letter, but none came. You mus'nt stand on your dignity, little one in these piping times." He mentioned a plan to come to New York and sent her "an arm *full* of kisses." The next brief undated note gave more details about coming to New York, where "I will call to see you as soon as I arrive." He was somewhat doubtful, however, about when he could make the trip: "I am not quite as well & hearty as before my illness."

A brief note on April 2 shows that Carrie had not been remiss in her writing to him; the delayed letters for which he had longed had finally arrived. His postscript suggests that they planned to go to Albany together: "Will it be in time for your visit to Albany if we leave New York Monday the 16th of April one week after my arrival in N. Y.?"

It was a pleasant plan. If Ellsworth arrived in New York

on April 9, possibly he and Carrie could celebrate his twenty-fourth birthday together on April 11. But now the fateful month of April, 1861, had come to the nation. Ellsworth probably did not leave Washington in the face of the crisis. On April 12 the Confederates fired on Fort Sumter. On April 15 President Lincoln issued a call for seventy-five thousand troops.

By April 16, the day two happy lovers had planned to journey to Albany, the country was at war.

22

The Fire Zouaves

Ellsworth went into action so promptly that it is evident he had already decided what he would do if war came. He would resign his commission as lieutenant in the regular army, go at once to New York, and try to raise a regiment of Zouaves from the New York Fire Department. He knew many of its men; besides, having worked with the Fire Department in Chicago, he thought firemen in general had the qualities to make good soldiers. This regiment would respond to President Lincoln's call for volunteers "to maintain the honor, the integrity, and the existence of our National Union, and the perpetuity of popular government." It would be a far greater service than a lieutenant could possibly render.

On the same day on which Lincoln issued the call for troops, he wrote a letter for Ellsworth to aid him in his plan to serve. Addressed to Col. E. E. Ellsworth, it was the kind of letter which he could use as a recommendation or credential. It stated that Ellsworth was a highly valued personal friend of whose military talent the President "had a very high estimate." Lincoln told Ellsworth in this letter, "I have been, and still am anxious for you to have the best position in the military which can be given you, consistently with justice and proper courtesy towards the older officers of the army. I can not incur the risk of doing them injustice, or a discourtesy, but I do say they would personally oblige me, if they could, and would place you in some position, or in some service, satisfactory to yourself."

Ellsworth carried this letter with him when he went to New York, where he set out to do what would have been impossible to any individual who did not have his power to "control the minds of men." He was born for action and leadership and it was probably a great relief to him, after his weeks of political tangles, to plunge into the work he loved most, enlisting and preparing men for military service.

On the day of his arrival he went to see Horace Greeley, editor of the *New York Tribune*, showing him President Lincoln's letter and asking his aid. An editorial in that paper later told about this interview, how this young man "of an unusually fine physique, of frank and attractive manners, and of great intelligence" called and said: "I want the New-York firemen, for there are no more effective men in the country, and none with whom I can do so much. They are sleeping on a volcano at Washington," Ellsworth added, "and I want men who can go into a fight now."

They were indeed sleeping on a volcano at the nation's capital. Washington lay exposed to attack by the Confederates until Union troops from the North could come to protect it. The city was holding its breath with fear. It was during this critical period, from April 15 to April 25 (when the New York Seventh arrived in Washington), that Ellsworth was working feverishly to raise his Zouave regiment in New York. Haste was terribly necessary.

The Fire Department enthusiastically agreed to his plan at once. Many of its members knew Ellsworth and enlistments quickly went over the required number. There were numerous difficulties to be surmounted (and as usual Ellsworth tried to attend to most of them himself), but by Saturday, April 20, the well-worked-out details of organization for the regiment of Fire Zouaves appeared in the New

York papers. The Zouave drill uniform was too conspicuous for the kind of fighting which was ahead, so, according to the *New York Commercial Advertiser* of that date, one similar to the United States Army regulation uniform was adopted. The regiment, however, retained the Zouave scarlet in their shirts.

A member of the regiment recalled an incident about the designing of the new uniform. A New York hatter came in with the drawing of a cap and asked if it would do. "No," said Ellsworth, "See here," and taking a pencil he made half a dozen strokes in a flash and there was the pattern of the cap he wanted.

Five days after President Lincoln issued his call for troops, the New York regiment of Fire Zouaves had organized and chosen its officers. Ellsworth was unanimously elected colonel. On that same day, Saturday, April 20, John Hay at Washington, sitting in the White House, where troops were quartered in the great East Room because of the fear of Confederate attack, wrote in his diary: "Ellsworth telegraphs that his regiment has been raised, accepted. . . . Much is hoped from the gallant Colonel's Blood-tubs. They would be worth their weight in Virginia currency at Ft. McHenry tonight." Hay mentioned that one of the "feverish rumours" was that Fort McHenry in Baltimore harbor expected an attack.

The State of New York could not equip the regiment quickly enough; money for rifles and uniforms was raised by the people of the city. The following Ellsworth had won on his tour the summer before stood the regiment in good stead now. To the popular adoration he and his Zouaves had then received was added the flame of patriotism which spreads with the outbreak of war.

New York, like Washington, had suddenly assumed a martial aspect: barracks were being erected in Central Park, the flag was waving on all sides, soldiers marched in the streets. The Fire Zouaves were drilling and parading to the loud hurrahs of the crowds. Ellsworth, as John Hay wrote, was "the idol of the Bowery and the pet of the Avenue." Ovation followed ovation.

The day the Fire Zouaves departed for Washington, Monday, April 29, was one of intense emotions and colorful scenes. A reporter from the *New York Tribune* went that day to the Devlin Building on Canal Street, where the Zouaves were quartered, and described what he saw. Outside he found policemen busy keeping out all except relatives of the men and the press. "Inside the building," he wrote, "everything wore a military business-like air; many soldiers were packing their knapsacks, fitting their belts and uniforms, while others were undergoing a preliminary drill, under the directions of their enterprising captains." The colored servants of the regiment, fourteen in all, he continued, "were rushing frantically about, conveying messages from one officer to another, or picking up small articles that were 'lying around loose.' "

The newspaperman sketched the leader of the Fire Zouaves: "The busiest man of the whole regiment, however, was Col. Ellsworth himself. Ten days devoted to the arduous task of forming, equipping, and providing for a regiment of 1,100 hardy men, seems to have had no effect whatever upon him; but his step was as brisk and his voice as deep and sonorous as when New Yorkers first beheld him at the head of his famous company of Chicago Zouaves." The reporter spoke of the remarkable way in which "the little Colonel" managed the recruits: "One moment he was marching at the head of an enthusiastic company of butcher boys, the next he would be assisting a colored servant to carry a box of muskets across the room, or buckling the knapsack to the broad shoulders of some volunteer who 'hadn't exactly got the hang of the infernal contrivance.' " The "little Colonel" introduces another nickname, an affectionate one destined to be much used. John Hay with an air wrote it "*le petit* Colonel."

Prominent city officials and two well-known gentlemen, General John A. Dix and the Honorable Cassius M. Clay of Kentucky, entered the Devlin Building that morning to express their appreciation of and wish godspeed to the departing Fire Zouaves. As two o'clock approached there began the heartbreaking good-bys of fathers, mothers, sweethearts and wives to their loved ones going off to war, the same brave, pitiful good-bys which were now being said all over the land, North and South.

One does not know whether Ellsworth saw Carrie this time in New York. His last available letter addressed to her there was dated April 2, in which he wrote about their going to Albany together on April 16. He was to address a letter to her at Rockford on May 10; the events between are hidden.

It is related, however, that he did say one tender good-by on that day of departure for war. A tiny, frail, dark-eyed woman from Mechanicville was at the Astor House; Mrs. Ellsworth had come to bid her son good-by. "I hope God will take care of you, Elmer," were her last tremulous words to him and he answered, "He will take care of me, mother. He has led me in this work, and He will take care of me."

At two o'clock the Zouaves formed in the street for the final ceremonies. The President of the Fire Department, Mr. W. H. Wickham, in behalf of that organization, presented the regiment with a huge white silk flag bordered with deep red, white, and blue fringe. Hooks, ladders, and other firemen's tools were worked into its design; its staff was crowned with the fireman's ax.

Mr. Wickham used an appropriate analogy in his words of presentation: "When the fire-bell rings in the night, the citizen rests securely, for he knows the New-York firemen are omnipotent to arrest the progress of destruction. You

are now . . . called to quench the flames of rebellion. . . .
Our hearts are with you, at all times and in every place."
Colonel Ellsworth made a fitting response.

Then General Dix brought forward a great crimson silk
banner given to the regiment by Mrs. John Jacob Astor, Jr.,
who was among those at the scene. The General read her
letter of presentation of the flag to the men "whose heads
are moved by a generous patriotism to defend it, and whose
hearts feel now more deeply than they have ever done that
the honor of their country's flag is sacred and precious to
them as their own."

A third flag was the gift of the actress Laura Keene, who
four years later would be playing in a comedy at the Ford
Theatre on the evening of April 14, 1865, when President
Lincoln was shot. Her letter of presentation began "Brother
Soldiers." Still other banners were given until, as the *New
York Tribune* put it the next day, "Col. Ellsworth and his
entire staff can wrap themselves up in American flags if
they choose."

Ceremonies concluded, the regiment began the march
which would end at the pier where the steamship *Baltic* was
waiting to receive them. The *Baltic* would take them to
Annapolis and they would proceed from there to Washington by rail. With band playing, the Fire Zouaves paraded
through the principal streets while the great crowds cheered
themselves hoarse. New York was saying a tremendous
good-by to her heroes.

It was a triumphant hour for Colonel Ellsworth in the
state of his birth. Fate, however, at all points seemed to provide the opposition and conflict which make his story so dramatic. On the march, orders came from the Governor that
the regiment was not to embark. It was the third such order
that day, the excuse being a mere technicality — that the
companies exceeded the regulation number of men. Evidently antagonistic forces were at work again.

The Fire Zouaves halted, their faces full of question. As one of them, Francis E. Brownell, told it later, "At the corner of Canal stood Gen. Wool, then in command of that department." This was the same General John E. Wool whom Ellsworth and his Chicago Zouaves had met at Troy when they were on their tour the previous July. Ellsworth showed him the order from the Governor and asked what he should do.

According to Brownell, General Wool said, "Go on, it don't make any difference if you've got 1,100 men." On marched the regiment to the crowded, bewildering scene at the pier. All the remaining members of the Fire Department were there and each, said the *New York Tribune* the next day, "felt it to be his bounden duty to shake the hand of every soldier." These good-bys lasted for two hours, then cannon boomed a parting salute as the *Baltic* steamed down the bay on her way to Annapolis.

Meanwhile at Washington a rumor started that the Fire Zouaves were going by way of Baltimore. This was a matter of worry to President Lincoln, knowing as he did that such a route could result in fruitless bloodshed. The Sixth Massachusetts Regiment had been assaulted by a mob when passing through that city shortly before, a fact that made most of the belligerent Zouaves extremely anxious to go that way. When word came that the Zouave regiment was on its way by ship, John Hay wrote in his diary on May 1: "Ellsworth's whereabouts pleased the Tycoon as it enabled him to correct a funk of Scott's that the Firemen were cutting their way through Baltimore." ("Tycoon" was Hay's affectionate nickname for Mr. Lincoln.)

Hay's spicy diary almost carries the story at this time. On May 2, 1861, he wrote, "Tonight Ellsworth & his stalwart troup arrived." Then follows a description of the new Zouave uniform and equipment: Ellsworth "was dressed like his men, red cap, red shirt, grey breeches, grey jacket. In his belt, a sword, a very heavy revolver, and what was still more significant of the measures necessary with the turbulent spirits under his command, an enormously large and blood-thirsty-looking bowie knife, more than a foot long in the blade and with body enough to go through a man's head from crown to chin as you would split an apple." The *New York Post* had given a further description of this formidable weapon a few days before — it was sixteen inches long and was called, with a sort of frontier humor, an "Arkansas toothpick."

Hay's keen dark eyes, looking at his friend, took in all details. Ellsworth's hair was cut short, his face was "thin from constant labor and excitement." His voice, continued Hay, "had assumed that tone of hoarse strength that I recognized at the end of the triumphant trip last year. He seemed contented and at ease about his regiment. He indulged in a little mild blasphemy when he found that no suitable quarters had been provided but was mollified by the proffer of the 69th's rooms & the Capitol."

John Hay went up that evening to Capitol Hill to see the Zouave regiment, which was being quartered in the House of Representatives. "It was a jolly, gay set of blackguards," he wrote with his usual light, youthful cynicism. He reported that the Firemen "were in a pretty complete state of don't care a damn, modified by an affectionate and respectful deference to the Colonel. He thought only of his men." Ellsworth was busy at the moment making provision for their supper. Later he and John talked together and the diary mentions that he "spoke with honest exultation" of the fruitless attempt made to prevent the embarkation of the regiment at New York.

Hay had made his usual neat choice of words when he called the Fire Zouaves "turbulent spirits." Here were eleven hundred men whom he further described in his diary as "the largest, sturdiest, and physically the most magnificent men I ever saw collected together. They played over the sward," he continued, "like kittens, lithe and agile in their strength." These soldiers, keyed up for heroic deeds when they reached Washington, were suddenly thrown into a state of inactivity, except for some drilling and parading. By May 5, as the *Chicago Tribune* noted, many of them were saying "they don't see what they were brought here to the 'war' for, as they can have more fighting any time in New York!" It could have been predicted that they would invent some activities of their own and furnish lively copy for the newspapers. They were, as one paper put it, "spiling for a fight."

The first inquiry one of the Fire Zouaves made on getting out of the train was: "Can you tell us where Jeff Davis is? we're lookin' for him." Another joined in, "Yes, we're bound to hang his scalp in the White House before we go back." A third called a citizen to his side and inquired, "Is there any secession flags about here?" The *Washington Star* continued this account: "Somebody remarked to one of the b'hoys that his hair was cut *rayther* short. 'O yes,' was the reply, 'we all had our heads *filed* before we left New York.'"

The *Philadelphia Press* went into the results of these circumstances and attitudes. The "b'hoys" chased imaginary secessionists through the streets pell-mell, terrifying all the old ladies in the neighborhood. They went into restaurants and ordered sumptuous meals, then when the bill was presented told the owners to charge it to the U. S. Government or the Southern Confederacy. Being quartered in the House of Representatives gave them a bright idea: they abolished the existing body of Representatives and set up a new House of Representatives of their own, electing their speaker, clerk, and other officers. They then went into session, dissolved the Union and reconstructed it according to their own ideas!

The staid citizens of Washington received daily shocks.

They saw the Firemen "walking the parapets of the capitol, rifle on shoulder, leaping fences, knocking down sentinels, turning aside indignant bayonets, hanging like monkeys from the outer edges of the dome, some two hundred feet above the firm-set earth."

A few of the offenses were more serious than this horseplay and of course the rumor-mill worked overtime exaggerating these and inventing others. Colonel Ellsworth's correspondence contains samples of the letters he was receiving at the time: one from a restaurant owner whose food some of the Firemen had eaten without paying for it; another from General Joseph Mansfield, who was in command of the Department of Washington, reprimanding him because his men had burned some fences; a third from the Chief Engineer of the New York Fire Department, who was distressed at the notoriety the Firemen were getting and wanted the names of the offenders so they could be dismissed from the Department.

John Hay summed up Ellsworth's feelings and the whole situation in his diary for May 7. Speaking of the Zouave Firemen, Hay said: "Ellsworth has been intensely disgusted at the wild yarns afloat about them which are, for the most part, utterly untrue. A few graceless rascals have been caught in various lapses. These are in irons. One horrible story which has been terrifying all the maiden antiques of the city for several days, has the element of horror pretty well eliminated today, by the injured fair, who proves a most yielding seducee, offering to settle the matter for 25 dollars. Other yarns are due to the restless brains of the press-gang."

Ellsworth decided that the Zouaves who had been guilty of serious offenses should be expelled from the regiment and turned over to the civil authorities. Just how few they were appears in his letter to Carrie several days later. "The reports," he wrote, "that the men are bad & that 150 have been sent back is false. We have sent back but 6 — and the men do *well*." According to the account of Francis Brownell, the scrupulous Ellsworth paid out of his own pocket for the damage done by his men.

The other ten hundred and ninety-four Zouaves were behaving, as Ellsworth said, very well. Daily he proudly paraded them down Pennsylvania Avenue and past the White House, where the Lincoln family loved to watch them and took an enormous interest in what they did. When Willie Lincoln, now going on eleven, wrote a playmate in Springfield on May 3, 1861, he knew the important news in Washington. "I suppose," began the little-boy handwriting, "that you did not learn that Colonel, E. E. Elsworth had gone to New York and organized a regiment, — divided into companys, and brought them here, & to be sworn in — I dont know when. Some people call them the B,hoys, & others call them, the firemen."

Willie wrote his letter on a Friday. The date of the swearing in of the Zouave regiment, which he did not know, was the following Tuesday, May 7. On the afternoon of that day Colonel Ellsworth formed his men in a hollow square on the east front of the Capitol. The correspondent of the *New York Tribune* described the event, including the arrival of "President Lincoln's coach" with a footman who seemed "some ten feet high, standing behind." From this stately carriage emerged "his Excellency, accompanied by 'Little Tad,' in straw hat" to join the great crowd which had assembled. John Hay was also present.

The newspaperman summarized Colonel Ellsworth's speech but he could not equal the salty prose in which Hay recorded it in his diary that evening. Hay said it was "a great speech." "There was more commonsense, dramatic power, tact, energy, & that eloquence that naturally flowers into deeds in *le petit* Colonel's fifteen-minute harangue," he continued, than there was in all the "spread-eagle" speeches recently heard in Congress put together. Hay said Ellsworth "spoke to them as men. Made them proud in their good name; spoke bitterly & witheringly of the disgrace of the recreant." Ellsworth "contrasted with cutting emphasis" the enlistment of other regiments for "thirty days" only while the Fire Zouaves were enlisting "for the war."

The newspaperman noticed that at this announcement "Some of the men blinked, but a vast majority seemed ecstatic with delight." They kept interrupting Colonel Ellsworth with clappings and cries of "Bully for you," "Good boy," and "You're my man."

Hay wrote that Ellsworth "closed with wonderful tact and dramatic spirit by saying, 'Now laddies, if anyone of you wants to go home, he had better sneak around the back alleys, crawl over fences, and get out of sight before we see him,' which got them again." Hay commented, "He must have run with this crowd sometime in his varied career. He knows and handles them so perfectly."

So, in front of the unfinished dome of the Capitol and in the presence of President Lincoln, the Fire Zouaves took the oath administered by General Irvin McDowell and were sworn into the service of the United States. They had become the New York Eleventh Regiment.

◈
◈
◈

23

EXCITEMENT AT CAMP LINCOLN

THE Zouaves were soon to remove from the public mind the last traces of the unfavorable impression produced by six transgressors. To accomplish this, fate selected a means which could not possibly have suited the Firemen better — a fire. The very sight of a fire engine made them homesick ever since they had been in Washington.

Before daybreak on the morning of May 9, fire broke out in a house almost next door to the Willard Hotel. Efforts made to extinguish it by those present only resulted in a waste of valuable time, and the flames got such a start that help was urgently needed to save the hotel. General Mansfield sent an SOS to Colonel Ellsworth at the Capitol.

Ellsworth quickly detailed ten men from each company and led them in a run down Pennsylvania Avenue in the dim light of dawn. The rest of the Zouaves began leaping out of the windows of their quarters to race after them. Nothing could keep the whole regiment from attending that fire!

Zouave Brownell, corporal of the guard, just returning to the Capitol from some special duty, saw the light of the fire and men running. He shoved his gun under some boxes and ran with them to the engine house. "When I reached the old Franklin engine house," he said, "some of the boys were already there, and they needed just one more hand. We soon had that engine out and at work."

The Zouaves were taking over the fire-fighting apparatus willy-nilly, much to the disgust of the Washington Fire Department. But they got the engines to the scene of the fire in double quick time and began playing streams of water on the swiftly mounting flames. In the two-hour struggle to bring the fire under control, the mass of spectators saw Ellsworth's Zouaves for the brave and skillful men they were. Onlookers held their breath as they saw two of them standing on the roof which was enveloped in flames. Each was holding by the leg a comrade who hung head downward over the edge of the burning building, trying desperately to reach a hose-pipe extended from the end of a too short ladder. Finally he succeeded and the Willard Hotel, which had been in grave danger, was saved.

There was some friction with the Washington Fire Department, which, of course, did not relish the part of looking on. Colonel Ellsworth, having been officially appealed to by General Mansfield, naturally took charge. He seized the trumpet from a Washington fireman, who remonstrated, insisting upon his right to command. "Well," said Ellsworth, "if you have more men here than I have, you can take it."

When the fire was extinguished there were warm, welcome words of praise from General Mansfield (the same gentleman who had reprimanded them for burning fences). Mr. Willard gratefully invited the regiment to breakfast after which the Zouaves gave three cheers (perhaps "Tig-a-r cheers"), sang "Dixie," and marched back to their quarters in perfect order. "Dixie" seems a strange choice for these staunch Unionists but in a belligerent sense each man did "wish I was in Dixie." Brownell recalled that a purse of five hundred dollars was made up and presented to the regiment.

Ellsworth's letter to Carrie on May 10 from "Head Quarters 1st Zouaves U. S. Capitol" told her about the fire and the ceremony of taking the oath. "My Regt was the first sworn in for the War," he said proudly, "& Ranks first *now*. The President & the Sec of War . . . *now* are giving me everything I ask for — & say my Regiment *is without exception* the best in the service of the U. S." The late small unpleasantness had blown over; the Zouaves were more than ever in the floodlight of public interest.

There was an example of this in the White House itself. Willie and Tad Lincoln with a handful of playmates organized a "soldier company" called "Mrs. Lincoln's Zouaves." Tad had his picture taken in the small Zouave uniform provided by the indulgent parents who, gravely and with due Presidential dignity, reviewed the company and presented it with a flag.

Zouave dolls, irresistible in their tiny scarlet trousers and blue jackets, appeared on the market. Willie and Tad received one as a present, named him Jack, and executed various warlike maneuvers with him. Advertisements for Ellsworth's *Manual of Arms* appeared: "HOW TO BE A SOLDIER! THE BEST BOOK OF STUDY FOR A YOUNG RECRUIT!"

While the Fire Zouaves were quartered at the Capitol, Ellsworth found it very convenient to walk down Pennsylvania Avenue (where he was doubtless much stared at) and drop in at the White House. Probably the first thing he did was to hurry up the stately stairs and go into the office of George Nicolay and John Hay, for Ellsworth was having Carrie send her letters to him in care of J. G. Nicolay at the Executive Mansion — he would not risk the loss of such precious letters in the avalanche of mail that came to his regiment.

One already knows how close Ellsworth was to John Hay. The measure of his friendship with George Nicolay appears in a letter written by the secretary. "I had been with him daily — almost hourly for the six months past," wrote Nicolay of Ellsworth the following month. "I had talked over with him his plans, hopes and aspirations, and had learned to know so well his great talents as well as his great goodness." The quiet, thoughtful Nicolay who chose his words carefully said that he loved Ellsworth more than a brother.

There were many things for these three companionable young men to talk over as they sat together in the secretary's room upstairs in the White House. They were at the very storm center of the nation which was gearing itself for a life and death conflict. One inevitable topic filled them with almost intolerable indignation — it was that Confederate flag which was waving over the principal hotel in Alexandria, Virginia, across the Potomac. It had been flaunting itself from the roof of the Marshall House ever since Ellsworth returned from New York with his Fire Zouaves.

Nicolay and Hay would tell later in their *Life of Abraham Lincoln* how this "rebel flag" was "in plain view from the windows of the Executive Mansion in Washington." They had looked at it, and so had Ellsworth, with fury in their hearts. It is said that President Lincoln remarked to Ellsworth that that flag was an insult. How the high-spirited Colonel must have longed to do something about it.

There was a good reason why nothing could be done yet. The Virginia legislature had passed an ordinance of secession on April 17, two days after President Lincoln's call for troops. The ordinance would not be final, however, until ratified by popular vote, and this voting was not to take place until May 23. In the meantime no move could be made, though Union forces were quietly preparing to occupy Alexandria as soon as the expected ratification took place and Virginia thus formally joined the Confederacy.

That Confederate flag was a sore subject when Ellsworth came to the White House as to a home. The brief chats with the President, who took such a fatherly interest in his plans, and the way in which Mrs. Lincoln's face lighted up when she saw him, warmed his heart. He formed pleasant friendships with other people who were much seen around the great white mansion. There was a third secretary named William O. Stoddard, a pleasant young newspaperman who, like Ellsworth himself, had worked vigorously for Mr. Lincoln's election in Illinois. Young Stoddard was very likable, as was Julia Taft, a shy, petite, appealing girl of sixteen whose younger brothers, "Bud" and "Holly" Taft, were playmates of Willie and Tad Lincoln. Mrs. Taft sent Julia along with the boys with instructions to see that "those young rascals don't tear down the White House." Julia, like John Hay, was keeping a diary of events in the Executive Mansion. She liked and admired Colonel Ellsworth very much and his name would appear in her diary.

His visits were brief, yet Nicolay and Hay remembered how "the echoes of his cheery and manly voice seemed . . . to linger in the corridors and rooms of the Executive Mansion." After May 11 it was not so convenient for him to go there; the regiment had moved. Ellsworth told Carrie about the plans in his letter of the 10th. "To morrow we go into Camp 4 miles out — on the road toward Alexandria," he said. Now that Washington had an ample number of soldiers for protection, it was a good idea for him to take his "turbulent spirits" (who had recently acquired the ironic nickname of "Pet Lambs") out of the city. The letter had a postscript which inevitably chilled Carrie's heart: "We expect a fight within 10 days. My Regt is promised a post of honor."

Ellsworth told her further details about the camp in his next message. Perhaps he was the one who had given it its name, Camp Lincoln. "We are doing well," he said, "are encamped in a beautiful place on the bank of the Potomac in sight of Alexandria & Washington."

It was truly a picturesque location with all the landscape beauty of hills and river in which his artist's heart rejoiced. Approaching it from Washington, one had a long gradual climb to the heights on which stood the walled Insane Asy-

lum, the same structure which has so sad a reference in the
Lincoln story. The following year President Lincoln would
lead his wife, wild in her grief over the death of Willie, to a
south window in the White House, point to the distant view
and say, "Mother, do you see that large white building on
the hill yonder? Try and control your grief, or it will drive
you mad, and we may have to send you there."

Beyond the Insane Asylum the road led through fields of
grain and woodland into a dense, dark forest from which
one emerged into an open space upon the heights and there,
far below, lay Camp Lincoln upon the river's bank.

Ellsworth continued his description of life at the camp
with almost telegraphic brevity: "Have to work night & day
— Sleep on straw & ground — Havent seen Butter or any
other like luxury." He disclosed a Civil War soldier's menu
at this time: "Regular food — breakfast beef steak dry bread
coffee, *dinners* coffee, beef, bread, supper bread coffee
beef."

He told Carrie he had not heard from her. Getting mail
through to each other was proving difficult under war conditions. He added, "Have no chance to go to Washington."
Even then there might be a letter waiting for him in Nicolay's hands at the White House. About the plans of the regiment he said, "No idea where we are to go. Everything in
a mist."

Friends rode or drove out from Washington to visit the
camp of the Fire Zouaves, now the New York Eleventh
Volunteers. One of the first was John Hay, who wrote in
his diary the evening of Sunday, May 12, "We spent this
afternoon at Camp Lincoln, the habitation of Ellsworth's
'pet lambs.' " Presumably the "We" means that Nicolay and
perhaps others went with him. Hay said that the men
"seemed very comfortable and happy," adding, "Ellsworth
was playing ball with them as we approached looking fine
and blouzy in his red shirt. We went to his tent."

Sunday seemed to be visitors' day at camp. One week later, on Sunday, May 19, Julia Taft was recording her visit to Camp Lincoln in her diary. She attended religious services there, she wrote, hearing "a fine sermon. . . . The soldiers sang 'I would not Live Alway' so heartily we could hardly hear the band." Her words create a moving scene: these hundreds of fine young soldiers who were soon to go into battle singing that particular hymn which said they did not ask for longer life in a stormy world. One can almost hear Ellsworth's magnificent voice as he sang the line, "I would not live alway; I ask not to stay . . ."

If John Hay had heard Ellsworth sing this line, he might well have been reminded of what he had heard him say about a month before. John knew how ready Ellsworth was, in the selflessness of his patriotism, to die for his country. The two had been talking together when Ellsworth was still ill in bed with measles at his room in the Willard Hotel and John was sitting at his bedside. The Sumter crisis was pending and John mentioned that some had doubts of the loyalty of the people if war broke out.

Ellsworth did not have this doubt. Like Mr. Lincoln, he had faith in the people. He said to John: "I can only speak for myself. You know I have a great work to do, to which my life is pledged; I am the only earthly stay of my parents; there is a young woman whose happiness I regard as dearer than my own; yet I could ask no better death than to fall next week before Sumter. I am not better than other men. You will find that patriotism is not dead, even if it sleeps."

Perhaps Ellsworth told John Hay then his plans in case war came. At all events, when Fort Sumter was fired upon and Lincoln called for troops, Ellsworth turned to John and "took all the money we both had, which was not much," when he started for New York to raise his regiment.

On Sunday, May 19, Ellsworth came into Washington, going, of course, to the White House. He found the upstairs empty; the Lincolns and Nicolay and Hay were elsewhere. As he was waiting in the President's office a voice came: "Hullo, Ellsworth, are you here?" It was the White House secretary, William Stoddard. Ellsworth answered cheerfully, "Yes, I'm all the President there is on hand this morning. I got away from camp to run over and see him and the boys."

The secretary was delighted to see Ellsworth for a special reason. Stoddard had enlisted in April in the United States Volunteers and here was the best possible person to give him some pointers on drilling. The two found a rifle and Ellsworth was demonstrating the drill when both young men had a surprise. "He was standing too near the south window," said Stoddard, "and the order which brought the butt of that piece against his shoulder sent the muzzle of it through a pane of glass."

The two stared at the shattered glass in dismay for a moment. Then, because they were not much more than "boys," as Stoddard said, they began to fix up a tale to tell Nicolay and Hay when they came in. They would say "that some assassin, lurking in the shrubbery down yonder, must have mistaken Colonel Ellsworth for the President," and tried to shoot him. Stoddard added that it was only "a passing jest" but it illustrated "the strong hold which the idea of possible assassination" had on the minds of those near the President.

On Wednesday evening of that week Ellsworth came to the White House again. There Nicolay handed him what he had been hoping for — a letter from Carrie.

Thursday, May 23, was a day of tense waiting for the results of the voting in Virginia. If the Virginians ratified the ordinance of secession, Alexandria would have to be taken by Union troops immediately. All was in readiness.

It was perhaps to keep his men occupied on that day of tension that Ellsworth put them through a special gymnastic drill. Visitors came out from Washington to watch the per-

formance. Among them was Surgeon Charles Sabin Taft,
Julia's older brother, whose life was destined to cross Lincoln's at a tragic moment. He would attend Ford's Theatre
that fatal evening of April 14, 1865; he would be the first
doctor to climb into the box after Lincoln was shot. All that
terrible night he would stand at the bedside of the dying
President in the Peterson house while the fragrance of the
lilacs blooming in the yard outside drifted into the room, and
ever after the scent of lilacs would turn him sick and faint.

Surgeon Taft brought with him to Camp Lincoln a young
party consisting of his sister Julia, his younger brothers, and
Willie and Tad Lincoln. Julia remembered with what gaiety
Colonel Ellsworth put his men through their drill, calling
them "his monkeys," and how agile as monkeys they were.
When they left, she said, "As he stood at the corner, waving
his cap and calling, 'Come again,' he looked very bright and
handsome."

By evening the die was cast; Virginia had seceded. The
news was like the push of a button which sets in motion a
vast, scheduled activity. Colonel Ellsworth had talked with
General Mansfield the day before and, believing that a
movement against Alexandria was inevitable, had asked that
his regiment, the first volunteer regiment sworn in for the
whole war, be given a foremost part. Camp Lincoln was
plunged suddenly into a fever of preparation.

With the impending military action newspapermen were
busy too. The correspondent of the *New York World* in
Washington walked the four miles out to Camp Lincoln to
get the story. It was a perfect summer evening, mild and
clear with a full moon. He described what he saw as he
came out of the forest into the open space on the heights and
looked down through the darkness upon the camp "some half
mile below me and upon the river's bank. A more beautiful
scene is not often looked upon," he said. "Imagine a hundred bell-shaped tents, each from its inside illumination ap-

pearing like an enormous transparency; look down upon
them in the stillness of night, while at their right, upon a
little eminence, the lurid flames of twenty or thirty camp
fires ascend, with the figures of grotesquely attired soldiers flitting about among them, and the mirror, moonlit
surface of the Potomac waves glistening in a silver expanse
beyond."

The newspaperman made his way with some difficulty
down the rugged hillside into camp. Ellsworth in a short
speech had informed his men that there was to be a movement against Alexandria in a few hours and that they would
go by steamer. "All that I can tell you," he said, "is to prepare yourselves for a nice little sail, and, at the end of it, a
skirmish." He gave his men one caution which requires
explanation. It was the wish of those in charge that Alexandria should be taken with as little bloodshed as possible.
A message under flag of truce would be sent ahead giving
the Confederate soldiers an hour to get out of the city. It
was said that the people of Alexandria had requested that
the Zouaves not be among those sent to take over. Ellsworth
felt that his regiment was on trial. "When we reach the place
of destination," he said, "act as men; do nothing to shame
the regiment; show the enemy that you are men, as well as
soldiers, and that you will treat them with kindness until
they force you to use violence. I want you to kill them with
kindness."

"Go to your tents," was his further advice, "lie down and
take your rest till two o'clock, when the boat will arrive, and
we go forward to victory or death."

Sleep, however, was the last thing the men were thinking
of; they were "in high glee," talking, laughing, and singing
patriotic songs. They seemed to feel "a triumphant delight
at the thought that the monotony of camp life was to be
broken by real action."

The reporter sought out Colonel Ellsworth in his tent and

was greeted, he said, "with that cordial grasp of the hand
. . . which I think no one can have felt without experiencing a kind of electric sympathy that at once inspired admiration and led you right into the inner sanctuary of his great
and noble heart." He seems to have followed Ellsworth
around and the colonel, he wrote, "was everywhere. . . .
Now in his tent conversing with his officers, now dashing
across the camp . . . now out upon the bluff looking earnestly across the waters to the Navy Yard, or down toward
Alexandria to catch a glimpse of any signal which might be
made, or any indication of movement, then back to his tent
to confer again with his staff."

The correspondent continued that when Ellsworth was
sitting with his officers he was "full of humor and wit, and
in most excellent spirits." Someone inquired, "Colonel, are
we to be quartered in Alexandria to morrow?"

"No," was the quick answer, "*quartered*, no; you
wouldn't think of being *quartered*, I hope, while you had a
thing like that at your command," and he pointed to the
sword at his side. The men laughed at the pun.

Midnight was approaching and perhaps the others had left
Ellsworth's tent. There was something more he must do, not
as a colonel in charge of a regiment but as a sensitive, understanding man who gave tender consideration to his loved
ones. He knew how great would be the anguish of his father
and mother and of Carrie if anything should happen to him
at Alexandria. Probably to every soldier there that night
came the thought that in a few hours he might be killed.
There were Confederate soldiers in Alexandria. Ellsworth
wanted to write two letters, one to his parents and one to
Carrie, letters that would give them what comfort was possible in case his voice was silenced.

This is the letter he wrote Carrie that night in his tent at
Camp Lincoln while his watch was ticking off the minutes
until his departure toward Alexandria:

My own darling Kitty,

My Regiment is ordered to cross the river & move on Alexandria within six hours. We may meet with a warm reception & my darling among so many careless fellows one is some what likely to be hit.

If anything should *happen — Darling just accept this assurance, the only thing I can leave you — the highest happiness I looked for on earth was a union with you. You have more than realised the hopes I formed regarding your advancement — and I believe I love you with all the ardor I am capable of. You know my darling any attempt of mine to convey an adequate expression of my feelings must be simply futile. God bless you as you deserve and grant you a happy & usefull life & us a union hereafter.*

Truly your own,
ELMER.

My own darling Kitty.

My Regiment is ordered to cross the river & move on Alexandria within six hours. We may meet with a warm reception & my darling among so many careless fellows one is some -what likely to be hit.

If anything _should_ happen— darling just accept this assurance, the only thing— I can leave you — the high -est happiness I looked for on earth was a union with you— You have more than realised the hopes I formed regarding your advance -ment— and I believe I love

"IF ANYTHING SHOULD HAPPEN"

First page of Ellsworth's final letter to Carrie, written in his tent at Camp Lincoln the night before he was killed. (Courtesy of the Illinois State Historical Library)

24

Tragedy at Alexandria

At midnight Captain John A. Dahlgren of the Navy Yard, who was in command of the three steamers which would transport the regiment down the river, arrived at Camp Lincoln. He reported at once, he said, to Colonel Ellsworth who told him everything was in readiness. Ellsworth had attired himself in a handsome uniform which, according to one of his captains, he had selected with great care, making a remark about choosing the clothes in which he was to die. This captain also remembered Ellsworth saying he had a feeling that his country would require his blood immediately. In this mood he had fastened upon his breast the gold badge with the Latin inscription which means "Not for ourselves alone but for country." When he was dressed and ready, he was again gay and full of jest.

The special correspondent of the *New York World* by this time had left the camp. He had gone to the Georgetown hospital, where other grim preparations were taking place. There the surgeons and nurses were laying out surgical supplies and making ready four hundred beds for bodies which at the moment were young, strong, and whole. At midnight this reporter was on the streets of Washington watching the regiments march by on their way to Long Bridge. About thirteen thousand Union troops were converging on Alexandria and Arlington Heights that night.

Wild rumors, as always in warfare, were afloat: the Confederates were going to burn the bridges across the river; they had masked batteries on Arlington Heights ready to open fire. The soldiers moved under the fear of a surprise attack.

Meanwhile another excellent journalist, Edward H. House, special correspondent of the *New York Tribune*, had come to Camp Lincoln. As he approached across the Potomac he heard the Zouave regiment burst with indescribable fervor into the song "Columbia, the Gem of the Ocean." The sound of these young men's voices coming over the moonlit water was something he would long remember.

Shortly before two o'clock the three steamboats appeared in the river, the *James Guy*, the *Baltimore*, and the *Mount Vernon*. A long line of rowboats was at the water's edge ready to carry the men out to the steamers. Captain Dahlgren had "pointed out" to Colonel Ellsworth, he said, "the difficulty of getting the men embarked" and the "danger in the very voyage itself with so many men crowded into a small vessel," but he added that Ellsworth's Zouaves, under his direction, "behaved with all the confidence and steadiness of veterans."

At two Ellsworth gave the order to "form." The companies quickly put themselves in line and marched in "double quick" down to the shore. Mr. House of the *New York Tribune* described the scene: the men on the beach "some being wrapped from head to foot in their great red blankets . . . the peaks of the tents, regularly distributed, all glowing like huge lanterns from the fires within them; the glittering rows of rifles and sabres; the woods and hills and the placid river . . . all these suffused with the broad moonlight." The soldiers once aboard, the great paddles of the steamboats began to revolve and the regiment was moving down the Potomac.

Meanwhile troops and horses were pouring across the river on the three bridges, the Long Bridge at Washington, the Aqueduct at Georgetown, and farther away, the Chain Bridge. The moon was serving as floodlight for a drama on a vast stage that night. Its light glittered on muskets and bayonets as the men moved in silence across the river, breaking step so that the solid beat of their marching feet would not put a strain on the bridges. There were the suppressed commands of the officers, the clatter of the cavalry, the rumbling of artillery.

Mr. House of the *New York Tribune* was with Ellsworth's regiment on the steamers. They drew near Alexandria, he said, "just as the dawn began to shine over the hills and through the trees." They ran alongside the wharf under cover of the guns of the federal steamer *Pawnee* which had been anchored there some days, its men fuming at the sight of that Confederate flag fluttering from the top of the Marshall House. The *Pawnee* had already sent a flag of truce to the rebel forces, giving them an hour to withdraw from the town. As the steamers had approached, a few Confederate sentinels had fired their guns into the air and fled. Alexandria lay quiet in the light of dawn. Without resistance the regiment landed in double-quick time at about five o'clock, each company forming on the street facing the river.

Colonel Ellsworth at once detailed Company E to destroy the railroad track leading to Richmond. This done, he himself, leaving Lieutenant Colonel Noah P. Farnham to command the regiment, set out with a small file of men for the center of the town for the purpose of cutting the wires in the telegraph office. With him were his aide, Lieutenant H. J. Winser, military secretary of the regiment, the chaplain, Reverend E. W. Dodge, Edward H. House, correspondent of the *New York Tribune*, Corporal Francis E. Brownell, and three other corporals. They had not gone far before Ellsworth added to the party Sergeant Frank B. Marshall from the first company.

"We passed quickly through the streets," said House, "meeting a few bewildered travelers . . . when the Colonel first of all caught sight of the Secession flag, which has so long swung insolently in full view of the President's House." "Boys, we must have that down before we return," he exclaimed. At this point he sent back Sergeant Marshall with an order for the advance of Company A. Ellsworth seems then to have hesitated an instant, torn between the necessity of cutting the telegraph wires and the burning desire he had felt for many days to tear down that intolerable flag. With a sudden decision, he started rapidly toward the three-story hotel from which the flag was flying.

On entering the hotel with his seven companions, he met a man in shirt and trousers and demanded of him, "Who put that flag up?" The man answered in great agitation, "I don't know; I am a boarder here." The colonel posted one of the corporals at the door, another on the first floor, and a third at the foot of the stairs; then with the rest of his party he sprang up the two flights of stairs which led to the attic. From the attic Ellsworth and Winser climbed up the roof on a ladder which they found there, to reach the flagstaff.

The colonel handed Winser his revolver to hold, borrowed the other's knife to cut the halyards, and hauled down the huge flag. Descending the ladder, they re-entered the attic, where two men (whom no one had noticed before) had been in bed and were now getting up in great amazement. Ignoring them, the party started down the stairs in this order: Corporal Brownell first, Colonel Ellsworth next with his eyes on the big flag which he was folding, House just behind him with his arm on Ellsworth's shoulder, and Winser last. Whether the chaplain went all the way to the attic is not clear.

As Brownell reached "the first landing-place or entry," he saw a man jump out from a dark passage on the second floor and aim a double-barreled shotgun at the colonel's breast. Ellsworth did not see him, as he was occupied in folding the flag. Brownell made a quick pass to turn the weapon aside, but the civilian's hand was firm and he discharged one barrel straight to its aim, the slugs entering Ellsworth's breast. House, whose arm was resting on Ellsworth's shoulder said, ". . . he seemed to fall almost from my grasp. He was on the second or third step from the landing, and he dropped forward with that heavy, horrible, headlong weight which always comes of sudden death inflicted in this manner."

The man then turned quickly to give the contents of the other barrel to Brownell. But Brownell knocked the gun aside so that the buckshot missed him and hit the panels of a bedroom door. "Simultaneously with this second shot, and sounding like an echo of the first," continued House, "Brownell's rifle was heard, and the assassin staggered backward. He was hit exactly in the middle of the face. . . . Brownell did not know how fatal his shot had been, and so before the man dropped, he thrust his saber bayonet through and through the body. . . ." The man fell with his face to the floor.

Someone said, "My God!" Winser from above was crying, "Who is hit?" For a moment the little group stood paralyzed, staring at the bodies and the blood which flooded the stairs and passageway. Brownell automatically reloaded and as he did so, he noticed that the door which had received the slugs intended for him was slowly opening. He instantly leveled his rifle at the occupants, two travelers who had lodged at the hotel, and said he would shoot if they stirred. "From the opening doors," said House, "and through the passages, we discerned a sufficient number of forms to assure us that we were dreadfully in the minority."

They were only seven in all, with one — House — un-armed, and they did not know but what this bloodshed was part of a general resistance. Brownell and the other three corporals posted themselves so as to command the corridors and threatened to shoot the first man who showed his face outside the rooms.

Winser, House, and Chaplain Dodge then bent over Colonel Ellsworth, so unbelievably, it seemed, lying on his face in his own blood. The chaplain gently turned him over and House stooped and called his name. He thought he heard an inarticulate murmur in reply but could not be certain. With careful hands House and Winser lifted the bleeding form and carried it into a nearby bedroom, laying it upon the bed. They had nothing to cover him with but the rebel flag wet with his blood. They unbuttoned his coat and saw the dreadful, fatal wound in his breast. They wanted to get a surgeon, but they did not know where one could be found nor could they leave Ellsworth's body alone in that house of violence. They must wait until Company A, for which he had sent, arrived. Meanwhile they tried, House said, to remove "some of the unsightly stains from the Colonel's features, and composed his limbs. His expression in death was beautifully natural."

At last the detachment was heard approaching and the surgeon was sent for. Then Mr. House remembered Colonel Ellsworth's earnestness about the telegraph seizure. Borrowing a revolver from Winser, he obtained permission to guide a squad of Zouaves to the telegraph office to cut the wires.

"When I returned to the hotel," continued House, "there was a terrible scene enacting. A woman had run from a lower room to the stairway where the body of the defender of the Secession flag lay and recognizing it, cried aloud with an agony so heart-rending that no person could witness it without emotion. She flung her arms in the air, struck her brow madly, and seemed utterly abandoned to desolation and frenzy." She seemed almost unaware of the presence of the Union soldiers, who learned then that the man who had shot Ellsworth was her husband, James W. Jackson, proprietor of the Marshall House. "Winser was confident," said the reporter, that "it was the same man who met us at the door when we entered and told us he was a boarder." The young Zouaves, in pity, assured the woman that no harm would come to her children and finally she seemed to understand.

His men wrapped Ellsworth's body in one of their scarlet blankets, unhinged a door, and improvised a litter. Reverently a little group of them carried him to the river's bank and on board the steamer *James Guy*. Francis Brownell was one of the escort; he had grown up in Troy and had probably known Ellsworth a long time. They were taking the body to the Navy Yard.

The men at the Navy Yard had been holding themselves in readiness to march at a moment's notice if reinforcements were needed. Many of them had been up all night, but before breakfast word had come that Alexandria was taken without resistance and there was general relief and rejoicing. Then about an hour later they saw the *James Guy* approaching on the river with its flag at half-mast. The news of Ellsworth's death plunged them into bitter grief. Desire for vengeance on Alexandria flamed up as the men heard the story. There were cries of "Will we go?" "Was the place sacked?" "Are we to have a chance?" "Not a man should be left alive!" Yet these were not Ellsworth's own men; every effort was being made to keep the news from all of his regiment, except those who had come to the Marshall House, as long as possible.

When the tragedy could no longer be withheld from the Zouaves and they learned that their beloved leader was dead, they were beside themselves with grief. One of them with tears running down his face said, "Oh God bless him, God bless him! We'll never have another friend like him!" Another said to one who had just come up, "Our noble laddie's dead, Jim," and turned away weeping. It was almost more than Lieutenant Colonel Farnham could do to restrain them from setting fire to Alexandria. That night they would be kept on shipboard anchored out in the Potomac to make certain that some would not slip away to burn the city.

When Ellsworth's body arrived at the Navy Yard, it was placed in the engine house, which was quickly draped in mourning. As the terrible news passed from mouth to mouth in Washington, the church bells began to toll and one by one the flags were seen sliding down their staffs to half-mast. Telegraph wires began to send out the news over the North.

That morning in the quiet little town of Mechanicville in New York an anxious father had walked through the streets to the telegraph office. He and "Mother" were so anxious about the movement into Virginia in which they feared their son Elmer might be involved that they wanted to get the news about it as soon as it came. As he sat in the office listening to the clicking of the instrument, suddenly he saw the operator, receiving a message, burst into tears. It was in this way that Ephraim Ellsworth learned that his son had been killed. The light went out in the lives of the pathetic couple at Mechanicville with the receiving of a telegram that day, just as it did in the life of Carrie Spafford at Rockford.

That morning of May 24, an officer with a saddened face entered the White House. He had come to tell the tragic news to another man who loved Ellsworth with a father's love. In the library on the second floor he related to President Lincoln what had happened. As he left the room two visitors who had come on a pressing matter of public business entered the library. Mr. Lincoln, his back to them, stood looking out of a window toward the Potomac and did not move until they came quite close. Then, turning, he extended his hand and said, "Excuse me, but I cannot talk." The two gentlemen thought that perhaps a cold had affected his voice until suddenly they saw him burst into tears and cover his face with his handkerchief. "He walked up and down the room for some moments," said one of them, "and we stepped aside in silence, not a little moved at such an unusual spectacle, in such a man in such a place."

After Lincoln had regained his self-control somewhat, he invited his visitors to sit down with him. "I will take no apology, gentlemen," he said, "for my weakness; but I knew poor Ellsworth well, and held him in great regard. Just as you entered the room, Captain Fox left me, after giving me the painful details of Ellsworth's unfortunate death. The event was so unexpected, and the recital so touching, that it quite unmanned me."

Here Mr. Lincoln had to make another violent effort to control his feelings. After a pause, in a voice choked with emotion, he gave them the particulars of the tragedy. "Poor fellow," he said at the conclusion, "it was undoubtedly an act of rashness, but it only shows the heroic spirit that animates our soldiers, from high to low, in this righteous cause of ours. Yet who can restrain their grief to see them fall in such a way as this, not by the fortunes of war, but by the hand of an assassin." The two visitors, deeply moved, left without bringing up the matter of business they had come to discuss. Well might John Hay, sharing the anguish of his chief over Ellsworth's death, say that the President "mourned him as a son."

Mrs. Lincoln, as grief-stricken as her husband, drove out to the Navy Yard that afternoon. She learned, however, that the embalmers were there and that she could not view the body. She then asked for Francis Brownell. He stood with sad face beside the engine house; he was to be part of the guard of honor which would accompany Ellsworth's body home to Mechanicville. Mrs. Lincoln wanted to hear the full story from him and the two, both in tears, talked together quite a while. Then, leaving flowers, she returned to the White House.

Later in the afternoon she and her husband both came, wrote John Hay, "and gazed long and tearfully on the still face which had so often brought sunshine with it, into the Executive Mansion." Abraham Lincoln was heard to say brokenly: "My boy! my boy! was it necessary this sacrifice should be made!" The President said it was his wish that the funeral be held in the White House.

When Ellsworth's body was examined, certain things had been discovered. In a pocket were the last tender letters he had written the night before, one to his father and mother, one to Carrie. There was Carrie's picture which he had looked at so earnestly and then slipped into his bosom. Once he had said in his diary that he felt he had two natures; one part of him longed for the sweet normal relationships of life. This part wished to give love, tenderness and protection to those dear to him. The other nature was driven by an exalted spirit of self-sacrifice for others; it was the spirit of the humanitarian and dedicated patriot. The letters and picture symbolized the first nature. Fate had provided a dramatic symbol for the second. It was discovered that the bullets which ended Ellsworth's life had driven into his breast the gold circlet with the words "Non Solum Nobis sed Pro Patria."

25

"PURPOSE EVEN IN THE FATE"

EARLY the next morning, Saturday, May 25, Colonel Ellsworth's body was brought to the great East Room of the White House. It was fitting that he, his coffin draped in the Stars and Stripes, should lie in state in the mansion which was at the very core of the Union to which he had given his complete devotion. Through the morning hours there were the hushed voices and muffled tread of an endless stream of people who came to look for the last time on this young man. As John Hay said then, Ellsworth had had "the power of grappling to his heart with hooks of steel the affections of every man with whom he came in contact. . . . All classes seem to regard his death as a personal affliction."

Shortly after eleven the funeral services began. President and Mrs. Lincoln entered and were seated near the foot of the coffin with various members of the Cabinet around them. Mrs. Lincoln was unable to control her grief and at times Mr. Lincoln too wept. The great ones of Army, Navy, and Government were assembled to honor the country's hero.

The minister, the Reverend J. Smith Pyne, speaking of the way in which Colonel Ellsworth drew all hearts to him and ruled his soldiers by their affection for him, chose as his theme the power of love. "The Scripture," he said, "tells us of a man who approached our divine Saviour, and when he looked upon him, he loved him."

Moving incidents occurred. The grand old figure of General Scott, now nearing the end of his distinguished military career, paused long beside the bier of the brilliant young officer who had been cut down at the threshold of his. Julia Taft was asked to lay a wreath of white roses on Colonel Ellsworth's breast. The sight of the pale face which two days before she had seen so bright and full of life turned the young girl sick and faint. Mrs. Lincoln placed on the coffin a laurel wreath in wax encircling a picture of Ellsworth.

The great funeral procession which escorted the hearse to the depot was a model of ceremonial and splendor. It passed along Pennsylvania Avenue between crowds of weeping people. This was a military funeral; company after company paraded by. Behind the hearse which was drawn by four white horses was led Ellsworth's own horse with empty saddle. President Lincoln rode in a carriage with members of his Cabinet. In another carriage with other pall-bearers was George Nicolay, his face drawn with grief. Ellsworth's death, he said, "was to me more than a brother's loss." Francis Brownell, carrying the fatal Confederate flag, was a prominent figure in all of the three-day ceremonies. He was a hero now as "Ellsworth's Avenger."

At the station, to the sound of the tolling bells, Colonel Ellsworth's body was placed upon the special train which would bear him to New York. There would be similar tribute in that city and at Albany before he finally reached Mechanicville, his resting place.

The body reached New York early Sunday morning, May 26, and was taken to Room 41 at the Astor House where Ellsworth's father and mother were waiting with a small group of relatives to receive it. Robert Sears, the kind neighbor with whose children the boy Elmer had once played, had brought the sorrowing parents to New York. The mother bent and kissed the pale, cold lips, the father followed her example, and then both gave way to such an agony of grief they were gently led from the room.

Private services were held for family and friends in that room at the Astor House. Carrie could not come; an injury to her ankle in addition to the prostration of grief made the trip impossible for her. At these services the clergyman read aloud Ellsworth's last letter to his parents, the one written the night before he died and found upon his body. To them it must have seemed as if they could hear the loved voice speaking.

> *My dear Father and Mother*
>
> *The Regiment is ordered to move across ther river to-night. . . . I am inclined to the opinion that our entrance to the City of Alexandria will be hotly contested. . . . Should this happen my dear parents it may be my lot to be injured in some manner. Whatever may happen cherish the consolation that I was engaged in the performance of a sacred duty — and tonight thinking over the probabilities of the morrow & the occurrences of the past I am perfectly content to accept whatever my fortune may be, confident that he who notheth even the fall of a sparrow will have some purpose even in the fate of one like me.*
>
> *My darling & ever loved parents, good bye. God bless, protect & care for you.*
>
> ELMER.

Ellsworth's body was then taken to New York City Hall to lie in state — just as President Lincoln's body would be taken there four years later. Some ten thousand persons, many of them in tears, passed by the bier to gaze at the handsome young figure in its rich uniform. "Never," said the *New York Times* the next day, "has a man of Ellsworth's age commanded such national respect and regard in so short a space." The Governor's room at the City Hall in which he lay was draped in mourning as had been the entrance to the Astor House.

With continued parade and ceremonial Ellsworth's body was taken to Albany by steamer on his beloved Hudson River. At Albany he lay in state at the Capitol. The last stage of the journey was by special train from Troy to Mechanicville. The body of the Union's hero passed over the rails on which, just a few years before, rode a bright-faced train newsboy selling his papers.

Crowds lined the tracks of that homecoming journey to Mechanicville and a great multitude was waiting at the station. A storm was raging in the town as if to represent the grief and rage in the hearts of the friends who received Elmer Ellsworth home. Through wind and rain the hearse, adorned with heavy black plumes, toiled up a high hill overlooking the town. In the loftiest spot on that lovely hilltop, with highest military honors, Colonel Ellsworth was laid to rest.

On the day after his death two men who had loved him dearly sat writing in the White House. Mr. Lincoln with sad eyes was sending a letter of sympathy to the bereaved father and mother. Ellsworth had told him about them and what he so wished to do for them. The President's careful pen began the letter: "In the untimely loss of your noble son, our affliction here, is scarcely less than your own. So much of promised usefulness to one's country, and of bright hopes for one's self and friends, have rarely been so suddenly dashed, as in his fall."

With deep understanding Lincoln praised their son: "a boy only," yet with an extraordinary "power to command men." He spoke of Ellsworth's "fine intellect," "indomitable energy," and great military talent, of how "singularly modest" he had been and how much he had wished to help his beloved parents. "The honors he labored for so laudably, and, in the sad end, so gallantly gave his life, he meant for them, no less than for himself."

The letter ends: "In the hope that it may be no intrusion upon the sacredness of your sorrow, I have ventured to address you this tribute to the memory of my young friend, and your brave and early fallen child.

"May God give you that consolation which is beyond all earthly power. Sincerely your friend in a common affliction — A. Lincoln."

It is one of Abraham Lincoln's famous letters. But, being Abraham Lincoln, he did not stop there. He took it upon himself to give Ellsworth's parents the financial security the young man had longed in vain to give them; in November of that year the President commissioned Ephraim D. Ellsworth Captain in the Ordnance Department. Ellsworth's father was thereupon assigned to Fortress Monroe as military storekeeper. The duties, however (which perhaps involved heavy lifting), proved too much for Ephraim Ellsworth's frail health.

When word of this came to Lincoln he wrote the officer in charge: "I shall be very much obliged, if Mr. Ellsworth can be assigned to duty where the work will be lighter." The result was that Elmer's father was sent to a position at the Champlain Arsenal in Vergennes, Vermont, where he remained about nine years, retiring at the end of that time on a government pension. Then the couple returned to Mechanicville to live out the rest of their lonely days. Chester Denton, who had played with Elmer as a boy, cared for them, and President Lincoln had seen to it that they had something to live on.

Lincoln wrote his letter to Ellsworth's parents on May 25. On that same day John Hay too sat in the White House writing his tribute to his lost friend. He was preparing an article for the *Washington Chronicle* which would appear the next morning, Sunday, May 26. The words came crowding to his pen straight from his stunned and grieving heart.

He spoke first, as the minister had, of Ellsworth's supreme power to draw affection to him, of his personal lovableness. Hay sketched his friend's strange, involved, dramatic career and the courage and determination with which he met reverses until he finally rose in public notice to become the idol of the people. He spoke of the widespread sorrow: ". . . it is certain that no man could have died more deeply lamented than the young hero who is moving to-day in solemn grandeur toward the crushed hearts that sadly wait him in the North."

Thinking perhaps of the grief of Carrie in Illinois, of Ellsworth's parents in New York, of the Lincoln family, Nicolay, and himself in Washington, Hay continued: "Scattered over the land, severed by wide leagues of mountain and prairie, the few who knew him well are mourning in the utter abandon of irremediable anguish, as if all the earth had for them of bright or beautiful or brave, went out with his last breath." Ellsworth had seemed to these sorrowing ones, "not like the people one meets every day, but like a splendid type of the courtesy and valor that dignified the leal-hearted cavaliers of the great days that are gone."

This smaller circle, said Hay, "mourn him in tears as the truest, tenderest, most loyal-hearted man that ever died. . . . I do not remember but two faults that he had, and they were magnificent ones. He was too generous and too brave."

"Too brave!" Many people were saying this, in their awful regret that Ellsworth did not wait for the reinforcements he had sent for, before entering the Marshall House. Mr. Lincoln had called it "an act of rashness," adding in the same breath that it came from a "heroic spirit." He could well understand the effect that flag, which has so long been a source of irritation to all of them in the White House, had had upon the high-spirited young officer.

Those close to Colonel Ellsworth could guess at the motives which led to his quick decision to tear down the flag himself. His regiment was on trial at Alexandria, and to allow those "turbulent spirits" to see the flag might have led to bloodshed, even to the destruction of all in the house. He had told his men he would not ask them to go anywhere he would not go himself. He was used to attending to things without waiting for others. And he was young and impulsive. One of his men of Company A said later when he had reached the maturity of years: "We were all boys and it was the first taste we had had of war. . . . Foolish in Ellsworth to do that? Yes, undoubtedly . . . but then, you see, Ellsworth was only a boy!"

To the eighteen-year-old girl at Rockford it seemed, as John Hay said, that all the earth held for her "of bright or beautiful or brave" had gone out with Ellsworth's last breath. Carrie's life for some years would be one long grieving. Perhaps in the end it was Ellsworth's own words to his father and mother which helped her return to normal living: ". . . do not mourn," he had written — "God does not require it. . . . Let us . . . repay him by being happy."

Carrie in her twenties married Frederic E. Brett. In time she would hold her baby son in her arms and name him Charles for her father. Fate, however, seems to have marked Carrie for tragedy. It would be her sad destiny to look on the dead faces of her husband and of her son before he had reached full manhood. She would live on into the present century, fulfilling the wish which Ellsworth had written for her sixteenth birthday. "I will not wish for you," he had said, "a life of unclouded happiness, for that I fear can hardly be realised by any of us. But I will wish, dear Carrie, what may and I trust will be realised — that your life may be that of a true hearted, noble woman. . . ."

As always with a great shock and sorrow, it took time for the effect of Ellsworth's death to be fully understood. All over the North sermons, editorials, and private letters were pouring out an almost intolerable grief. The poet wrote in *Idylls of the King* that after the death of King Arthur there rose, "as it were one voice, an agony of lamentation." So the Northern people sorrowed over the loss of their knightly hero.

They praised him and spoke of his lasting greatness. They were so sure, these saddened, idolizing people that their loved hero would have everlasting fame. A *New York Times* editorial said: "His memory will be revered . . . and long after the Rebellion shall have become history . . . his name will be enrolled upon the list of our country's greatest patriots."

The editor of the *New York World* wrote with a warmth that seems to indicate personal attachment to Ellsworth. "He was a hero," said the *World* editorial, "in the fairest and most captivating sense of the word." It was recognized that few public figures were at one time so lovable yet so high-minded and noble. Ellsworth represented the idealism of the Civil War.

There was the terrible regret that his military genius had been lost to the Union. In time, after the war was over, it would be said that he might have been the Robert E. Lee of the North. One of Ellsworth's Chicago Zouaves, Joseph C. Barclay, who later fought on the side of the Confederacy, told what General Lee himself said when he heard of Ellsworth's death. Major Barclay was located at Camp Washington near Richmond, Virginia, when the news came. General Lee said to Barclay it was his belief that if Ellsworth had lived, he would have become the commanding general of the Union Army. General Lee also expressed the highest admiration for Ellsworth's military talents. Jefferson Davis, who introduced young Major Barclay to General Lee, regretted very much the manner in which Ellsworth had been killed.

The editorial about Ellsworth's death in the *New York*

World on May 25 concluded by saying that the public's grief "will pass from us to our descendants, so that generations hence children shall look with moist eyes upon the book wherein the story of the young Captain is written. The day last gone has added a knightly name to our list of heroes — one that will not be blurred so long as the record of our war of liberty survives."

Grieving took many forms. Numerous military companies wore crape for thirty days. Memorial envelopes with bright-colored pictures of the gallant Colonel on the left-hand side flooded the mails. Under the picture often were the words currently on many lips: "Remember Ellsworth." This phrase became the battle cry of Ellsworth's regiment in the Civil War; it rose from the bloody battlefield at the First Battle of Bull Run. As one of the poems to Ellsworth's memory said:

> *Brave Fire Zouaves! Your leader's name*
> *Is left you for a battle-cry;*
> *Let Ellwsorth's pure and spotless fame*
> *Lead you to conquer or to die.*

Poems like this about the young hero appeared in numerous newspapers. Songs were written in his praise. "Colonel Ellsworth's Funeral March" was composed in his honor and dedicated to Mrs. Lincoln. On the cover was a picture of Ellsworth in the bright red, blue, and gold of the Zouave uniform. Mrs. Lincoln asked Julia Taft to learn this composition and one day she played it before President and Mrs. Lincoln, their faces sorrowful with the loss of the young man they had loved.

Newborn babies were named for him, just as many of the baby crop of the year before had been named for Colonel Ellsworth of the Zouave Cadets. A fort at Alexandria became Fort Ellsworth. In time many streets and towns over the country would bear his name.

Along with this public sorrow went a vast rage and desire for vengeance. The divided country was awakening to the hatred which is always engendered by war. The Southerners, sincere in their own way of thinking, were to the Northern mind the most despicable of traitors. The first verse of a popular "Song on the Death of Colonel Ellsworth" called on all the sons and daughters of Columbia to join in this song:

> *To Ellsworth, our gallant Zouave,*
> *Who tore down the banner of treason,*
> *And perished our Union to save.*

There are seven verses of this song, all perhaps appalling in their mediocrity but completely faithful in expressing the feeling of the time. The sixth verse calls for revenge on "Secession's base Neros"— conveniently rhyming with the Union's "heroes." The Confederate banner was the *"rebel rag"* in the North, where James W. Jackson was being called by the basest of names. Yet the South was praising him in almost the same terms in which the North was praising Ellsworth, as the hero who had died in defense of the flag to which he had given his allegiance. The Southern people were raising a fund for the widow and children "of the martyr Jackson" at the same time the North was starting a fund for the parents of Colonel Ellsworth. Such was the tragedy — and vast pity — of our Civil War.

Ellsworth's was the first conspicuous death in that war; he was the first shining victim, just as Lincoln was the last. The two deaths punctuated the beginning and end of the tragic conflict. At the time Ellsworth was killed the North was not yet fully aroused to the all-out effort and sacrifice of war; some terrible event which would pierce the hearts of the people was needed to awaken them. The result of Ellsworth's death is expressed in a letter of sympathy which a young woman friend wrote Carrie four days after her lover died; she said in consolation: ". . . perhaps in a manner we cannot understand, God will accomplish more by his death than He would by his life. . . . Oh Carrie, darling, your grief is that of a nation: him you loved was the idol of the people & his death will consolidate the North as one man."

Preachers and editors on all sides were proclaiming the same idea. "We needed just such a sacrifice as this," declared one minister in his funeral sermon for Ellsworth. People would now say, he continued, "Let the war go on!" Enlistments would increase. Another minister said of Ellsworth, "It seemed as if God had chosen him out from among millions to be the honored martyr whose sacrifice should give climax to the . . . sentiment of the North."

Enlistments did increase; they fairly jumped. At Mechanicville a party of young men were playing ball when a friend came to tell them the news of Ellsworth's assassination. With their faces darkened in anger and grief, they stopped their game, and went off in a body to enlist. The Lake Forest Zouaves, when they heard the news, did the same thing. Incidents like this occurred all over the North.

In New York a new volunteer regiment was formed which became the Forty-fourth New York. The requirements were the same as for Ellsworth's Zouaves, splendid physique and high moral character. These men were called "Ellsworth's Avengers," and they fought bravely in the war. Thinking of such men and the far-reaching effect of Ellsworth's personality and death upon the battling North, William H. Burleigh wrote:

> He is — *not,* was: *The pulse that beat*
> *But yesterday within his frame,*
> *To-day is like a living flame*
> *In every manly breast we meet.*

John Hay, reflecting upon this last great service which his friend had given his country by his death, wrote sadly, "I believe that may solve the dark mystery why Ellsworth died."

Today he sleeps upon the high hill above the town of his boyhood. Over his grave has been erected a fitting monument for a patriot hero, a tall shaft of granite holding aloft a bronze American eagle. Ellsworth had said to John Hay that he "could ask no better death" than to die for his country. Did he, in that exaltation of self-sacrifice which he felt the night before he died, have a glimpse of what his death would do for the Union? On the base of his monument is this inscription, taken from his last letter to his parents written that very night: "I am content . . . confident that He who noteth even the fall of a sparrow, will have some purpose even in the fate of one like me."

Bibliographical Note

BIBLIOGRAPHICAL NOTE

MANUSCRIPTS

FEW biographies can be written so completely from manuscript sources as Elmer Ellsworth's. The most important of these is the collection of approximately one hundred Ellsworth letters at the Illinois State Historical Library at Springfield. The greater part of this collection consists of Ellsworth's letters to his fiancée, Carrie Spafford. Intimate, autobiographical, lengthy (one is fifteen pages long), these letters are ideal material for a biographer. This collection also contains Ellsworth's letters to Carrie's parents, Mr. and Mrs. Charles H. Spafford, and to several other persons, some letters written to Ellsworth (such as the notable letter of General Simon B. Buckner, February 18, 1861), two useful letters from J. G. Nicolay, one to Mr. Spafford, one to Carrie Spafford, and a few miscellaneous documents. The Illinois State Historical Library also has a number of Ellsworth's original drawings and the oil painting said to have been done by him at about nine years of age.

The question naturally arises, what became of the other side of this correspondence, Carrie Spafford's letters to Ellsworth? A letter written by Nicolay to Carrie Spafford from Washington on July 3, 1861, after Ellsworth's death, says: "I write this to inform you that when I was lately in Springfield, Illinois, in looking over Col. Ellsworth's effects which he left there, I found a considerable number of your letters to him, which I took charge of and brought with me here and have now in my possession. . . . I thought you yourself would prefer to have me take them, and return them directly to yourself and thus obviate entirely the danger of their falling into any hands but mine. I was the more convinced that such would be the case from the fact that your last letters to the Col. were enclosed to my care by yourself. . . . Please to write to me at once where I shall send them to you and whether by mail or express." (Original in the Godfrey Collection, see below.) A letter to Nicolay from Carrie Spafford written on August 13, 1861, says: "I received the package of letters by express yesterday." (Original at the Lincoln National Life Foundation.) Presumably Carrie, who later married Frederic E. Brett, destroyed her own letters to Ellsworth.

Other manuscripts used at the Illinois State Historical Library are the typed recollections of Edward P. Bartlett (whom Ellsworth had drilled at Lake Forest), a typed manucript entitled "In Memoriam" by Hon. Caleb Lyon, and two original letters from General T. W. Sherman to Captain John A. Dahlgren, Washington, May 24, 1861, about arrangements for the funeral of Colonel Ellsworth.

An extremely valuable manuscript source is what I call the Godfrey Collection. This is an accumulation of five hundred and seventy-nine papers which were collected by Ellsworth's fiancée, Carrie Spafford, and by her family. It is now in the possession of Miss Carolyn Godfrey, whose mother was Carrie's sister, and I have used it by Miss Godfrey's generous permission. The collection is a vast miscellany whose items have one thing in common: they all relate to Elmer Ellsworth and are therefore invaluable in writing a biography of him.

The Godfrey Collection contains many of Ellsworth's own papers which came to Carrie Spafford after his death. The letters to him are especially useful. It contains Carrie Spafford's papers including many letters to her. (Ellsworth's letters to her, which were sold to the Illinois State Historical Library, were once a part of this collection.) Among the various items is an assemblage of the sentimental souvenirs saved by these two young lovers — invitations to balls, dance programs, and the like, faded, mid-Victorian relics which bring the romance to life.

Unexpectedly one finds in the Godfrey Collection the research papers of Dr. Charles A. Ingraham used in the preparation of his book *Elmer E. Ellsworth and the Zouaves of '61*. Here are answers to letters which the elderly physician wrote to libraries, historical societies, and individuals to get information about Ellsworth. Here are his notes on interviews with Ellsworth's father and mother, with Chester Denton, Mrs. Ellsworth's half-brother, and other relatives. Here are the recollections of Mattie Sears Harris and Merritt Hutchins, playmates of Ellsworth, and of other old-timers of Mechanicville.

The Godfrey Collection includes a great number of contemporary newspaper clippings, some of them the very same clippings Ellsworth enclosed in his letters to Carrie Spafford. Loving hands during his life and after his death collected newspaper items and articles from all sides, thus making a most unusual newspaper coverage of Ellsworth's career.

Extremely interesting in its intimacy is Ellsworth's diary from April 11 to August 25, 1859. After Ellsworth's death his father gave this diary to Francis E. Brownell, "Ellsworth's Avenger." (Letter of Chester Denton to Dr. C. A. Ingraham, March 27, 1917, Godfrey Collection.) Brownell published extracts from the diary in various newspapers and the major part of it in the *Chicago Times*, October 28, 1883. (A clipping of this is in the Godfrey Collection.) John Hay quoted from the diary at some length in his article "A Young Hero," *McClure's Magazine*, March, 1896.

According to Chester Denton, Ellsworth's father tried to get the diary back from Francis Brownell to destroy it. (Notes on Denton's interview with Dr. C. A. Ingraham, March 22, 1917, Godfrey Collection.) By Denton's account Brownell was unwilling to give the diary back. However, what seems to have happened is that Brownell finally did return the diary to Ellsworth's father, retaining a copy. "Ellsworth's Diary was destroyed. We have the cover with his autograph," wrote a dealer in books and autographs at Wilder's Bookshop, Boston, to Dr. Ingraham, December 13, 1917. (Godfrey Collection.) Miss Jessie F. Wheeler of Mechanicville, librarian at the Troy Public Library, wrote Dr. Ingraham on August 10, 1918, about the diary: "I saw it and read it all. . . . It stopped just before Ellsworth's fame began." She had told Dr. Ingraham on January 11, 1918, that the diary had a red cover. (Both items from the Godfrey Collection.)

What is, in my opinion, a faithful manuscript copy of the original diary was presented about 1921 to the Minnesota Historical Society by Mrs. Edgar B. Barton, a stepdaughter of Francis E. Brownell. (An unidentified clipping in the Godfrey Collection gives this item taken from the *Minnesota Historical News.*) Though Ellsworth's handwriting varied greatly according to haste, mood, or other circumstance, the handwriting of this document, which is strongly individual, does not, in my judgment, bear resemblance to Ellsworth's writing in any of its phases. The greater part of the diary can be compared with the newspaper printing. What the diary tells dovetails perfectly with the letters Ellsworth was writing Carrie Spafford at the same time. Ellsworth's characteristic misspellings and other individual traits in writing appear throughout this copy of the diary.

Incidents of Ellsworth's boyhood are mostly taken from a forty-three-page manuscript, "Memoranda of his life; by his mother," at the New York State Library. It is in the handwriting of Mrs. Charity Louisa (Steadwell) Mabbitt. (The probable reason why Mrs. Ellsworth did not write it herself was that she, as her son mentioned in one of his letters, had palsy.) This manuscript, in addition to Mrs. Ellsworth's recollections, includes copies of two of Ellsworth's letters, the letter to him at the end of the tour from the mother of five sons, "Extracts from Elmers private papers," and fourteen pages of memorial poems sent to the parents of Ellsworth after his death.

I have also quoted from two other items at the New York State Library: a broadside of the instructions "To the committee of arrangements FOR THE RECEPTION OF THE PRESIDENT ELECT," and a broadside of the "Song on the Death of Col. Ellsworth."

Ellsworth's notable last letter to his parents is at the Chicago Historical Society, which also has a very fine exhibit of Ellsworth relics, including the *Album of Love*, from which I have quoted parts of Ellsworth's inscriptions. I have also quoted from two other items at the Chicago Historical Society, a handwritten manuscript called "Anecdote of Col. Elmer Ellsworth" (written by his cousin, Elmie Denton), and a typed manuscript called "G. H. Fergus tells of Tragedy," an account of Ellsworth's death by George Harris Fergus, a member of the Zouave regiment at Alexandria.

I have quoted from four very interesting letters to Nicolay at the Lincoln National Life Foundation: one written by Ellsworth himself; one by his father; one by Carrie Spafford; and one by her father, Charles H. Spafford.

The above are the main manuscript sources found in the documentation of this book. There are a few scattered items such as Ellsworth's last written orders for his men on the night of May 23, 1861 (from Lincoln College, Illinois) and a copy of a letter (in private hands) in which a soldier tells about the "suvays" and the death of Ellsworth.

BOOKS AND ARTICLES

THE following are the books and articles named in the annotations of my original manuscript. A special account must be given of Dr. Charles A. Ingraham's *Elmer E. Ellsworth and the Zouaves of '61*, published for the Chicago Historical Society by the University of Chicago Press in 1925. Dr. Ingraham was a physician who was in his seventies when his book was published. In a letter written December 22, 1933 (in the Godfrey Collection), he stated he was in his eighty-second year, which means he was born around 1852. He remembered the assassination of Colonel Ellsworth who became his boyhood hero. His book on the double subject of Ellsworth and the Zouaves stemmed from his great admiration of the Zouave Colonel.

Dr. Ingraham was most earnest and dedicated in writing his book but his approach to biography was that of the last century. In quoting Ellsworth's letters he edited them in a manner then considered proper, but regarded as inexcusable by present-day historians and biographers. He corrected misspellings and punctuation, he omitted and inserted words or phrases with nothing to indicate he was doing so, he rearranged the order of paragraphs, and constantly changed the wording to suit his own conventional taste. He had much of the Victorian idea that very personal matters should not be put into a biography, so he omitted most of the terms of endearment in Ellsworth's letters to Carrie Spafford and in other ways left out the personal flavor. One does not question his sincere belief that these changes were within his editorial right, but I have been careful never to quote anything from Dr. Ingraham's transcription of letters, newspapers or any other document; I have always gone to the original source. Nevertheless, I owe a great deal to Dr. Ingraham's book and to his research papers in the Godfrey Collection. He blazed a trail.

Arpee, Edward, *The History of Lake Forest Academy*, Chicago, 1944.

Basler, Roy P. *See* Lincoln, Abraham.

Bayne, Julia Taft, *Tad Lincoln's Father*, Boston, 1931.

"Colonel Elmer E. Ellsworth, First Hero of the Civil War," The One Hundredth Anniversary 1837-1937 (booklet), Mechanic-ville, New York.

Dennett, Tyler, ed., *Lincoln and the Civil War in the Diaries and Letters of John Hay*, New York, 1939.

Ellsworth, E. E., *Manual of Arms For Light Infantry*, Arranged for the U. S. Zouave Cadets. Published in early June, 1860. Foreword explaining use in place of Hardee's manual because of using Minie musket instead of rifle. First 110 pages devoted to drills, remaining 39 pages contain press notices of the U. S. Zouave Cadets.

Ellsworth, Col. E. E., *Manual of Arms For Light Infantry*, Adapted to the Rifled Musket . . . Arranged for the U. S. Zouave Cadets, Chicago, 1861. Revised edition.

[Ellsworth Monument Association] Exercises connected with the Unveiling of the Ellsworth Monument at Mechanicville, May 27, 1874, Albany, New York, 1875.

Farnum, George R., "Elmer E. Ellsworth," *American Bar Association Journal*, May, 1944, pp. 278 ff.

Grimsley, Elizabeth Todd, "Six Months in the White House," *Journal of the Illinois State Historical Society*, October, 1926-January, 1927, pp. 43-73.

Hay, John, "A Young Hero: Personal Reminiscences of Colonel E. E. Ellsworth," *McClure's Magazine*, March, 1896, pp. 354-361.

——, "A Young Hero," *New York World*, February 16, 1890.

——, "Colonel Ellsworth, As His Friends Knew Him," *Washington Chronicle*, May 26, 1861.

——, "Ellsworth," *Atlantic Monthly*, July, 1861, pp. 119-125 [Unsigned].

——. See also Dennett, Tyler, and Nicolay, J. G.

Ingraham, Charles A., "Colonel Elmer E. Ellsworth: First Hero of the Civil War," *Wisconsin Magazine of History*, June, 1918, pp. 349-374.

——, *Elmer E. Ellsworth and the Zouaves of '61*, Chicago, 1925.

Lincoln, Abraham, *The Collected Works of Abraham Lincoln* (8 vols. plus index vol.), Roy P. Basler, ed., New Brunswick, New Jersey, 1953.

McIlvaine, Mabel, comp., *Reminiscences of Chicago during the Civil War*, Chicago, 1914. Includes "Ellsworth's Zouaves," by Henry H. Miller.

Moore, Frank, ed., *The Rebellion Record*, New York, 1862, 1864. First 3 vols.

Nicolay, J. G., and Hay, John, *Abraham Lincoln: A History*, New York, 1890. Vol. 4.

Poore, Ben: Perley. *Perley's Reminiscences of Sixty Years in the National Metropolis*, Philadelphia, 1886. 2 vols.

Robinson, Luther E., "Ephraim Elmer Ellsworth, First Martyr of the Civil War," *Illinois State Historical Society Transactions*, 1923, No. 30, pp. 111-132.

W. B. S. [Walter B. Stevens], "Lincoln and Ellsworth," *St. Louis Globe-Democrat*, June 3, 1888.

Stoddard, William O., *Inside the White House in War Times*, New York, 1890.

Swain, Martha, "It Was Fun To Be a Soldier," *American Heritage*, August, 1956, pp. 12 ff.

Truesdell, Winfred Porter, *Catalog Raisonné of the Portraits of Elmer E. Ellsworth*, Champlain, New York, 1927.

Victor, Orville J., *Incidents and Anecdotes of the War*, New York, 1862, pp. 101 ff.

Waggoner, Madeline Sadler, *The Long Haul West*, New York, 1958.

Wilson, Rufus Rockwell, ed., *Intimate Memories of Lincoln*, Elmira, New York, 1945.

NEWSPAPERS

As stated above under *Manuscripts,* there are a great many newspaper clippings in the Godfrey Collection covering Ellsworth's enormous publicity in 1860 and 1861 and including later articles about him. Ellsworth's own *Manual of Arms* has a number of press notices. I have also collected a few photostats of pertinent articles not found in these sources. Material and quotations have been used from the following: *Adrian* (Mich.) *Daily Watchtower; Baltimore American; Boston Post; Boston Transcript;* (Carlinville, Ill.) *Macoupin County Enquirer; Chicago Daily Journal; Chicago Herald; Chicago Leader; Chicago Morning Post; Chicago Press and Tribune;* (Chicago) *Railroad Gazette; Chicago Times; Chicago Tribune; Cincinnati Commercial; Cleveland Morning Leader; Detroit Free Press; Illinois State Journal; Illinois State Register;* (Kenosha, Wis.) *Telegraph-Courier; Sunday Mercury* (unidentified); *New York Commercial Advertiser; New York Evening Post; New York Herald; New York Leader; New York Mail and Express; New York Tribune; New York World; Philadelphia North American and United States Gazette; Philadelphia Press; Pittsburgh Evening Chronicle; Pittsburgh Post; Rockford* (Ill.) *Register-Gazette; St. Louis Globe-Democrat; St. Louis Republican; Troy Daily Budget; Troy Times; Troy Whig; Washington Chronicle;* (Washington) *The National Republican;* (Washington) *The National Tribune; Washington Star.*

INDEX

INDEX